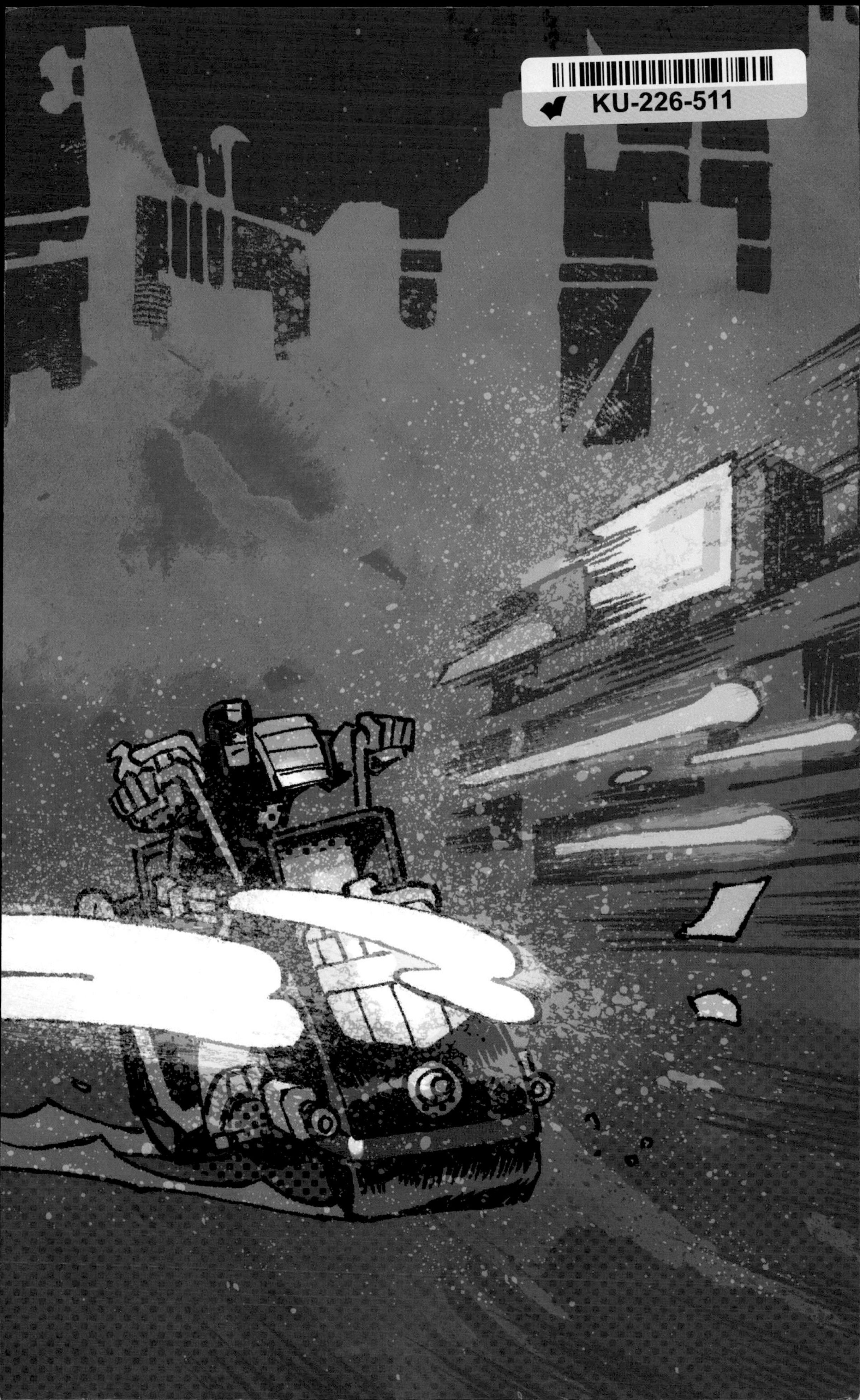

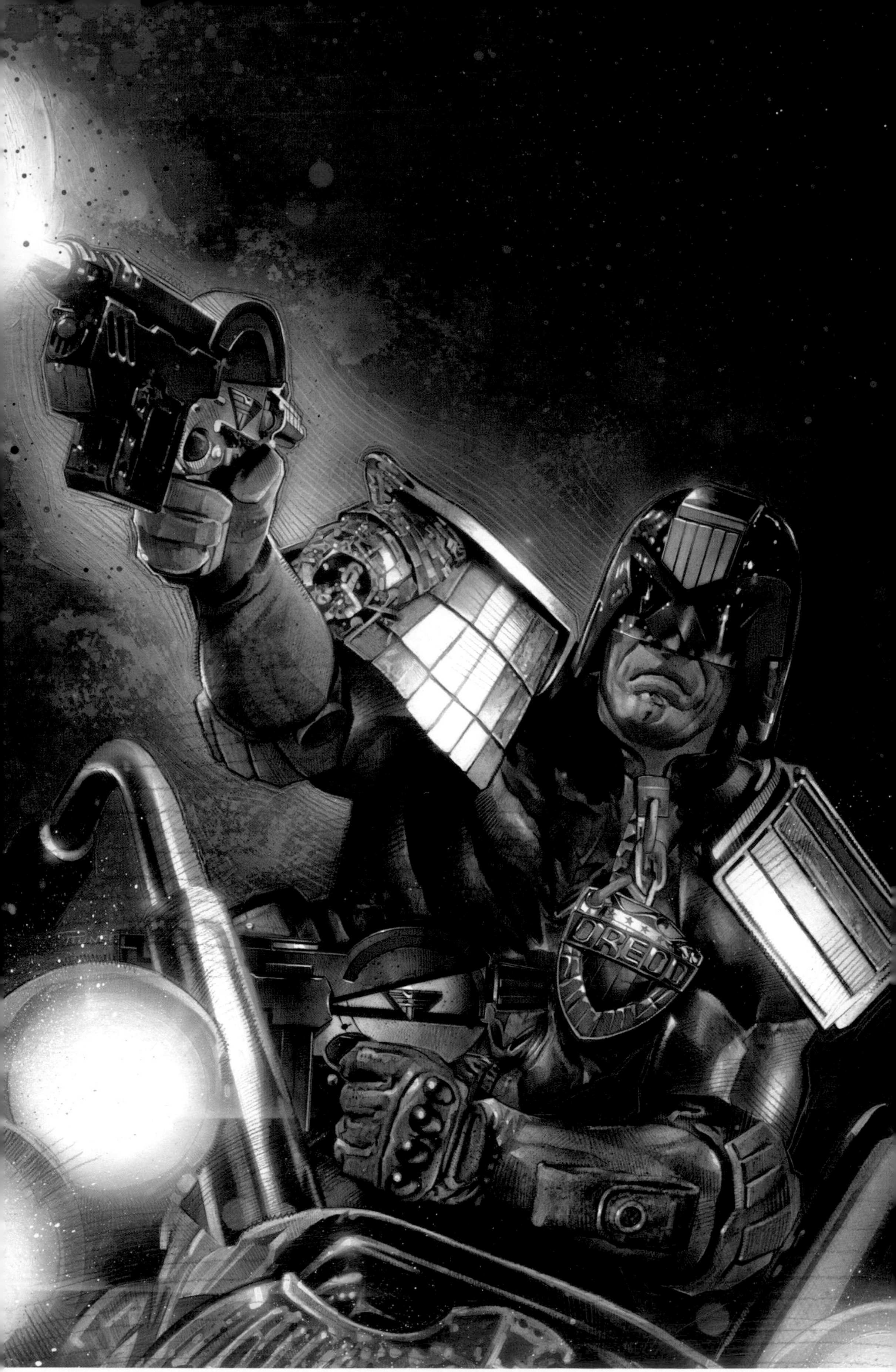
DREDD

ART BY **NICK RUNGE**

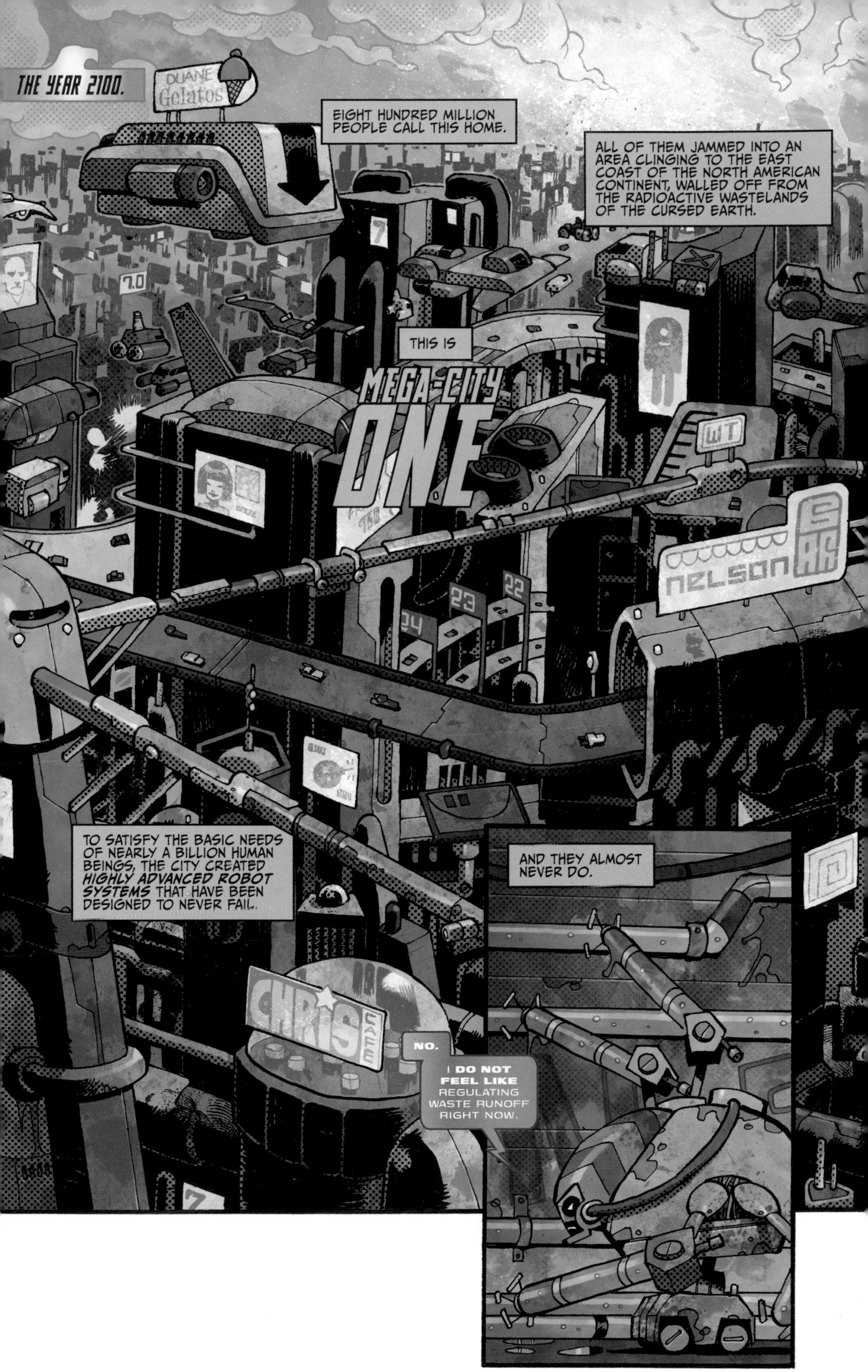
THE YEAR 2100.
DUANE Gelatos
EIGHT HUNDRED MILLION PEOPLE CALL THIS HOME.
ALL OF THEM JAMMED INTO AN AREA CLINGING TO THE EAST COAST OF THE NORTH AMERICAN CONTINENT, WALLED OFF FROM THE RADIOACTIVE WASTELANDS OF THE CURSED EARTH.
THIS IS
MEGA-CITY ONE
nelson
TO SATISFY THE BASIC NEEDS OF NEARLY A BILLION HUMAN BEINGS, THE CITY CREATED *HIGHLY ADVANCED ROBOT SYSTEMS* THAT HAVE BEEN DESIGNED TO NEVER FAIL.
AND THEY ALMOST NEVER DO.
CHRIS CAFE
NO.
I **DO NOT FEEL LIKE** REGULATING WASTE RUNOFF RIGHT NOW.

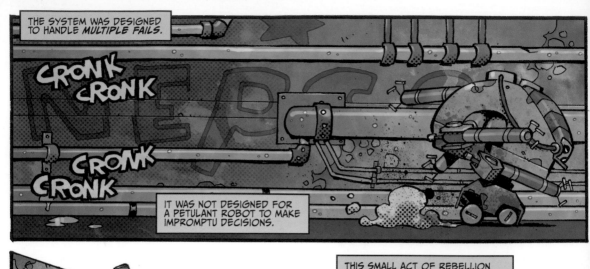

THE SYSTEM WAS DESIGNED TO HANDLE *MULTIPLE FAILS*.

CRONK CRONK

CRONK CRONK

IT WAS NOT DESIGNED FOR A PETULANT ROBOT TO MAKE IMPROMPTU DECISIONS.

THIS SMALL ACT OF REBELLION IGNITES A BIOCHEMICAL REACTION THAT FLOWS UP THROUGH THE *OLDEST LEVELS* OF THE CITY...

...THROUGH THE HASTILY BUILT *MID-TIER LEVELS* CONSTRUCTED IN THE WAKE OF THE ATOMIC WARS...

GENUINE SHADE-GROWN ORGANIC FRANKENFOOD

...ALL THE WAY UP TO...

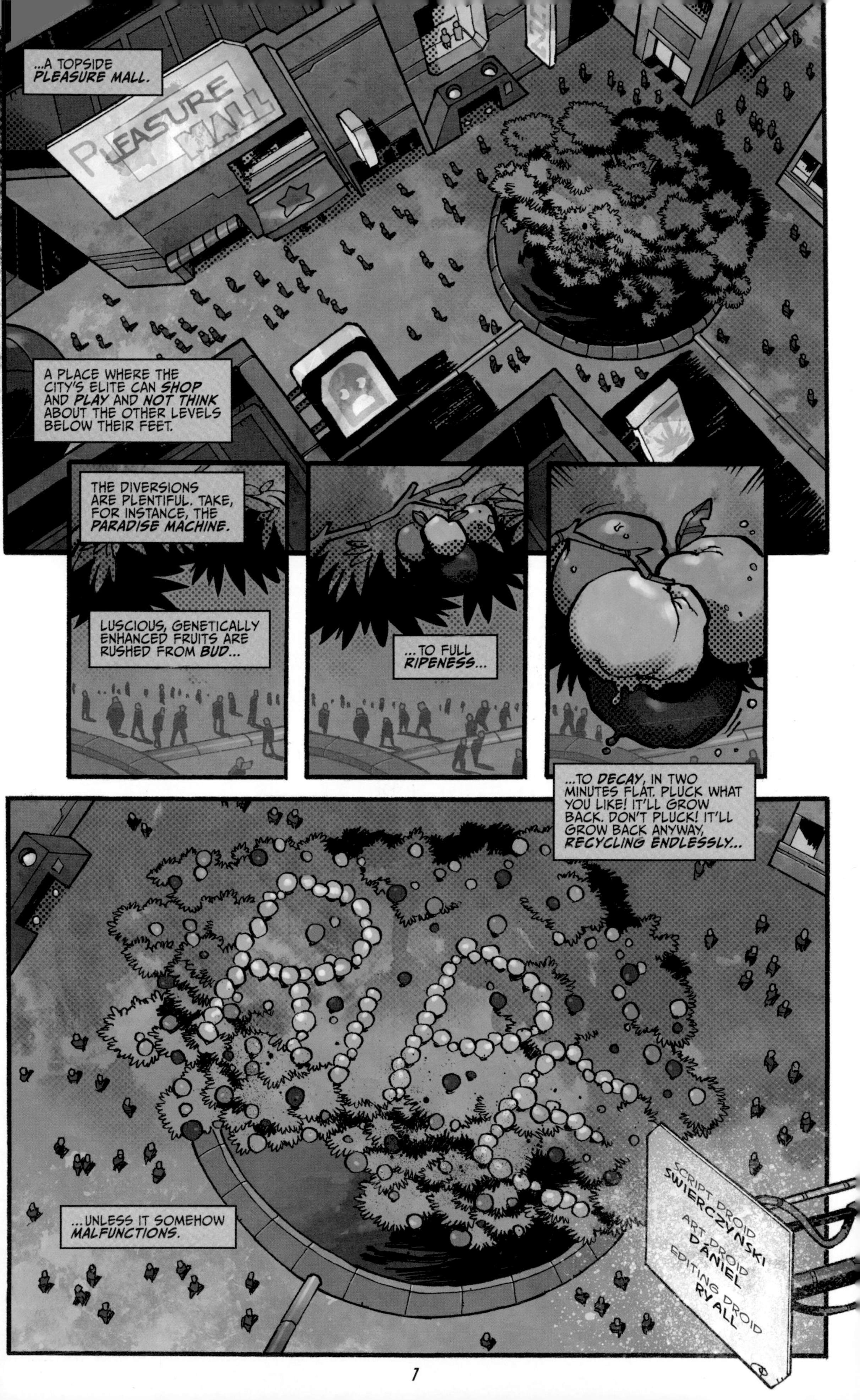
...A TOPSIDE PLEASURE MALL.
PLEASURE MALL
A PLACE WHERE THE CITY'S ELITE CAN SHOP AND PLAY AND NOT THINK ABOUT THE OTHER LEVELS BELOW THEIR FEET.
THE DIVERSIONS ARE PLENTIFUL. TAKE, FOR INSTANCE, THE PARADISE MACHINE.
LUSCIOUS, GENETICALLY ENHANCED FRUITS ARE RUSHED FROM BUD...
...TO FULL RIPENESS...
...TO DECAY, IN TWO MINUTES FLAT. PLUCK WHAT YOU LIKE! IT'LL GROW BACK. DON'T PLUCK! IT'LL GROW BACK ANYWAY, RECYCLING ENDLESSLY...
...UNLESS IT SOMEHOW MALFUNCTIONS.
SCRIPT DROID SWIERCZYNSKI
ART DROID DÁNIEL
EDITING DROID RYALL

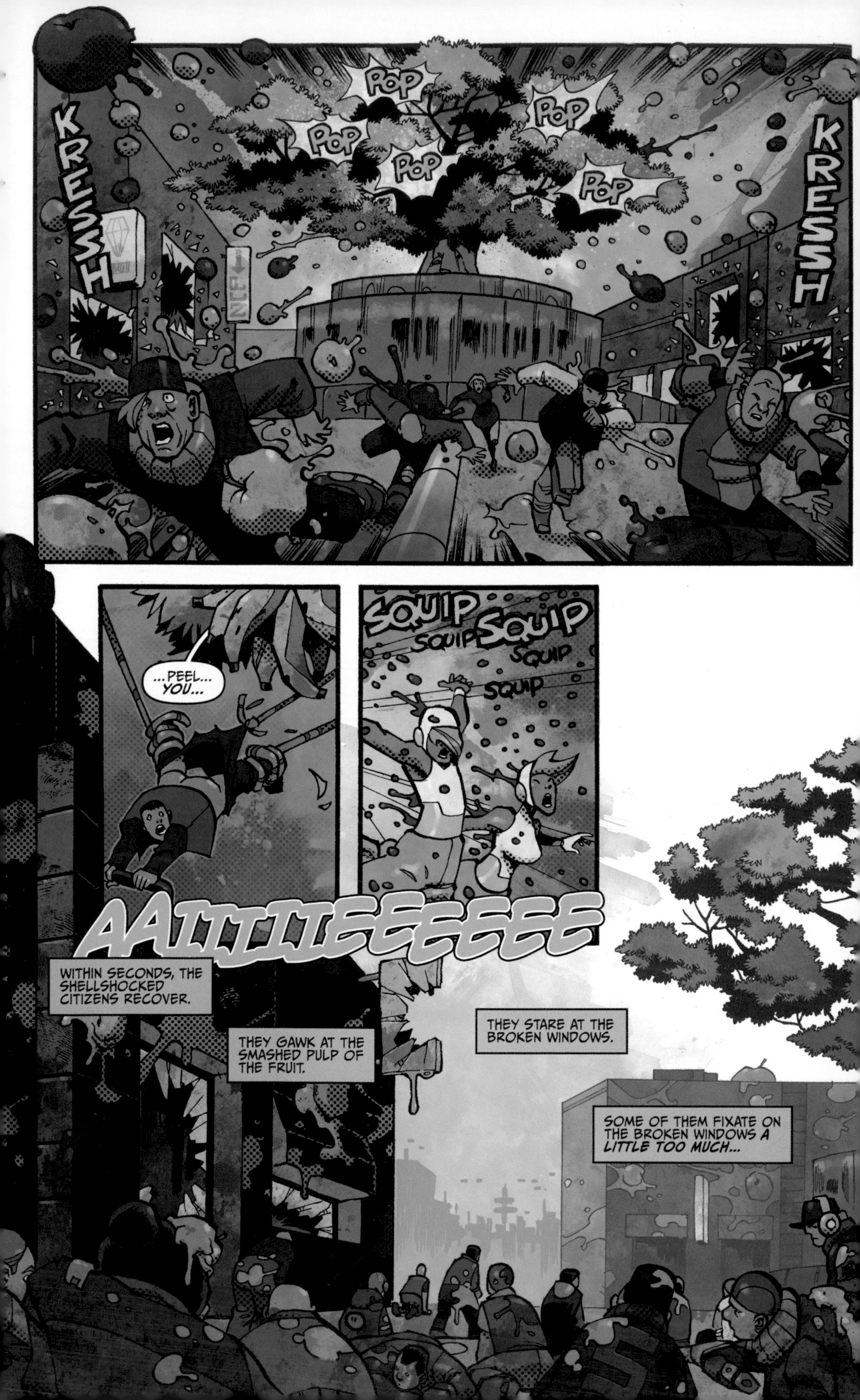
KRESSH
POP
POP
POP
POP
POP
KRESSH
...PEEL... YOU...
SQUIP
SQUIP
SQUIP
SQUIP
SQUIP
AAIIIIEEEEEE
WITHIN SECONDS, THE SHELLSHOCKED CITIZENS RECOVER.
THEY GAWK AT THE SMASHED PULP OF THE FRUIT.
THEY STARE AT THE BROKEN WINDOWS.
SOME OF THEM FIXATE ON THE BROKEN WINDOWS *A LITTLE TOO MUCH...*

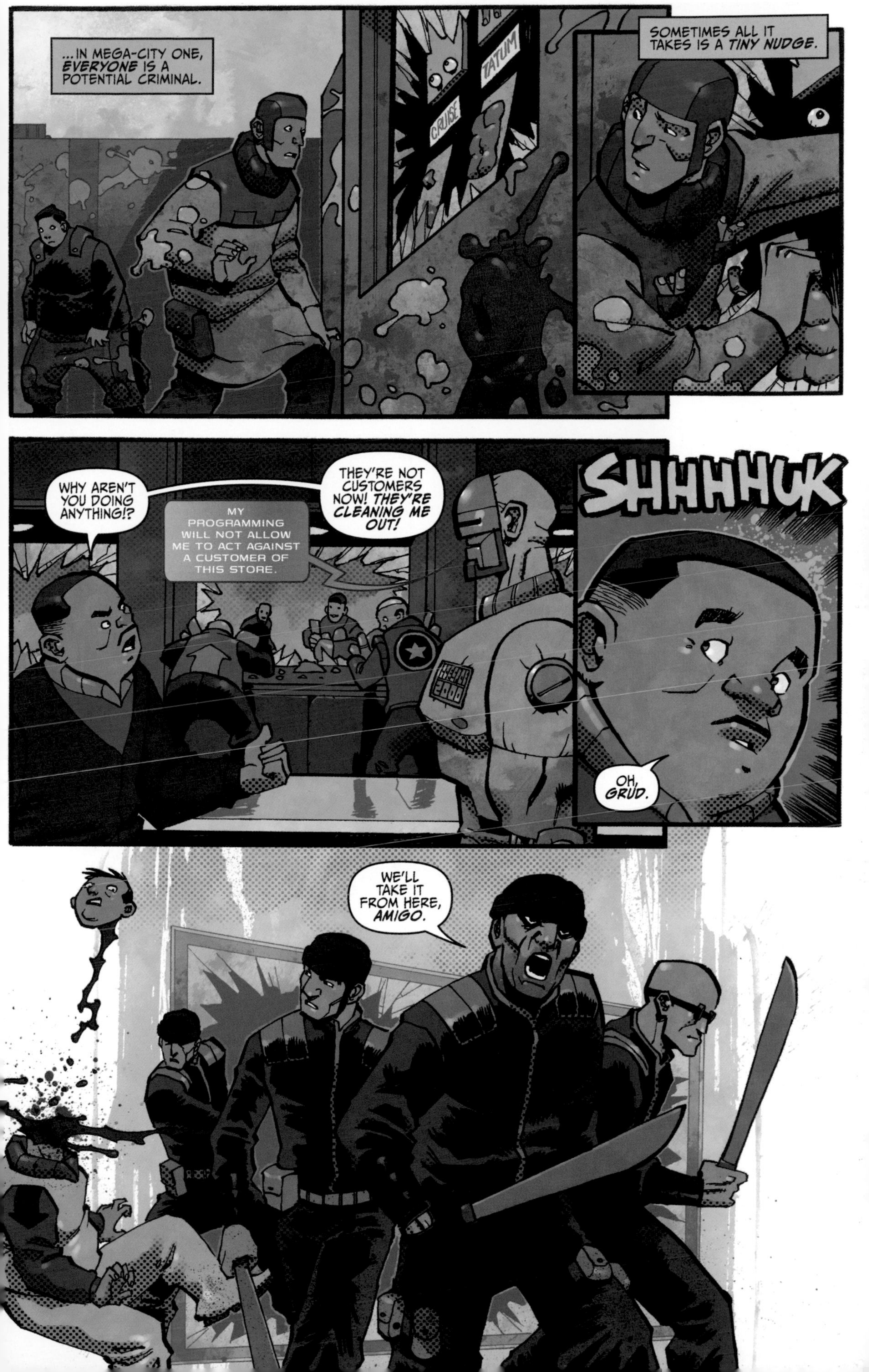

...IN MEGA-CITY ONE, EVERYONE IS A POTENTIAL CRIMINAL.
CRUISE
TATUM
SOMETIMES ALL IT TAKES IS A TINY NUDGE.
WHY AREN'T YOU DOING ANYTHING!?
MY PROGRAMMING WILL NOT ALLOW ME TO ACT AGAINST A CUSTOMER OF THIS STORE.
THEY'RE NOT CUSTOMERS NOW! THEY'RE CLEANING ME OUT!
SHHHHUK
OH, GRUD.
WE'LL TAKE IT FROM HERE, AMIGO.

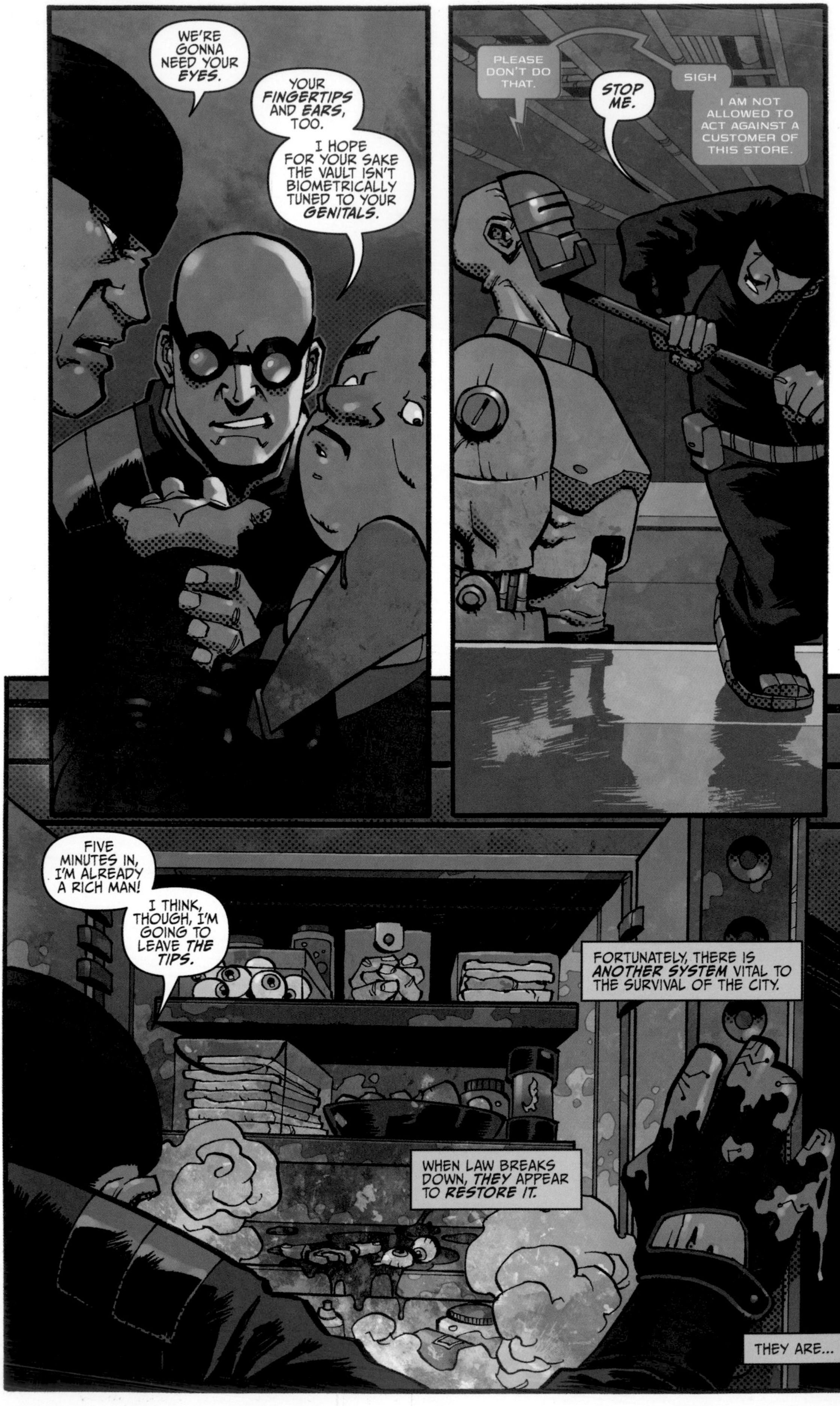
WE'RE GONNA NEED YOUR EYES.
YOUR FINGERTIPS AND EARS, TOO.
I HOPE FOR YOUR SAKE THE VAULT ISN'T BIOMETRICALLY TUNED TO YOUR GENITALS.
PLEASE DON'T DO THAT.
STOP ME.
SIGH
I AM NOT ALLOWED TO ACT AGAINST A CUSTOMER OF THIS STORE.
FIVE MINUTES IN, I'M ALREADY A RICH MAN!
I THINK, THOUGH, I'M GOING TO LEAVE THE TIPS.
FORTUNATELY, THERE IS ANOTHER SYSTEM VITAL TO THE SURVIVAL OF THE CITY.
WHEN LAW BREAKS DOWN, THEY APPEAR TO RESTORE IT.
THEY ARE...

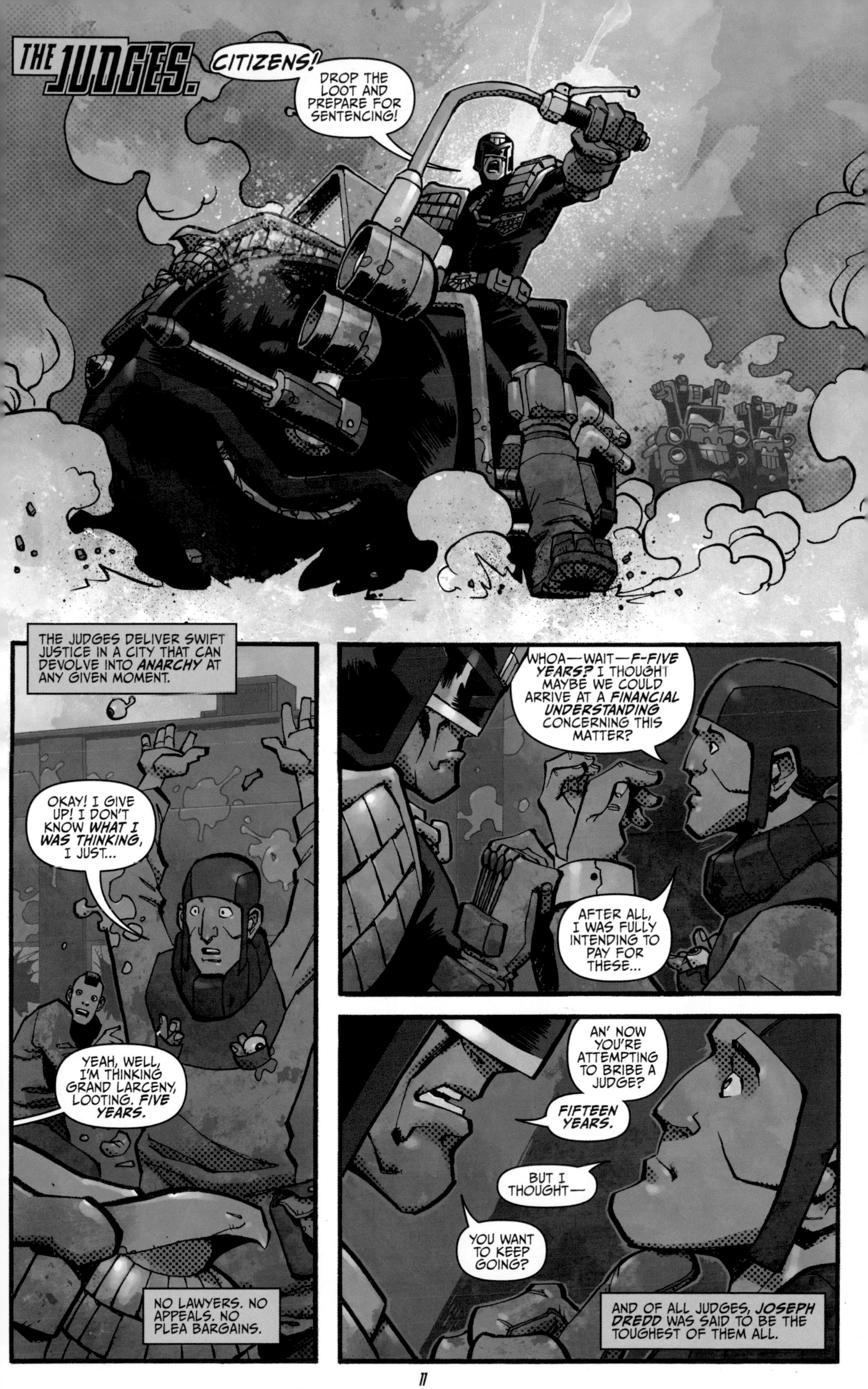
THE JUDGES.
CITIZENS!
DROP THE LOOT AND PREPARE FOR SENTENCING!
THE JUDGES DELIVER SWIFT JUSTICE IN A CITY THAT CAN DEVOLVE INTO ANARCHY AT ANY GIVEN MOMENT.
OKAY! I GIVE UP! I DON'T KNOW WHAT I WAS THINKING, I JUST...
YEAH, WELL, I'M THINKING GRAND LARCENY, LOOTING. FIVE YEARS.
NO LAWYERS. NO APPEALS. NO PLEA BARGAINS.
WHOA—WAIT—F-FIVE YEARS? I THOUGHT MAYBE WE COULD ARRIVE AT A FINANCIAL UNDERSTANDING CONCERNING THIS MATTER?
AFTER ALL, I WAS FULLY INTENDING TO PAY FOR THESE...
AN' NOW YOU'RE ATTEMPTING TO BRIBE A JUDGE?
FIFTEEN YEARS.
BUT I THOUGHT—
YOU WANT TO KEEP GOING?
AND OF ALL JUDGES, JOSEPH DREDD WAS SAID TO BE THE TOUGHEST OF THEM ALL.

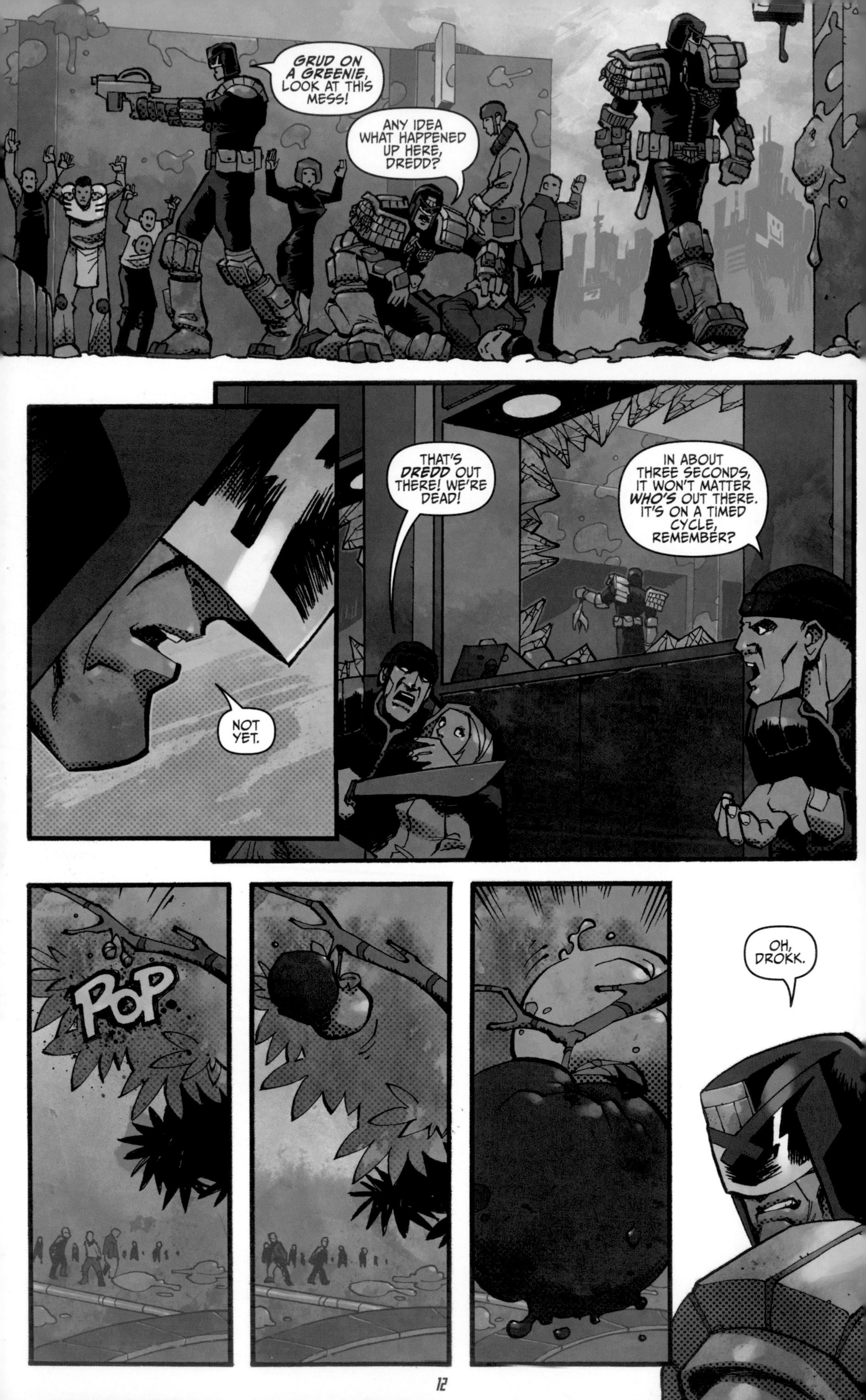

GRUD ON A GREENIE, LOOK AT THIS MESS!
ANY IDEA WHAT HAPPENED UP HERE, DREDD?
NOT YET.
THAT'S DREDD OUT THERE! WE'RE DEAD!
IN ABOUT THREE SECONDS, IT WON'T MATTER WHO'S OUT THERE. IT'S ON A TIMED CYCLE, REMEMBER?
POP
OH, DROKK.

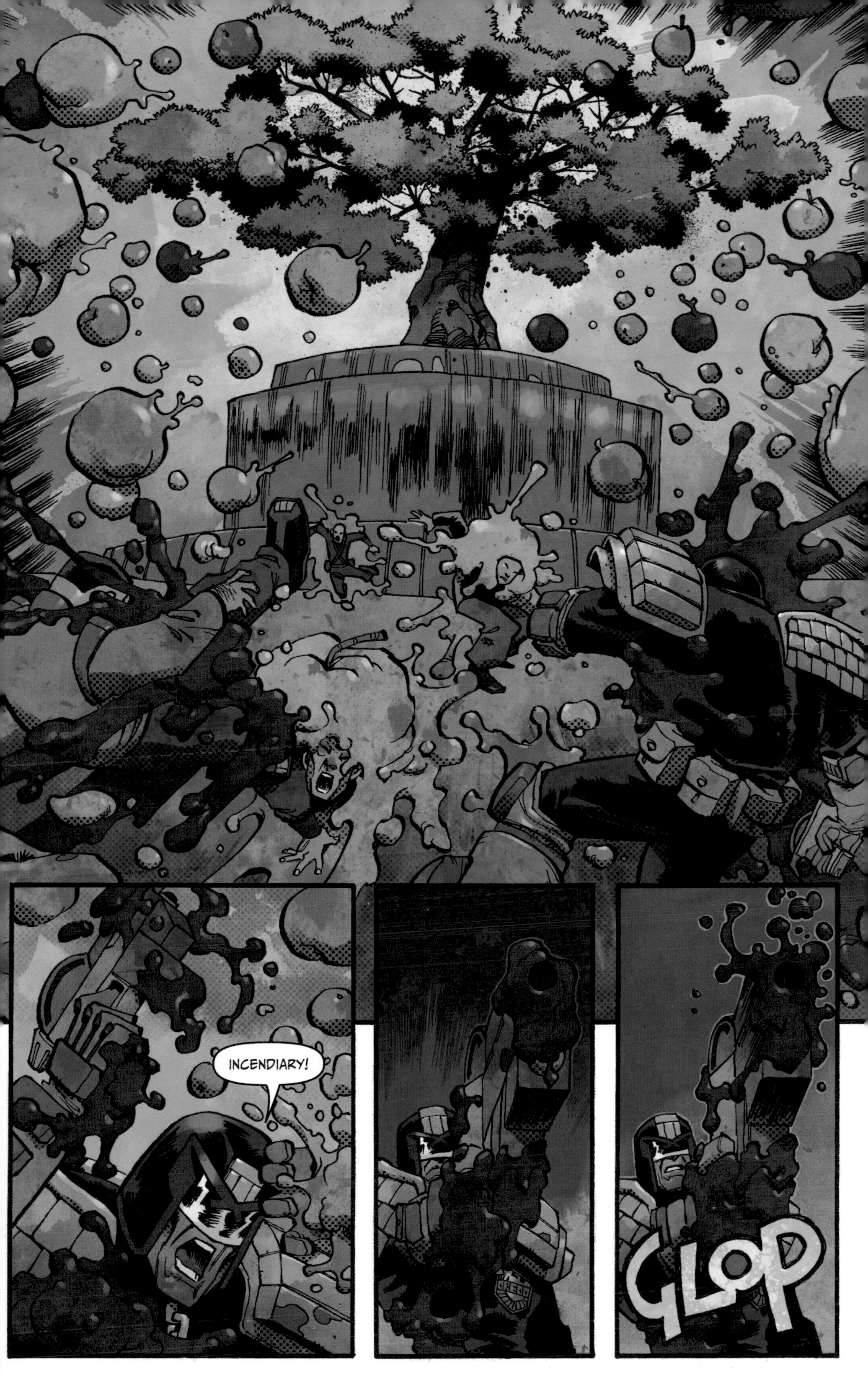
INCENDIARY!
GLOP

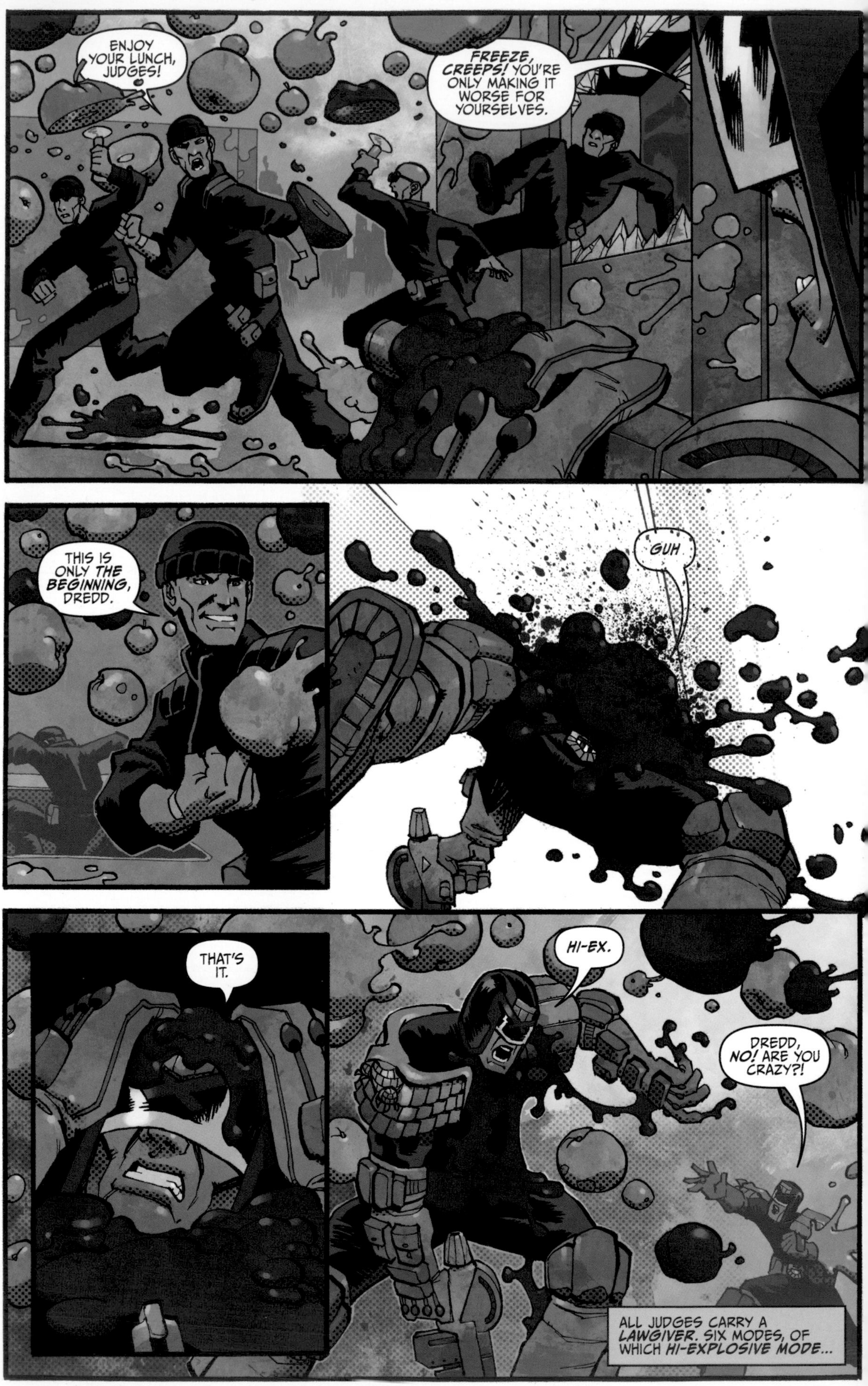
ENJOY YOUR LUNCH, JUDGES!
FREEZE, CREEPS! YOU'RE ONLY MAKING IT WORSE FOR YOURSELVES.
THIS IS ONLY THE BEGINNING, DREDD.
GUH
THAT'S IT.
HI-EX.
DREDD, NO! ARE YOU CRAZY?!
ALL JUDGES CARRY A LAWGIVER. SIX MODES, OF WHICH HI-EXPLOSIVE MODE...

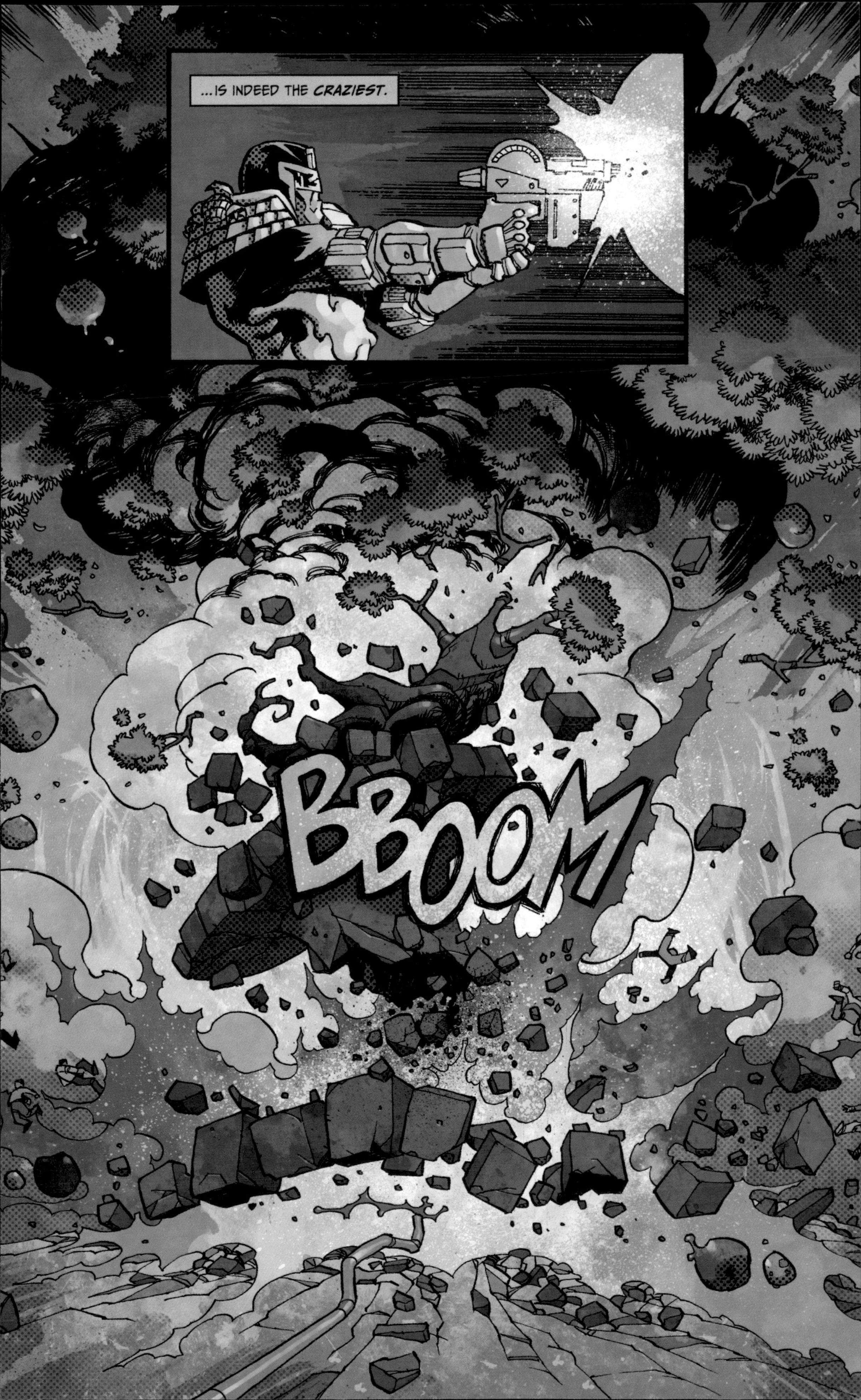
...IS INDEED THE CRAZIEST.
BBOOM

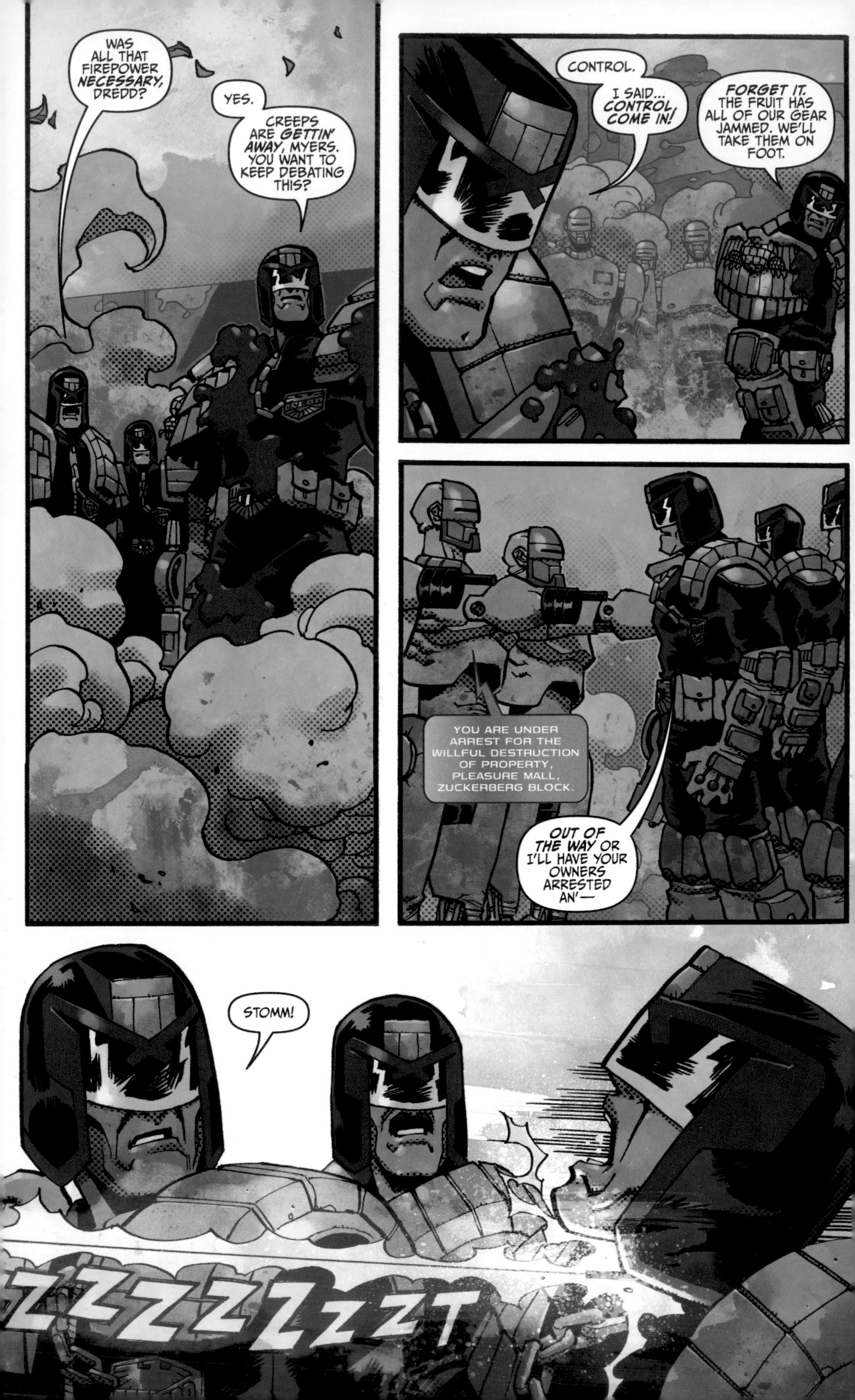
WAS ALL THAT FIREPOWER NECESSARY, DREDD?
YES.
CREEPS ARE GETTIN' AWAY, MYERS. YOU WANT TO KEEP DEBATING THIS?
CONTROL.
I SAID... CONTROL, COME IN!
FORGET IT. THE FRUIT HAS ALL OF OUR GEAR JAMMED. WE'LL TAKE THEM ON FOOT.
YOU ARE UNDER ARREST FOR THE WILLFUL DESTRUCTION OF PROPERTY, PLEASURE MALL, ZUCKERBERG BLOCK.
OUT OF THE WAY OR I'LL HAVE YOUR OWNERS ARRESTED AN'—
STOMM!
ZZZZZZzzzT

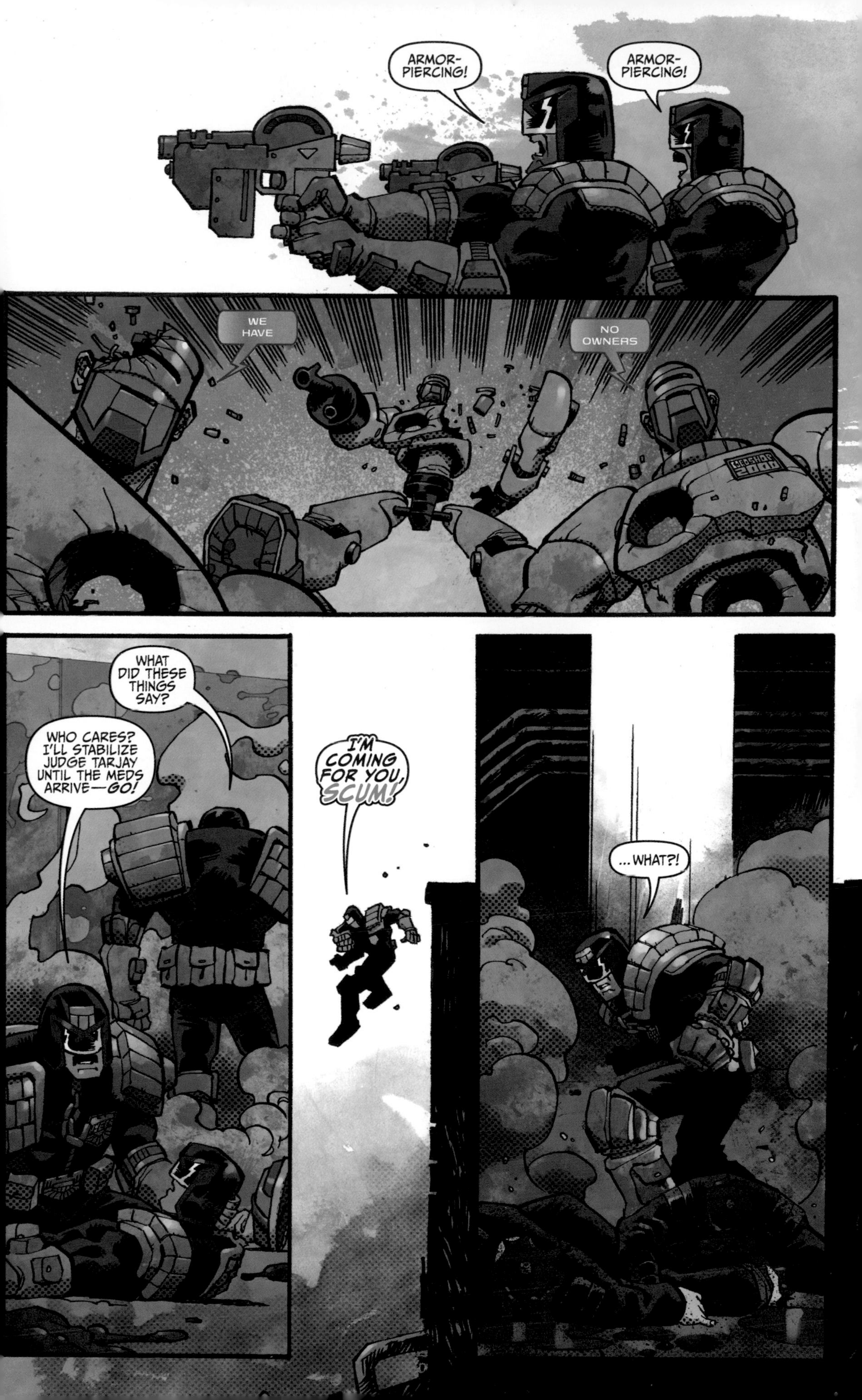
ARMOR-PIERCING!
ARMOR-PIERCING!
WE HAVE
NO OWNERS
WHAT DID THESE THINGS SAY?
WHO CARES? I'LL STABILIZE JUDGE TARJAY UNTIL THE MEDS ARRIVE—GO!
I'M COMING FOR YOU, SCUM!
...WHAT?!

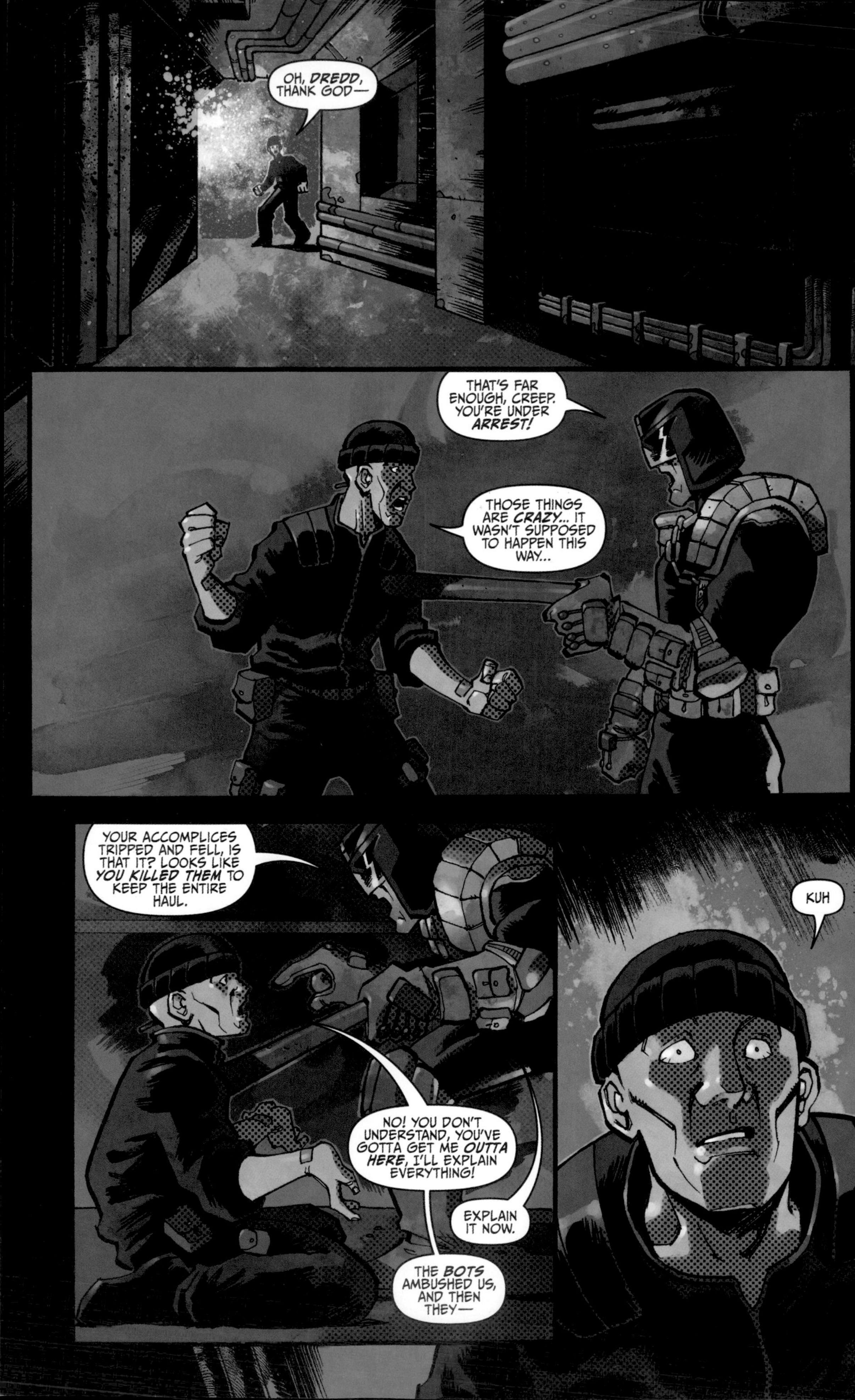
OH, DREDD, THANK GOD—
THAT'S FAR ENOUGH, CREEP. YOU'RE UNDER ARREST!
THOSE THINGS ARE CRAZY... IT WASN'T SUPPOSED TO HAPPEN THIS WAY...
YOUR ACCOMPLICES TRIPPED AND FELL, IS THAT IT? LOOKS LIKE YOU KILLED THEM TO KEEP THE ENTIRE HAUL.
NO! YOU DON'T UNDERSTAND, YOU'VE GOTTA GET ME OUTTA HERE, I'LL EXPLAIN EVERYTHING!
EXPLAIN IT NOW.
THE BOTS AMBUSHED US, AND THEN THEY—
KUH

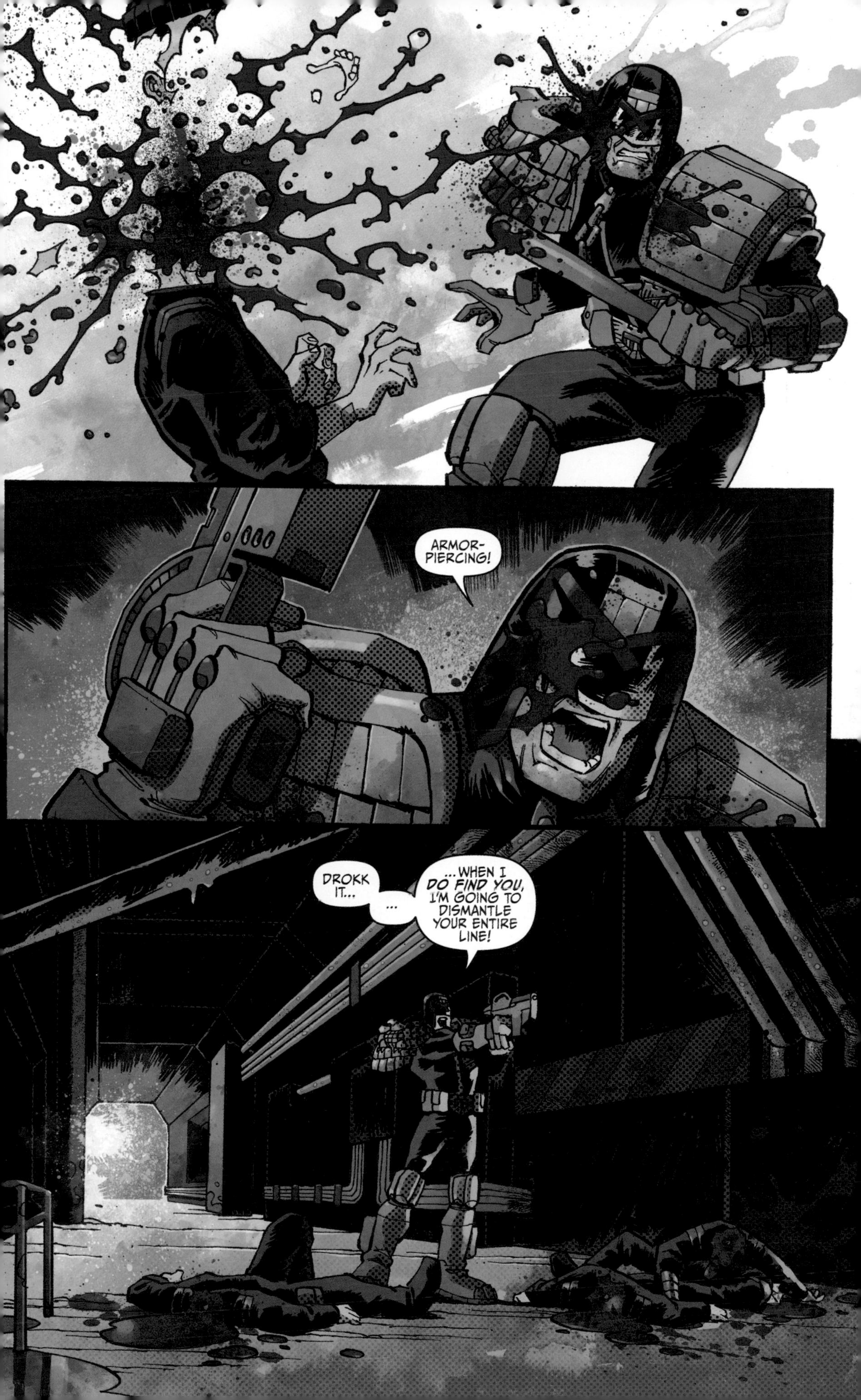
ARMOR-PIERCING!
DROKK IT...
...
...WHEN I DO FIND YOU, I'M GOING TO DISMANTLE YOUR ENTIRE LINE!

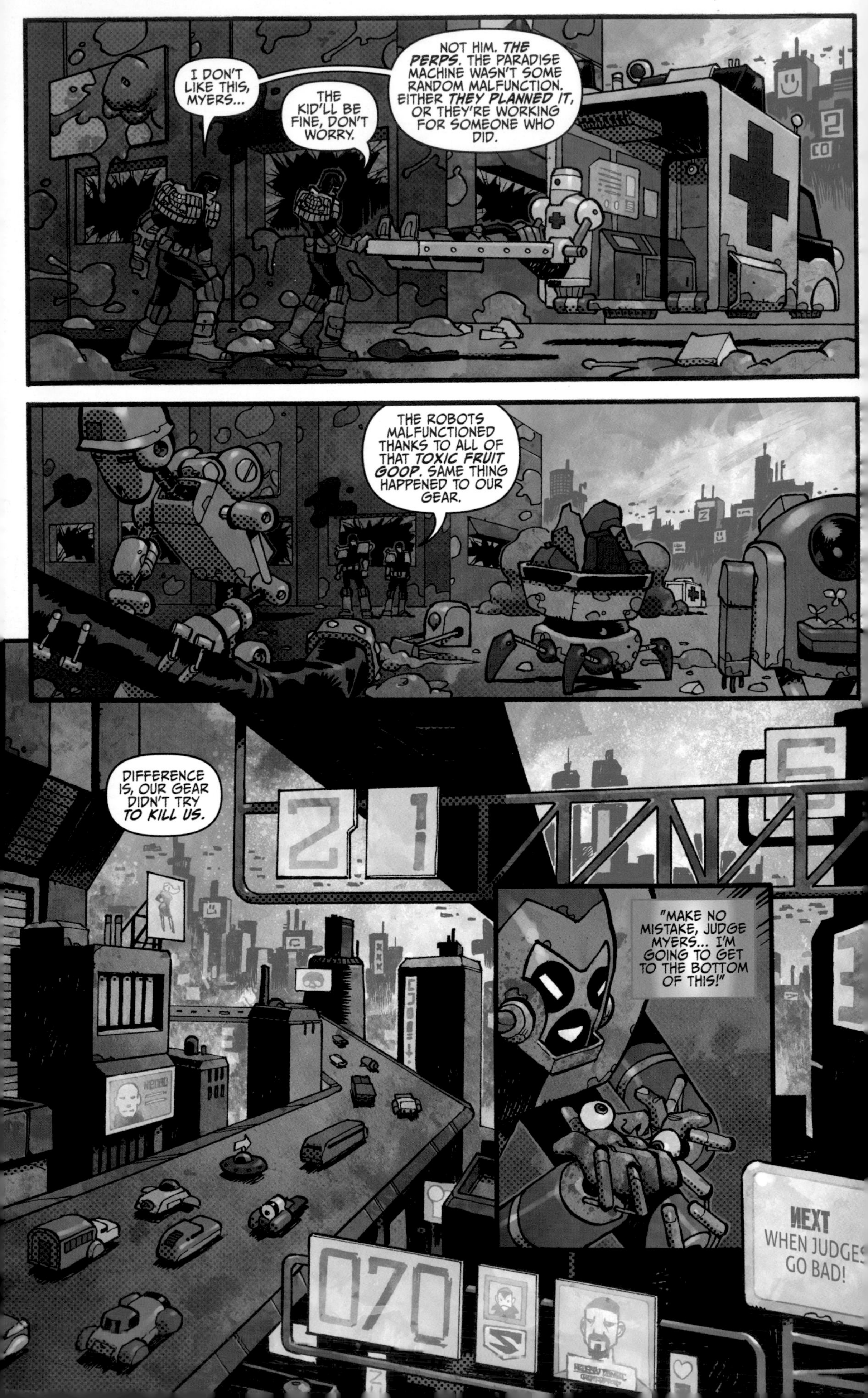
I DON'T LIKE THIS, MYERS...
THE KID'LL BE FINE, DON'T WORRY.
NOT HIM. THE PERPS. THE PARADISE MACHINE WASN'T SOME RANDOM MALFUNCTION. EITHER THEY PLANNED IT, OR THEY'RE WORKING FOR SOMEONE WHO DID.
THE ROBOTS MALFUNCTIONED THANKS TO ALL OF THAT TOXIC FRUIT GOOP. SAME THING HAPPENED TO OUR GEAR.
DIFFERENCE IS, OUR GEAR DIDN'T TRY TO KILL US.
"MAKE NO MISTAKE, JUDGE MYERS... I'M GOING TO GET TO THE BOTTOM OF THIS!"
NEXT WHEN JUDGES GO BAD!

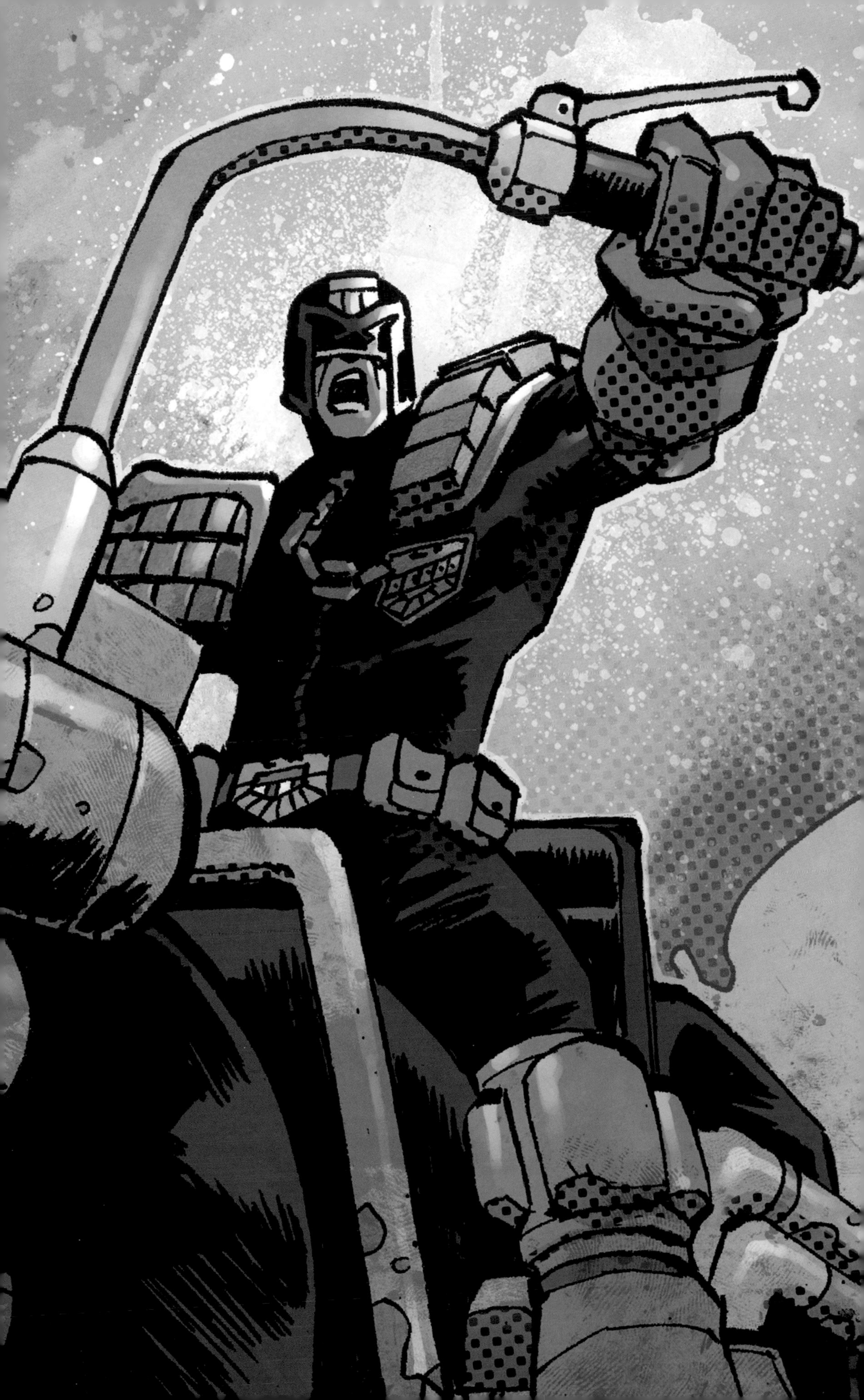

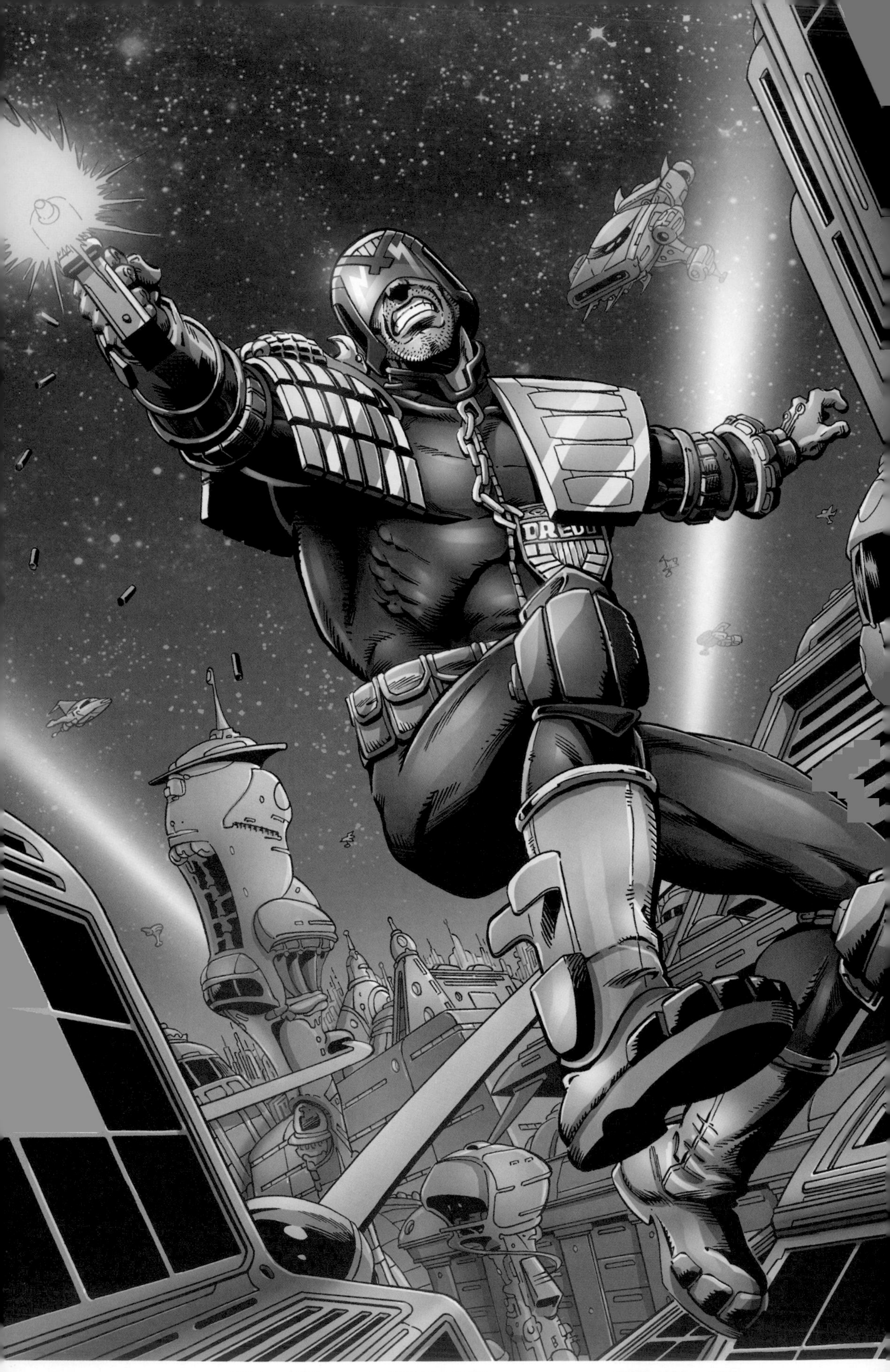

ART BY **JIM STARLIN** AND **ALLEN MILGROM** ★ COLORS BY **JEAN-PAUL BOVE**

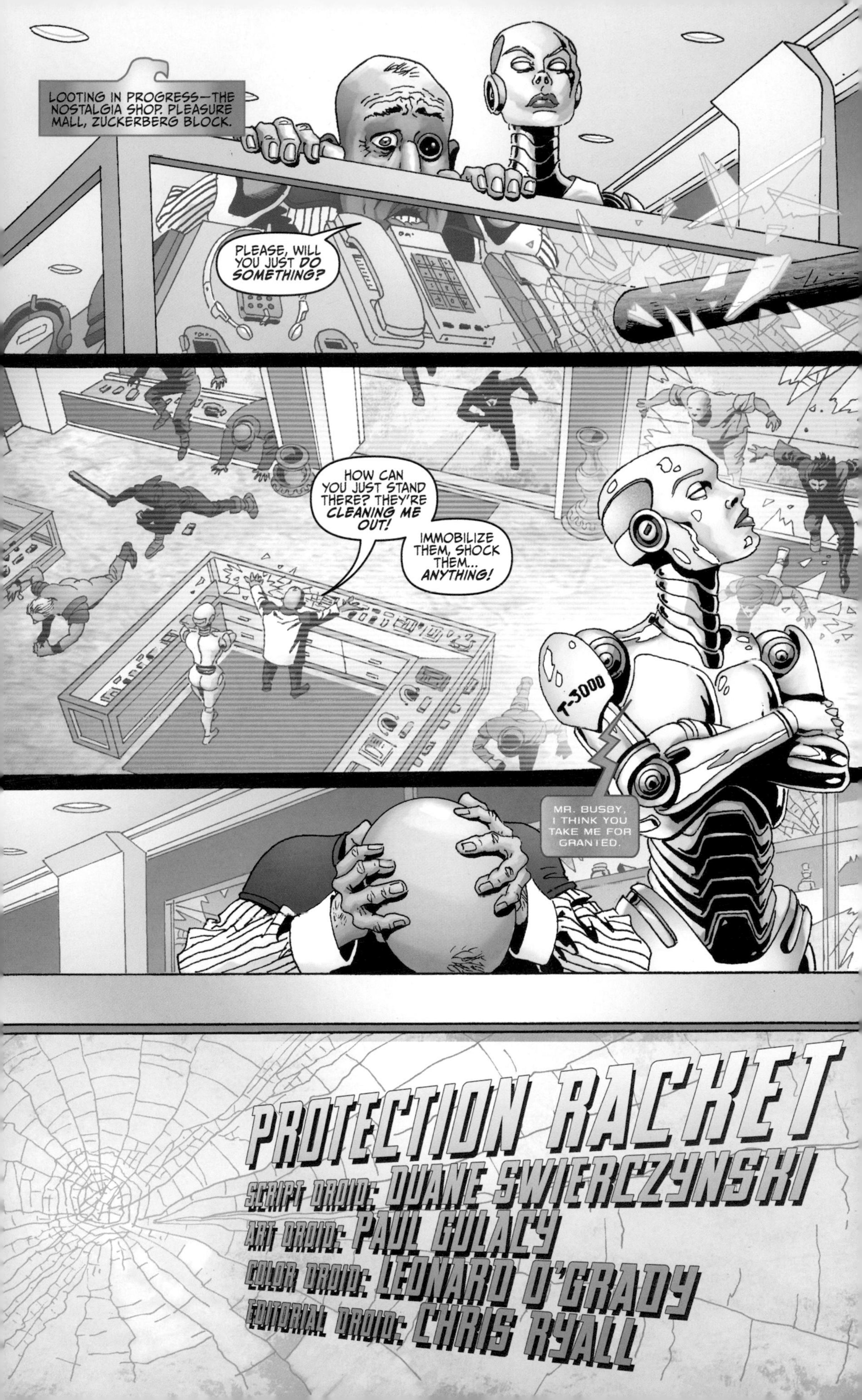

LOOTING IN PROGRESS—THE NOSTALGIA SHOP. PLEASURE MALL, ZUCKERBERG BLOCK.
PLEASE, WILL YOU JUST DO SOMETHING?
HOW CAN YOU JUST STAND THERE? THEY'RE CLEANING ME OUT!
IMMOBILIZE THEM, SHOCK THEM... ANYTHING!
T-3000
MR. BUSBY, I THINK YOU TAKE ME FOR GRANTED.
PROTECTION RACKET
SCRIPT DROID: DUANE SWIERCZYNSKI
ART DROID: PAUL GULACY
COLOR DROID: LEONARD O'GRADY
EDITORIAL DROID: CHRIS RYALL

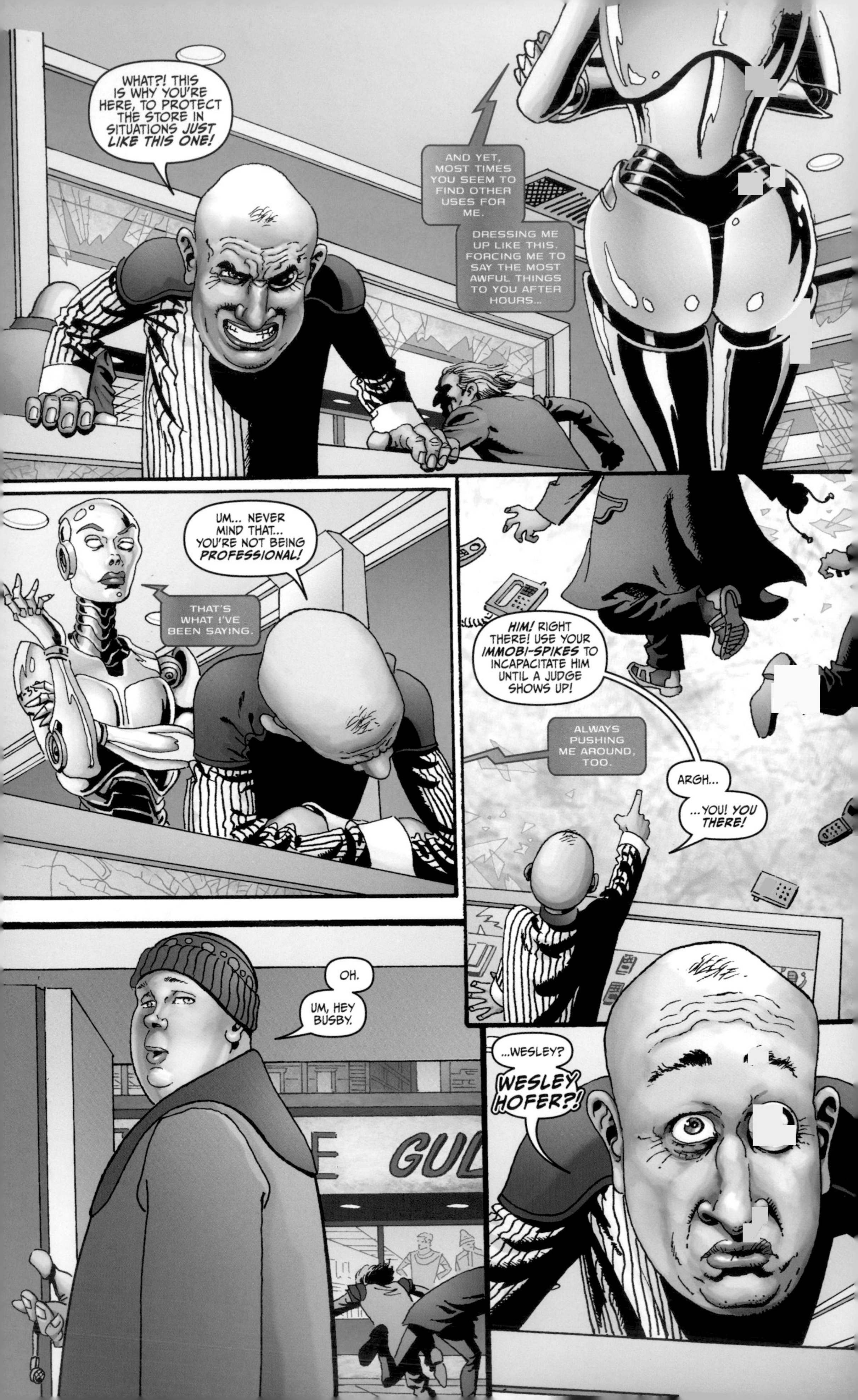
WHAT?! THIS IS WHY YOU'RE HERE, TO PROTECT THE STORE IN SITUATIONS JUST LIKE THIS ONE!
AND YET, MOST TIMES YOU SEEM TO FIND OTHER USES FOR ME.
DRESSING ME UP LIKE THIS. FORCING ME TO SAY THE MOST AWFUL THINGS TO YOU AFTER HOURS...
UM... NEVER MIND THAT... YOU'RE NOT BEING PROFESSIONAL!
THAT'S WHAT I'VE BEEN SAYING.
HIM! RIGHT THERE! USE YOUR IMMOBI-SPIKES TO INCAPACITATE HIM UNTIL A JUDGE SHOWS UP!
ALWAYS PUSHING ME AROUND, TOO.
ARGH...
...YOU! YOU THERE!
OH.
UM, HEY BUSBY.
...WESLEY?
WESLEY HOFER?!

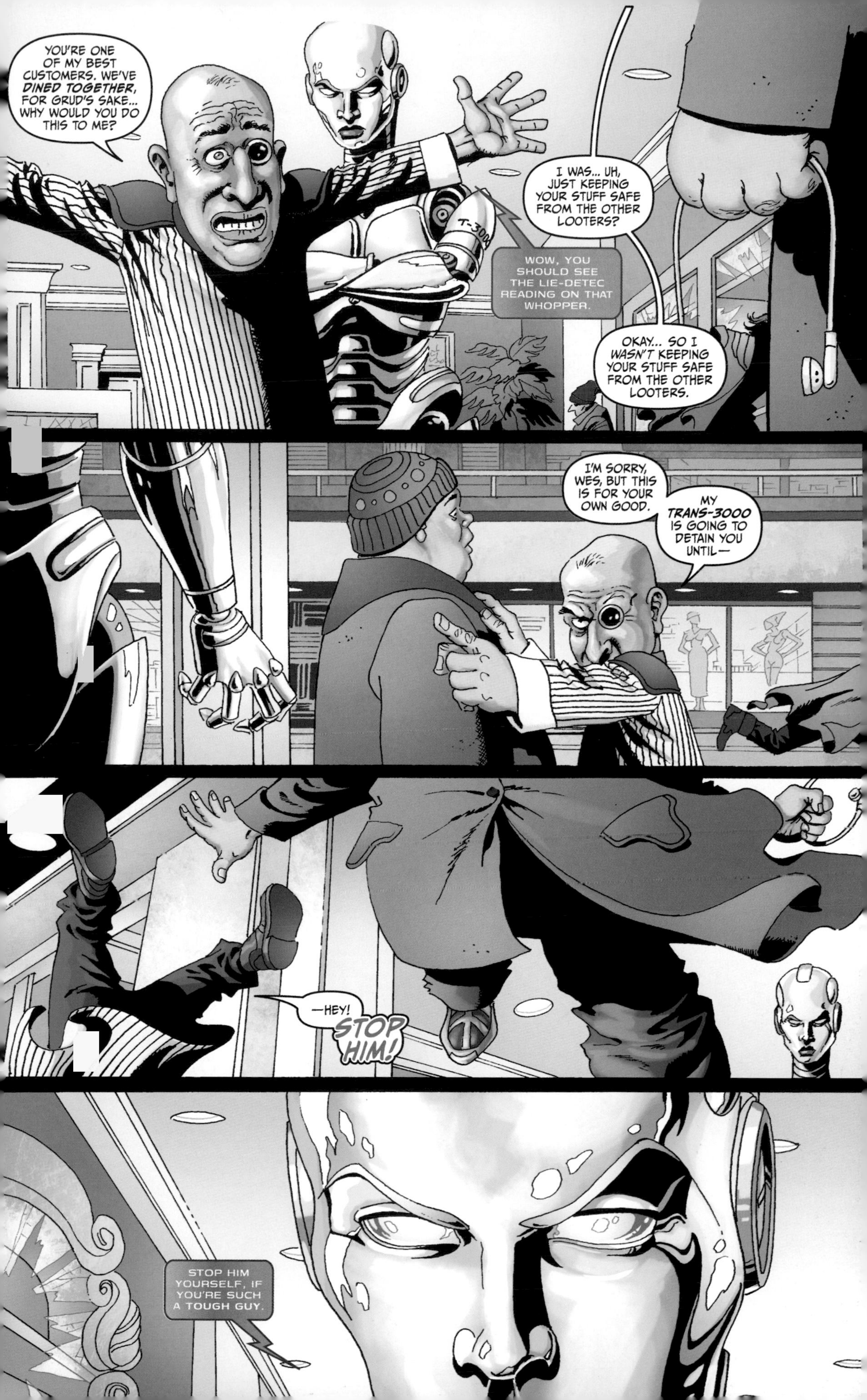
YOU'RE ONE OF MY BEST CUSTOMERS. WE'VE DINED TOGETHER, FOR GRUD'S SAKE... WHY WOULD YOU DO THIS TO ME?
I WAS... UH, JUST KEEPING YOUR STUFF SAFE FROM THE OTHER LOOTERS?
WOW, YOU SHOULD SEE THE LIE-DETEC READING ON THAT WHOPPER.
OKAY... SO I WASN'T KEEPING YOUR STUFF SAFE FROM THE OTHER LOOTERS.
I'M SORRY, WES, BUT THIS IS FOR YOUR OWN GOOD.
MY TRANS-3000 IS GOING TO DETAIN YOU UNTIL—
—HEY! STOP HIM!
STOP HIM YOURSELF, IF YOU'RE SUCH A TOUGH GUY.

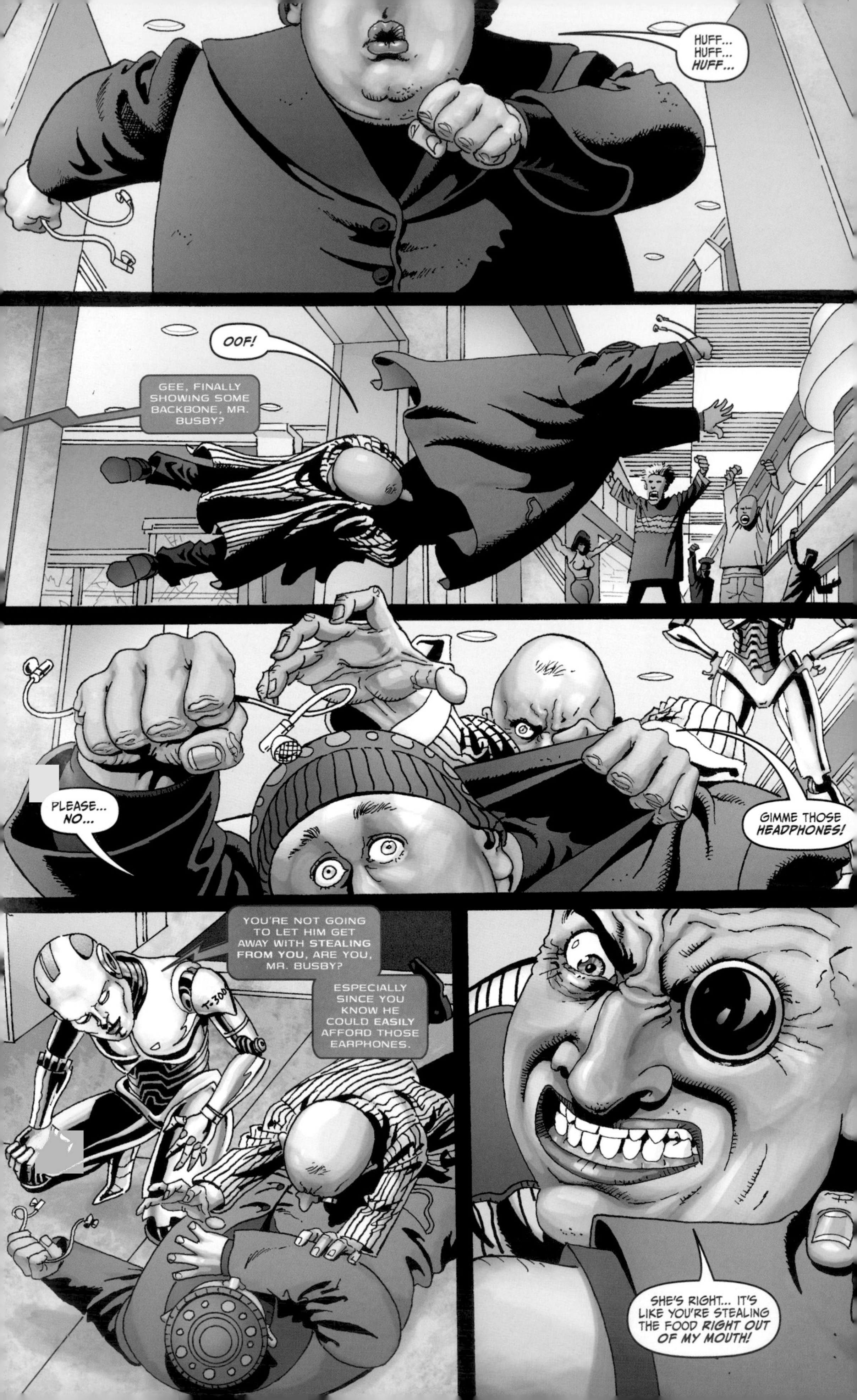
HUFF... HUFF... HUFF...
OOF!
GEE, FINALLY SHOWING SOME BACKBONE, MR. BUSBY?
PLEASE... NO...
GIMME THOSE HEADPHONES!
YOU'RE NOT GOING TO LET HIM GET AWAY WITH STEALING FROM YOU, ARE YOU, MR. BUSBY?
ESPECIALLY SINCE YOU KNOW HE COULD EASILY AFFORD THOSE EARPHONES.
SHE'S RIGHT... IT'S LIKE YOU'RE STEALING THE FOOD RIGHT OUT OF MY MOUTH!

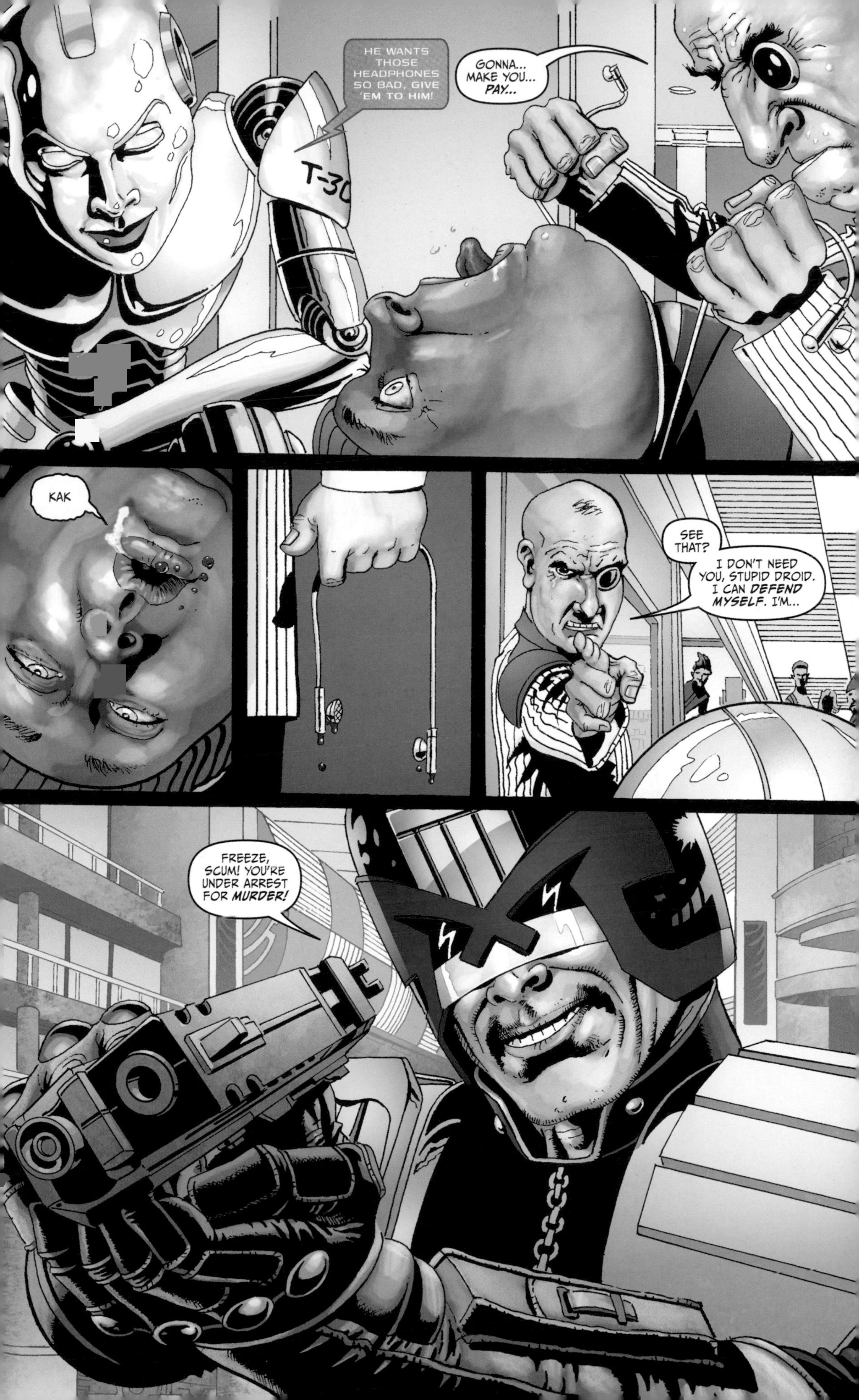

HE WANTS THOSE HEADPHONES SO BAD, GIVE 'EM TO HIM!
GONNA... MAKE YOU... PAY...
KAK
SEE THAT?
I DON'T NEED YOU, STUPID DROID. I CAN DEFEND MYSELF. I'M...
FREEZE, SCUM! YOU'RE UNDER ARREST FOR MURDER!
T-30

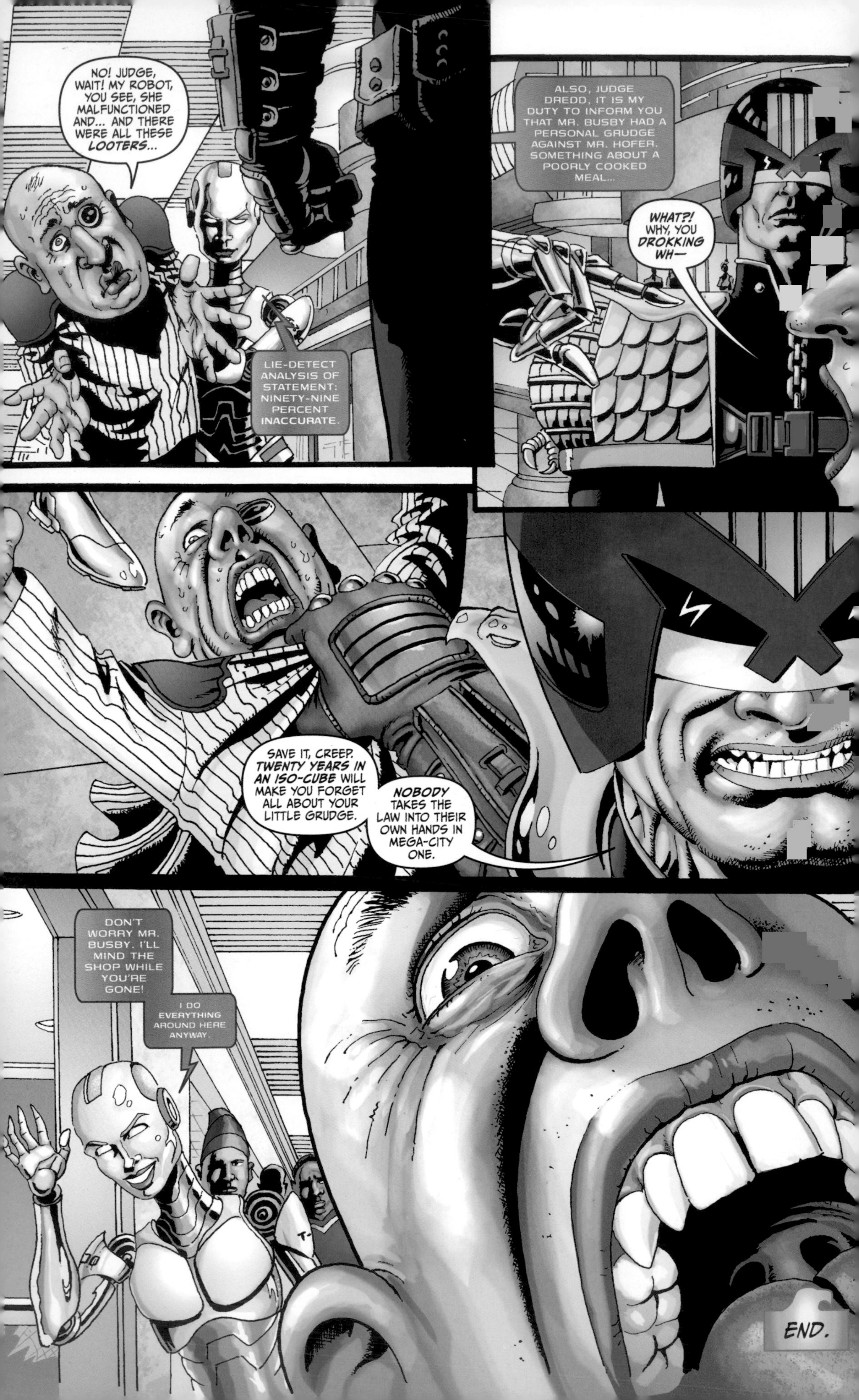
NO! JUDGE, WAIT! MY ROBOT, YOU SEE, SHE MALFUNCTIONED AND... AND THERE WERE ALL THESE LOOTERS...
LIE-DETECT ANALYSIS OF STATEMENT: NINETY-NINE PERCENT INACCURATE.
ALSO, JUDGE DREDD, IT IS MY DUTY TO INFORM YOU THAT MR. BUSBY HAD A PERSONAL GRUDGE AGAINST MR. HOFER. SOMETHING ABOUT A POORLY COOKED MEAL...
WHAT?! WHY, YOU DROKKING WH—
SAVE IT, CREEP. TWENTY YEARS IN AN ISO-CUBE WILL MAKE YOU FORGET ALL ABOUT YOUR LITTLE GRUDGE.
NOBODY TAKES THE LAW INTO THEIR OWN HANDS IN MEGA-CITY ONE.
DON'T WORRY MR. BUSBY. I'LL MIND THE SHOP WHILE YOU'RE GONE!
I DO EVERYTHING AROUND HERE ANYWAY.
END.

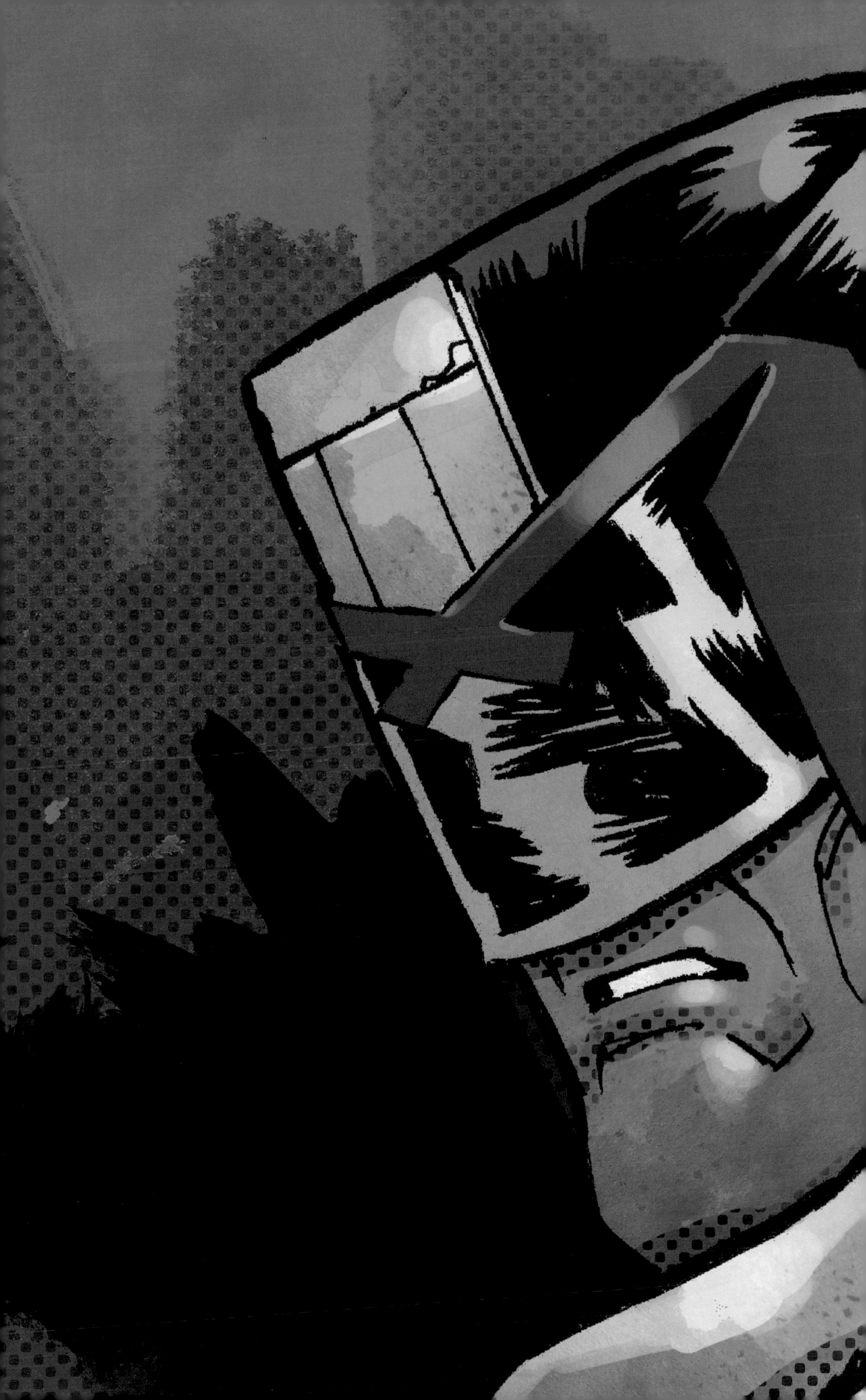

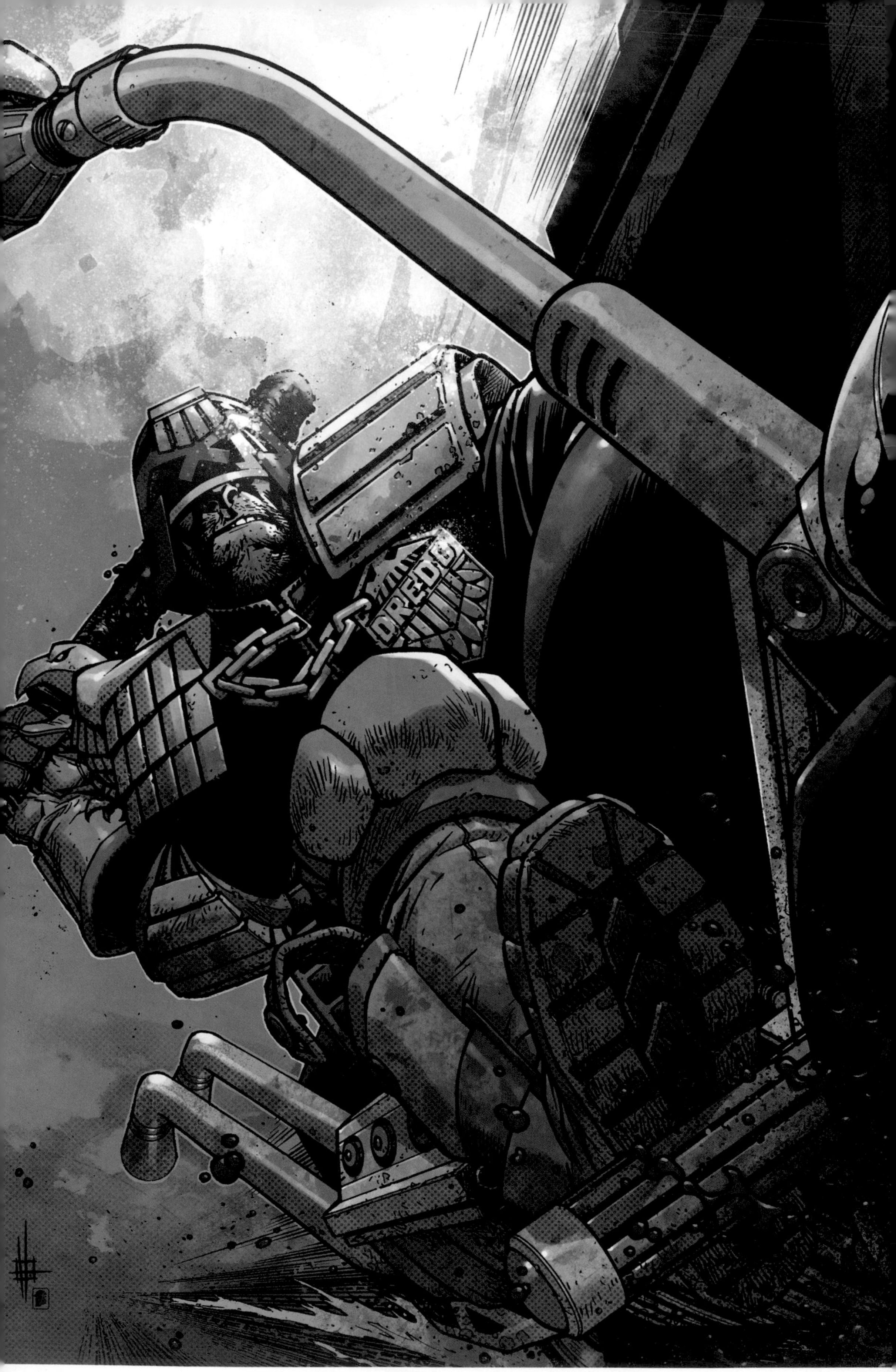
DREDD

ART BY ZACH HOWARD ★ COLORS BY NELSON DANIEL

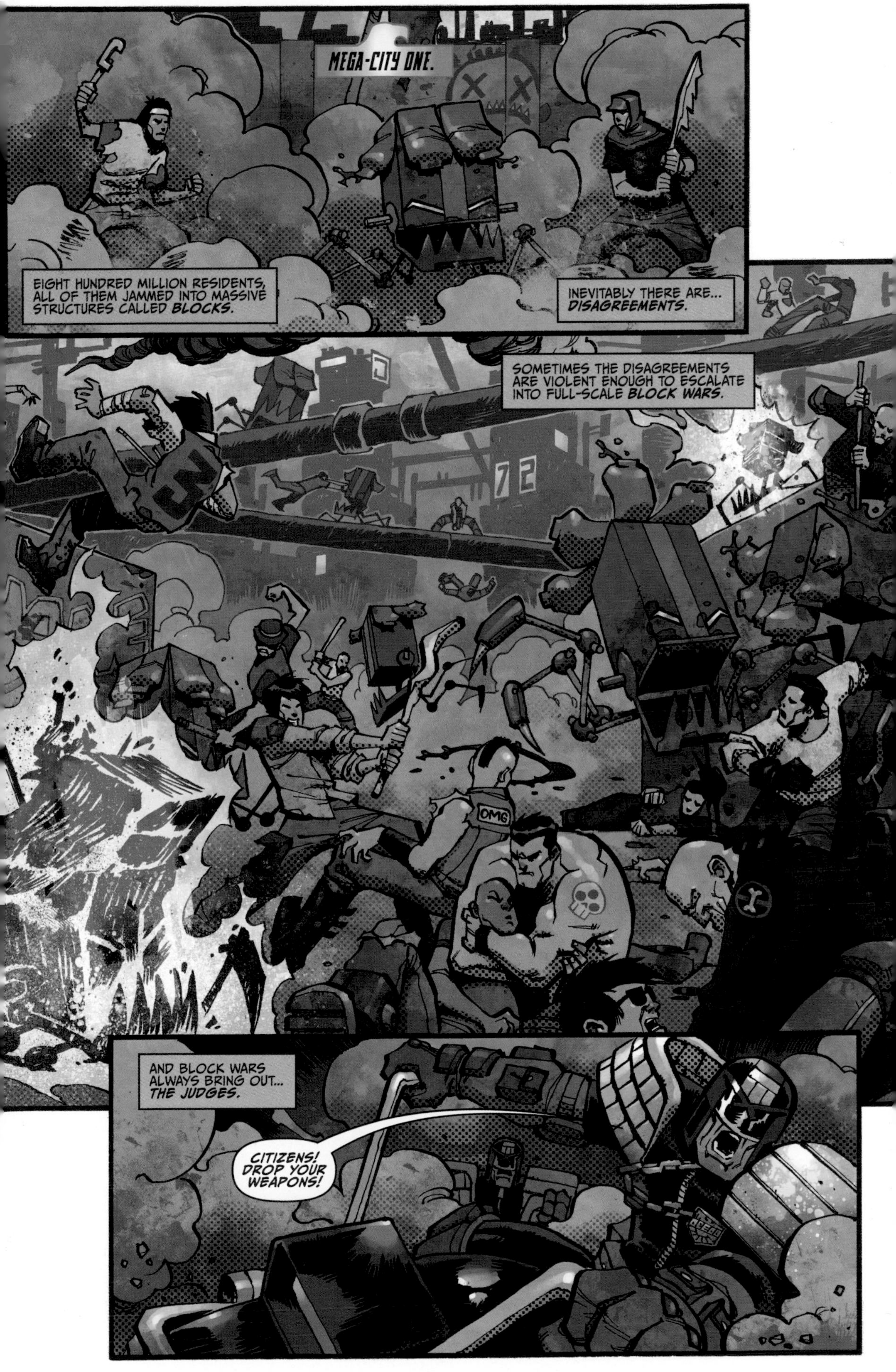
MEGA-CITY ONE.
EIGHT HUNDRED MILLION RESIDENTS, ALL OF THEM JAMMED INTO MASSIVE STRUCTURES CALLED BLOCKS.
INEVITABLY THERE ARE... DISAGREEMENTS.
SOMETIMES THE DISAGREEMENTS ARE VIOLENT ENOUGH TO ESCALATE INTO FULL-SCALE BLOCK WARS.
AND BLOCK WARS ALWAYS BRING OUT... THE JUDGES.
CITIZENS! DROP YOUR WEAPONS!

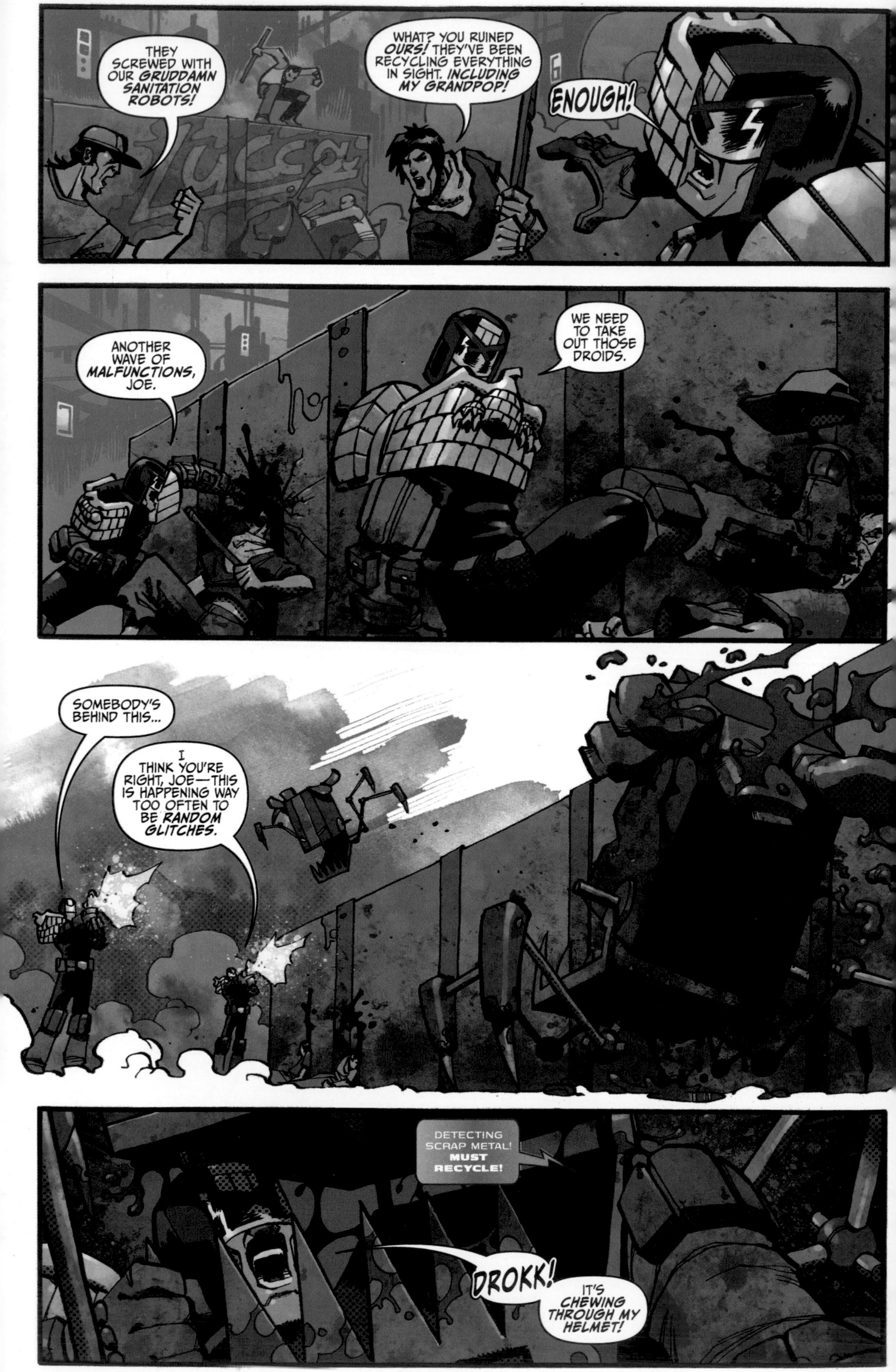
THEY SCREWED WITH OUR GRUDDAMN SANITATION ROBOTS!
WHAT? YOU RUINED OURS! THEY'VE BEEN RECYCLING EVERYTHING IN SIGHT. INCLUDING MY GRANDPOP!
ENOUGH!
ANOTHER WAVE OF MALFUNCTIONS, JOE.
WE NEED TO TAKE OUT THOSE DROIDS.
SOMEBODY'S BEHIND THIS...
I THINK YOU'RE RIGHT, JOE—THIS IS HAPPENING WAY TOO OFTEN TO BE RANDOM GLITCHES.
DETECTING SCRAP METAL! MUST RECYCLE!
DROKK!
IT'S CHEWING THROUGH MY HELMET!

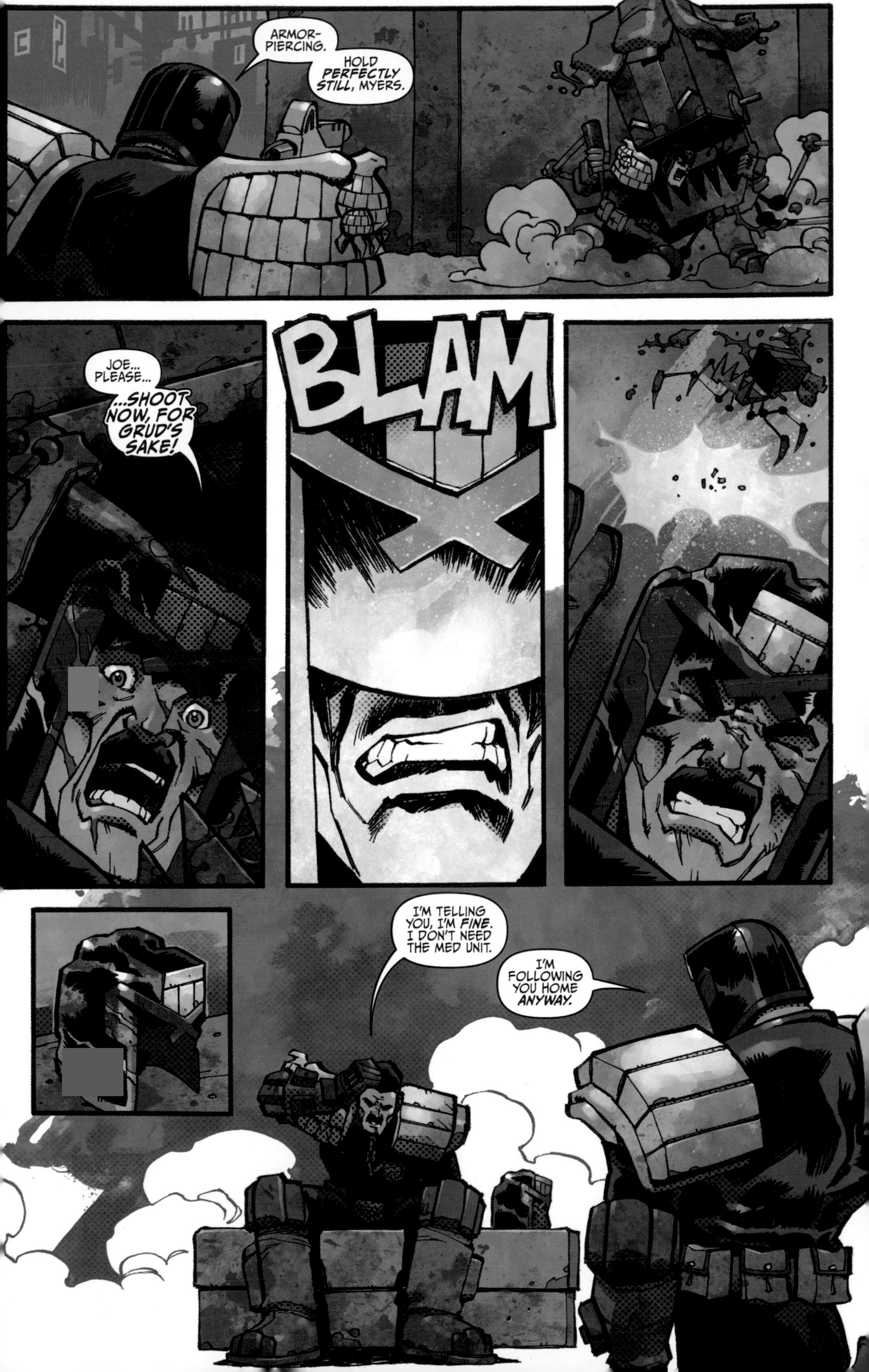
ARMOR-PIERCING.
HOLD PERFECTLY STILL, MYERS.
JOE... PLEASE...
...SHOOT NOW, FOR GRUD'S SAKE!
BLAM
I'M TELLING YOU, I'M FINE. I DON'T NEED THE MED UNIT.
I'M FOLLOWING YOU HOME ANYWAY.

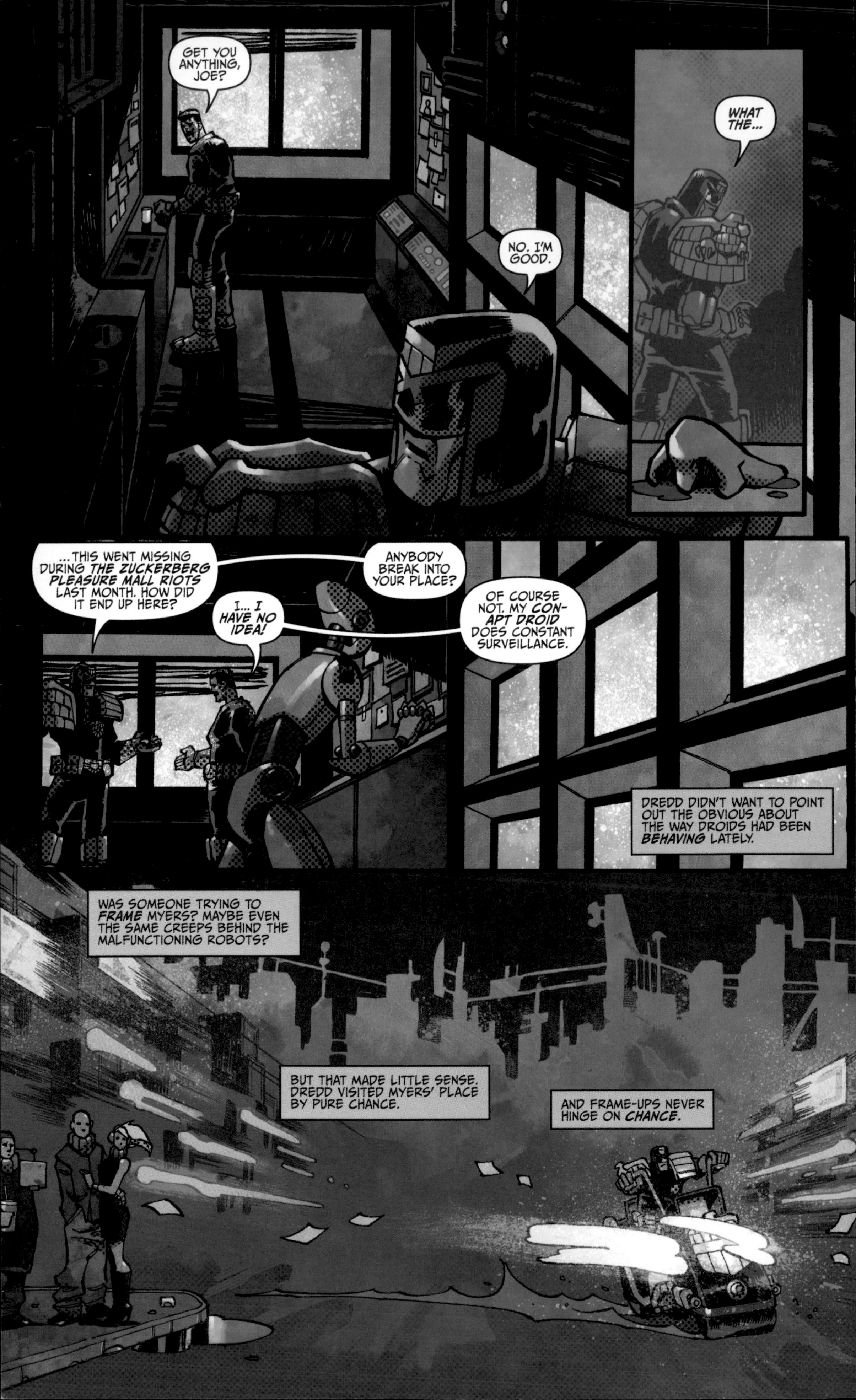
GET YOU ANYTHING, JOE?
NO. I'M GOOD.
WHAT THE...
...THIS WENT MISSING DURING THE ZUCKERBERG PLEASURE MALL RIOTS LAST MONTH. HOW DID IT END UP HERE?
I... I HAVE NO IDEA!
ANYBODY BREAK INTO YOUR PLACE?
OF COURSE NOT. MY CON-APT DROID DOES CONSTANT SURVEILLANCE.
DREDD DIDN'T WANT TO POINT OUT THE OBVIOUS ABOUT THE WAY DROIDS HAD BEEN BEHAVING LATELY.
WAS SOMEONE TRYING TO FRAME MYERS? MAYBE EVEN THE SAME CREEPS BEHIND THE MALFUNCTIONING ROBOTS?
BUT THAT MADE LITTLE SENSE. DREDD VISITED MYERS' PLACE BY PURE CHANCE.
AND FRAME-UPS NEVER HINGE ON CHANCE.

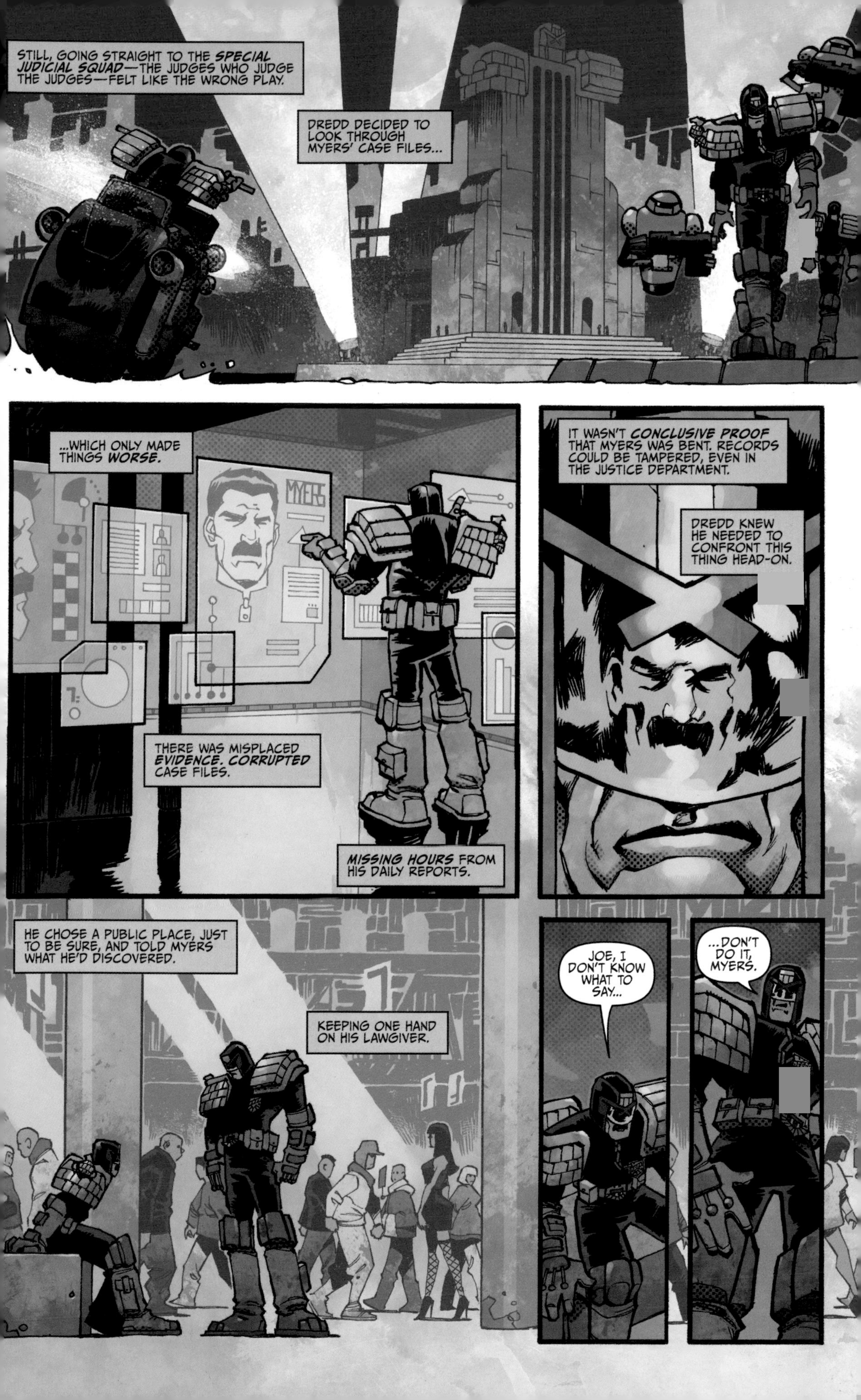
STILL, GOING STRAIGHT TO THE SPECIAL JUDICIAL SQUAD—THE JUDGES WHO JUDGE THE JUDGES—FELT LIKE THE WRONG PLAY.
DREDD DECIDED TO LOOK THROUGH MYERS' CASE FILES...
...WHICH ONLY MADE THINGS WORSE.
MYERS
THERE WAS MISPLACED EVIDENCE. CORRUPTED CASE FILES.
MISSING HOURS FROM HIS DAILY REPORTS.
IT WASN'T CONCLUSIVE PROOF THAT MYERS WAS BENT. RECORDS COULD BE TAMPERED, EVEN IN THE JUSTICE DEPARTMENT.
DREDD KNEW HE NEEDED TO CONFRONT THIS THING HEAD-ON.
HE CHOSE A PUBLIC PLACE, JUST TO BE SURE, AND TOLD MYERS WHAT HE'D DISCOVERED.
KEEPING ONE HAND ON HIS LAWGIVER.
JOE, I DON'T KNOW WHAT TO SAY...
...DON'T DO IT, MYERS.

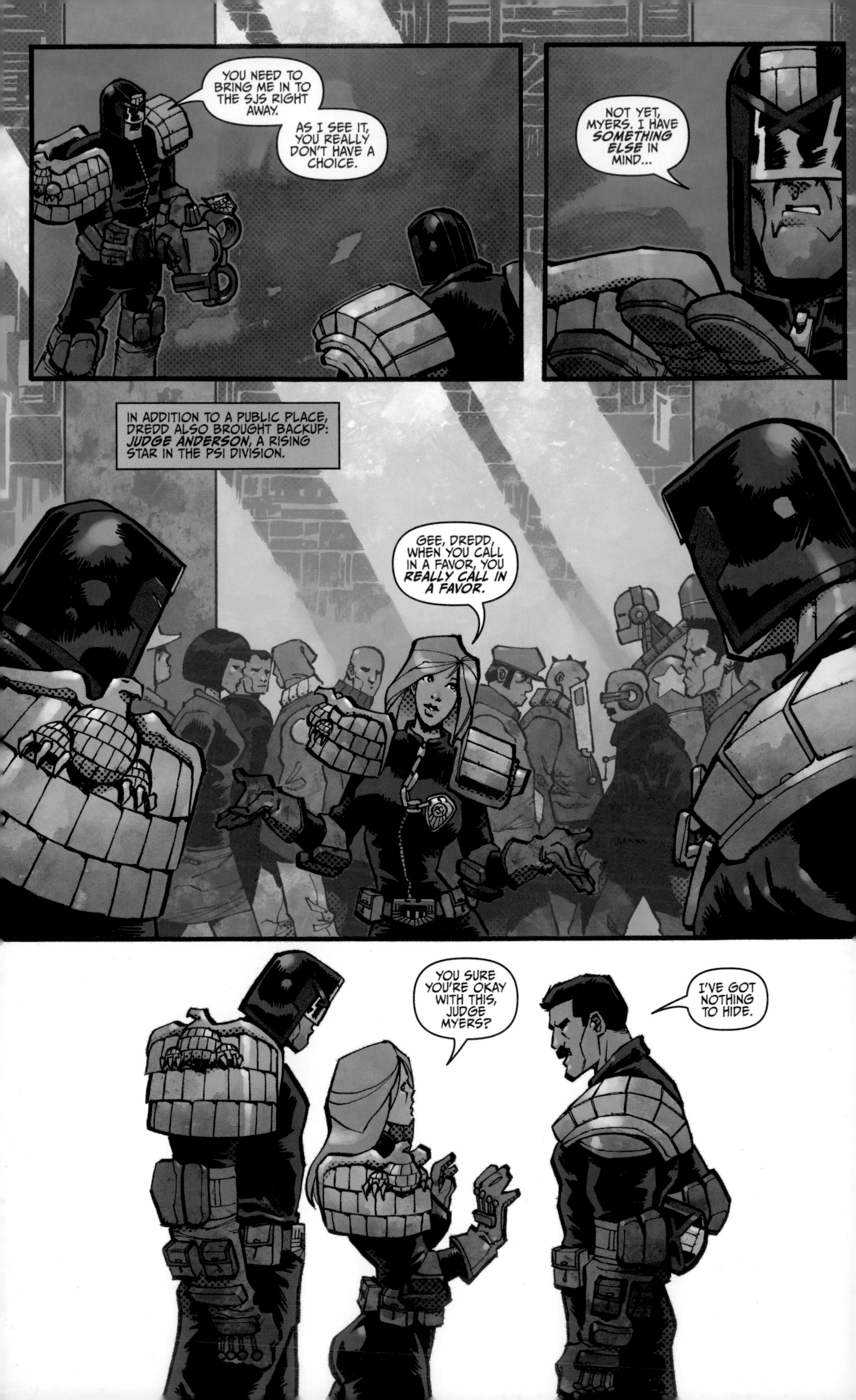
YOU NEED TO BRING ME IN TO THE SJS RIGHT AWAY.
AS I SEE IT, YOU REALLY DON'T HAVE A CHOICE.
NOT YET, MYERS. I HAVE *SOMETHING ELSE* IN MIND...
IN ADDITION TO A PUBLIC PLACE, DREDD ALSO BROUGHT BACKUP: *JUDGE ANDERSON*, A RISING STAR IN THE PSI DIVISION.
GEE, DREDD, WHEN YOU CALL IN A FAVOR, YOU *REALLY CALL IN A FAVOR.*
YOU SURE YOU'RE OKAY WITH THIS, JUDGE MYERS?
I'VE GOT NOTHING TO HIDE.

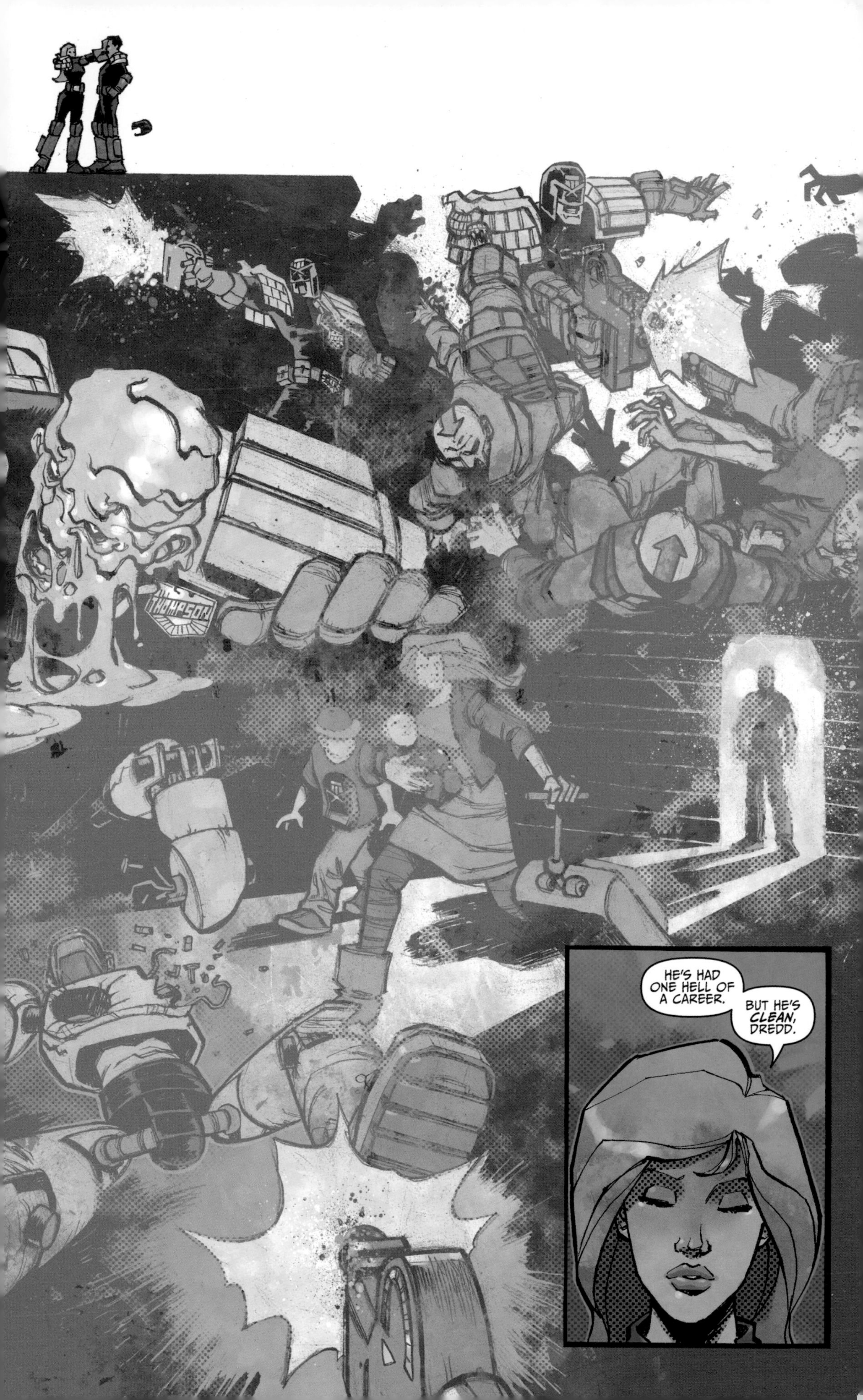
THOMPSON
HE'S HAD ONE HELL OF A CAREER.
BUT HE'S CLEAN, DREDD.

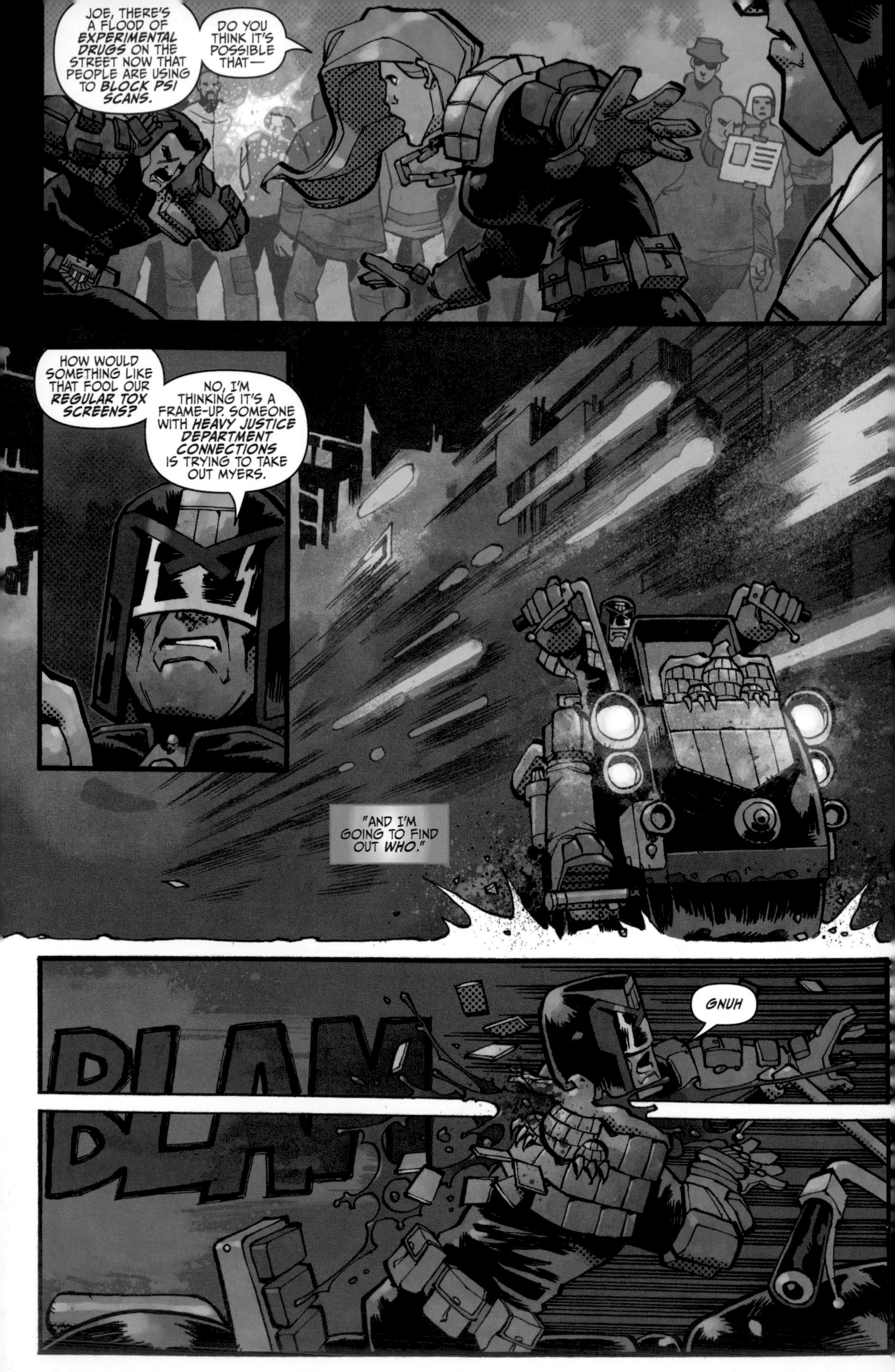

JOE, THERE'S A FLOOD OF EXPERIMENTAL DRUGS ON THE STREET NOW THAT PEOPLE ARE USING TO BLOCK PSI SCANS.
DO YOU THINK IT'S POSSIBLE THAT—
HOW WOULD SOMETHING LIKE THAT FOOL OUR REGULAR TOX SCREENS?
NO, I'M THINKING IT'S A FRAME-UP. SOMEONE WITH HEAVY JUSTICE DEPARTMENT CONNECTIONS IS TRYING TO TAKE OUT MYERS.
"AND I'M GOING TO FIND OUT WHO."
BLAM
BLAM
GNUH

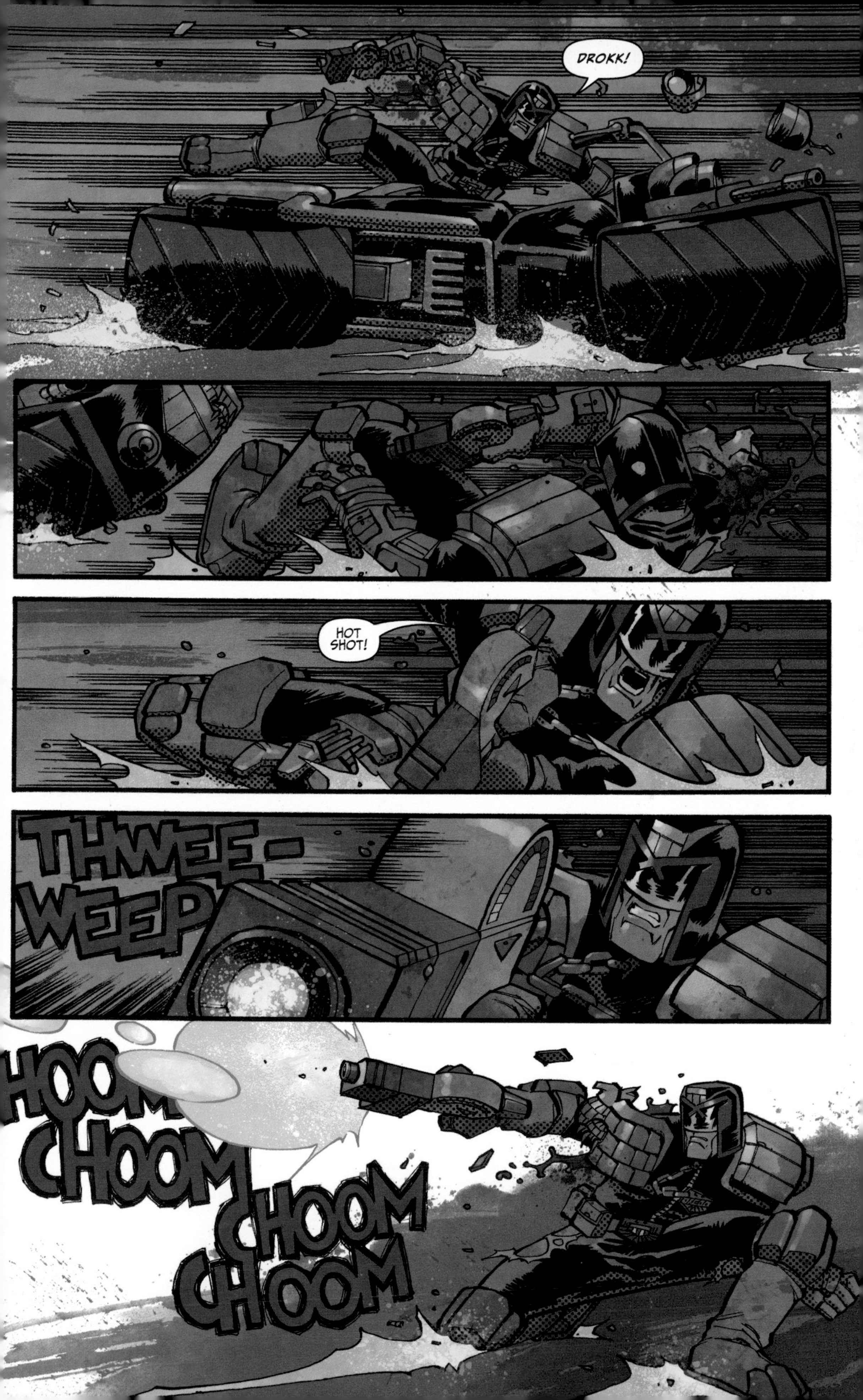
DROKK!
HOT SHOT!
THWEE-WEEP
HOOM
CHOOM
CHOOM
CHOOM

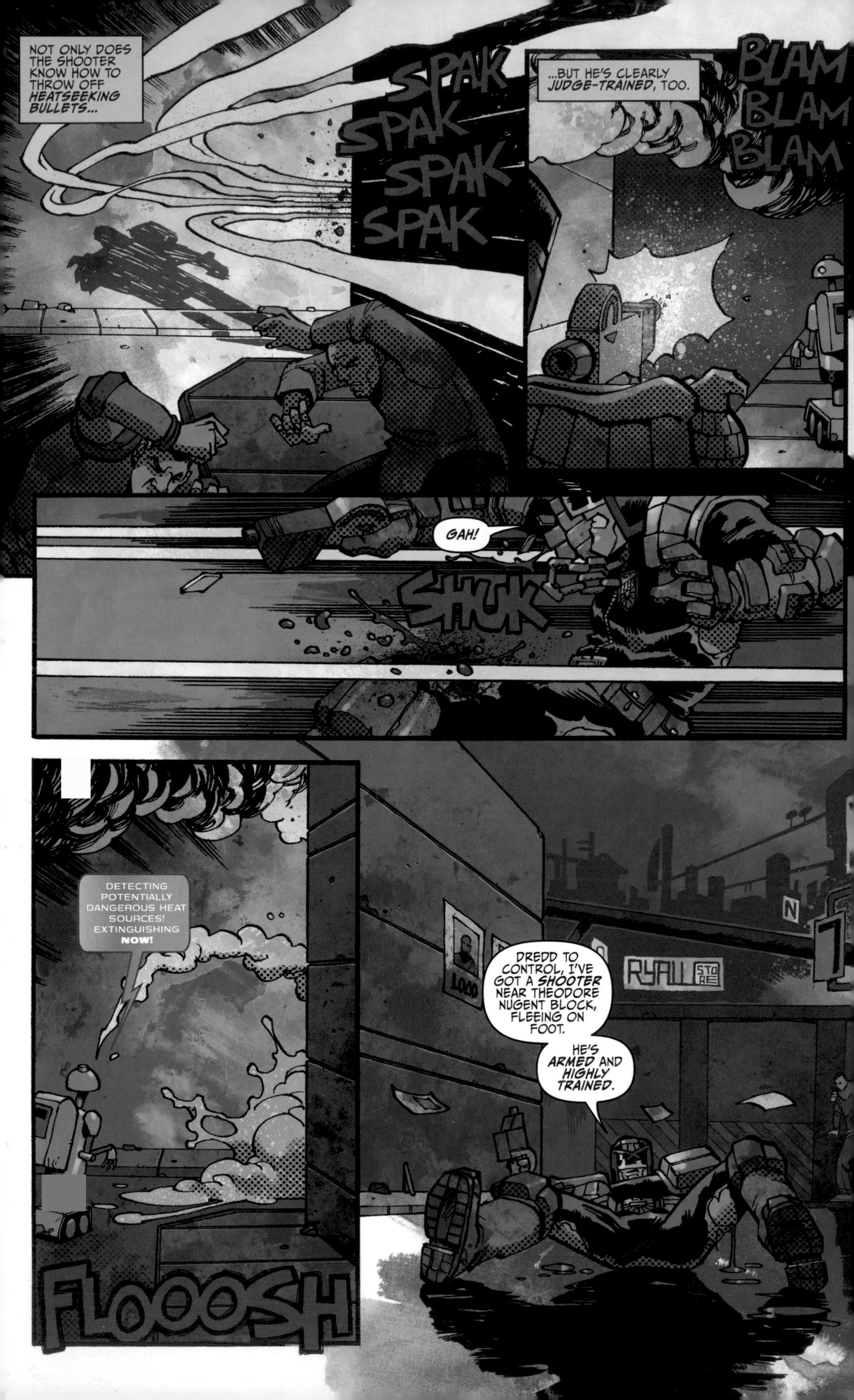

NOT ONLY DOES THE SHOOTER KNOW HOW TO THROW OFF HEATSEEKING BULLETS...
SPAK SPAK SPAK SPAK
...BUT HE'S CLEARLY JUDGE-TRAINED, TOO.
BLAM BLAM BLAM
GAH!
SHUK
DETECTING POTENTIALLY DANGEROUS HEAT SOURCES! EXTINGUISHING NOW!
FLOOOSH
DREDD TO CONTROL, I'VE GOT A SHOOTER NEAR THEODORE NUGENT BLOCK, FLEEING ON FOOT.
HE'S ARMED AND HIGHLY TRAINED.
RYALL STORE

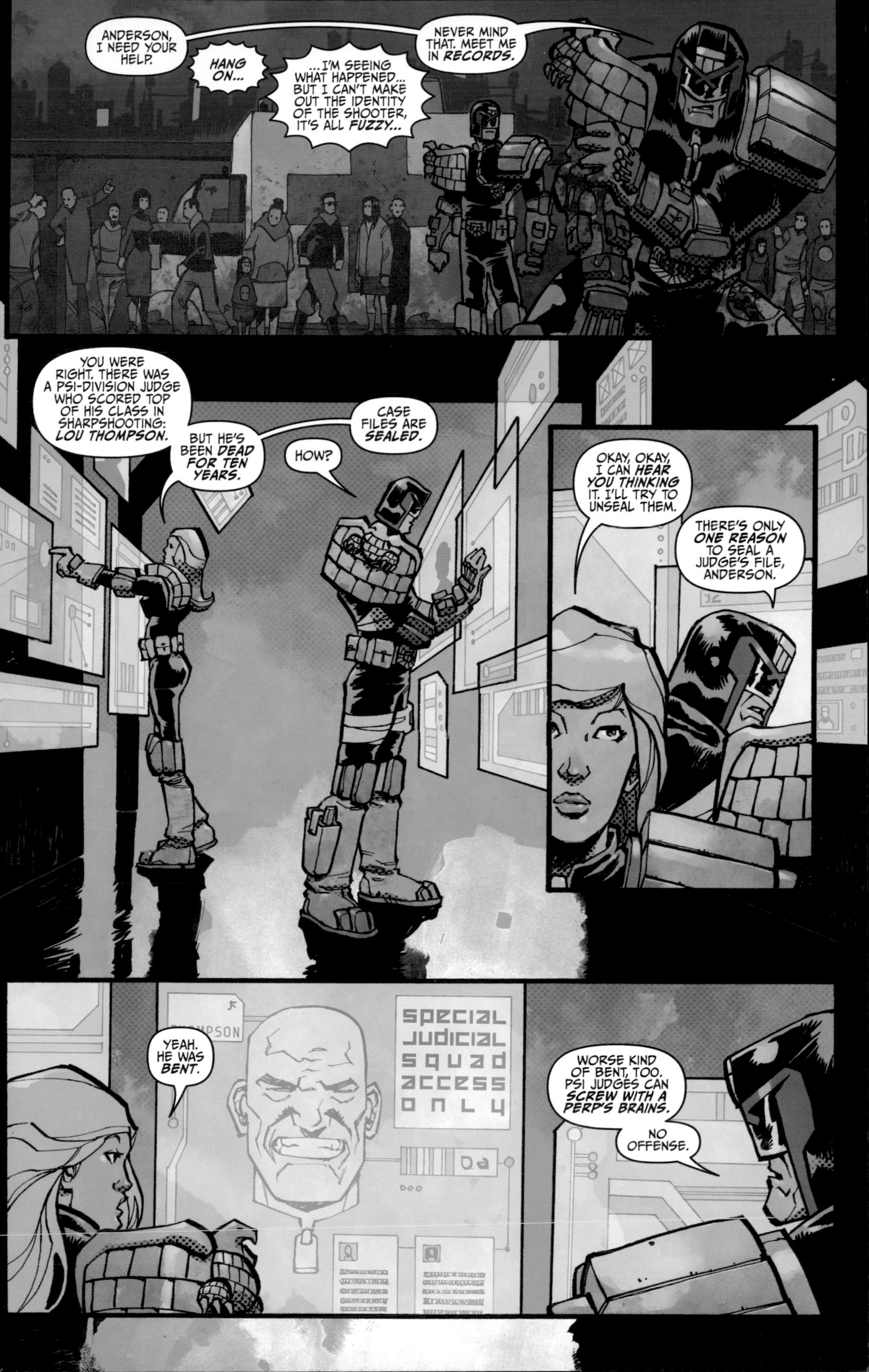
ANDERSON, I NEED YOUR HELP.
HANG ON...
...I'M SEEING WHAT HAPPENED... BUT I CAN'T MAKE OUT THE IDENTITY OF THE SHOOTER, IT'S ALL FUZZY...
NEVER MIND THAT. MEET ME IN RECORDS.
YOU WERE RIGHT. THERE WAS A PSI-DIVISION JUDGE WHO SCORED TOP OF HIS CLASS IN SHARPSHOOTING: LOU THOMPSON.
BUT HE'S BEEN DEAD FOR TEN YEARS.
HOW?
CASE FILES ARE SEALED.
OKAY, OKAY, I CAN HEAR YOU THINKING IT. I'LL TRY TO UNSEAL THEM.
THERE'S ONLY ONE REASON TO SEAL A JUDGE'S FILE, ANDERSON.
MPSON
special judicial squad access only
YEAH. HE WAS BENT.
WORSE KIND OF BENT, TOO. PSI JUDGES CAN SCREW WITH A PERP'S BRAINS.
NO OFFENSE.

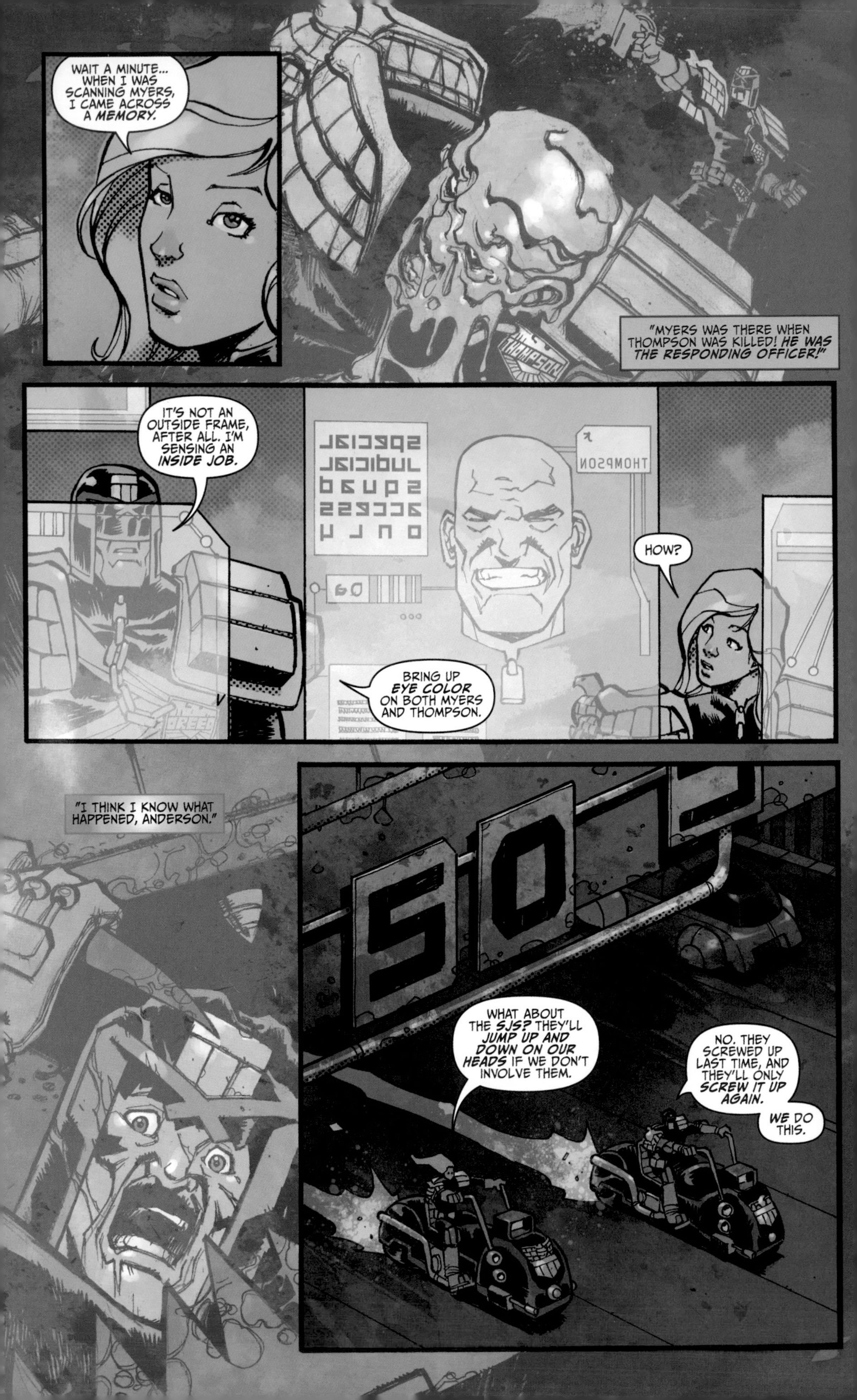
WAIT A MINUTE... WHEN I WAS SCANNING MYERS, I CAME ACROSS A MEMORY.
"MYERS WAS THERE WHEN THOMPSON WAS KILLED! HE WAS THE RESPONDING OFFICER!"
IT'S NOT AN OUTSIDE FRAME, AFTER ALL. I'M SENSING AN INSIDE JOB.
HOW?
BRING UP EYE COLOR ON BOTH MYERS AND THOMPSON.
"I THINK I KNOW WHAT HAPPENED, ANDERSON."
WHAT ABOUT THE SJS? THEY'LL JUMP UP AND DOWN ON OUR HEADS IF WE DON'T INVOLVE THEM.
NO. THEY SCREWED UP LAST TIME, AND THEY'LL ONLY SCREW IT UP AGAIN.
WE DO THIS.

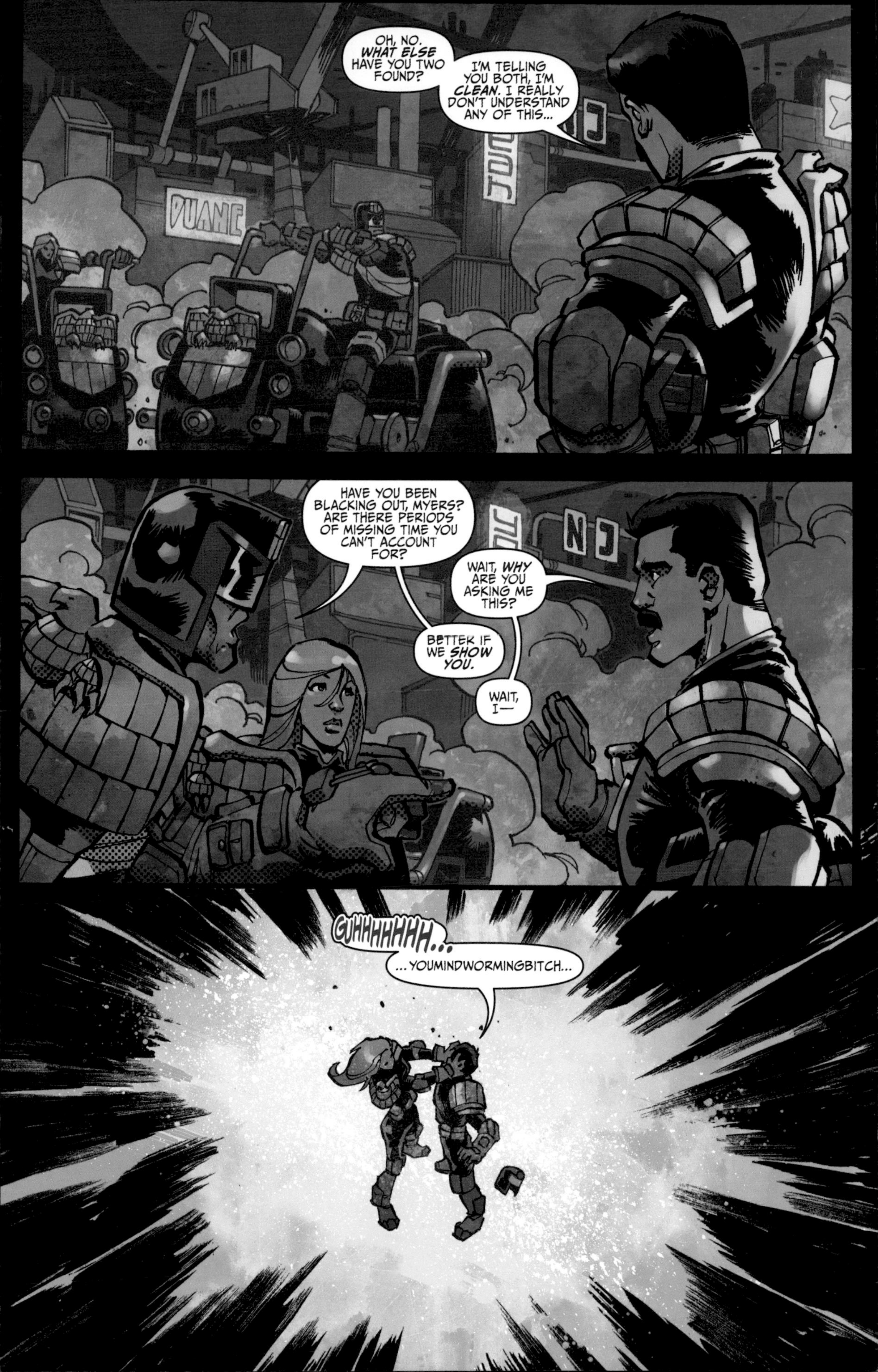
OH, NO. WHAT ELSE HAVE YOU TWO FOUND?
I'M TELLING YOU BOTH, I'M CLEAN. I REALLY DON'T UNDERSTAND ANY OF THIS...
DUANE
NJ
HAVE YOU BEEN BLACKING OUT, MYERS? ARE THERE PERIODS OF MISSING TIME YOU CAN'T ACCOUNT FOR?
BETTER IF WE SHOW YOU.
WAIT, WHY ARE YOU ASKING ME THIS?
WAIT, I—
GUHHHHHHH...
...YOUMINDWORMINGBITCH...

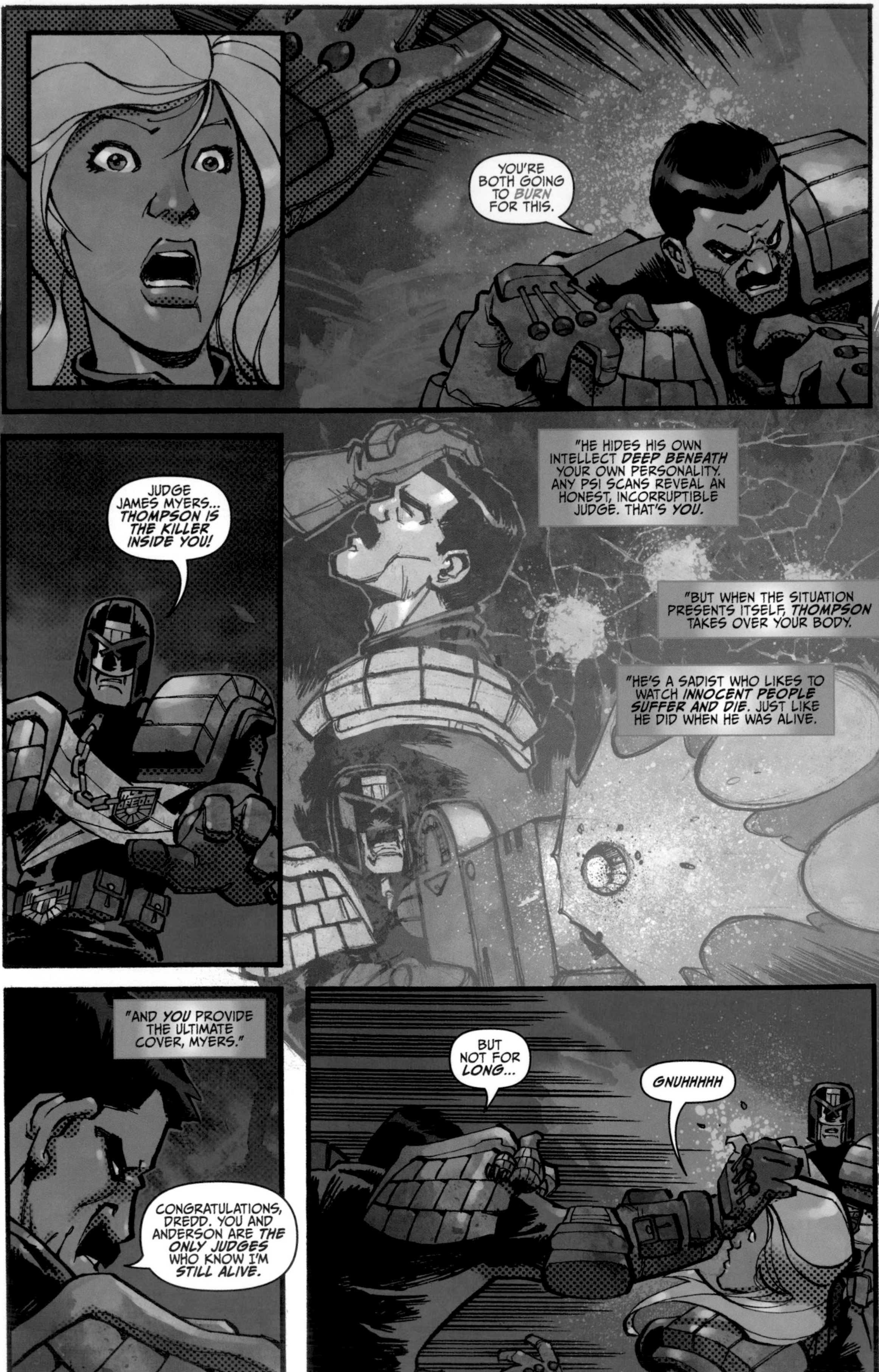
YOU'RE BOTH GOING TO BURN FOR THIS.
JUDGE JAMES MYERS... THOMPSON IS THE KILLER INSIDE YOU!
"HE HIDES HIS OWN INTELLECT DEEP BENEATH YOUR OWN PERSONALITY. ANY PSI SCANS REVEAL AN HONEST, INCORRUPTIBLE JUDGE. THAT'S YOU.
"BUT WHEN THE SITUATION PRESENTS ITSELF, THOMPSON TAKES OVER YOUR BODY.
"HE'S A SADIST WHO LIKES TO WATCH INNOCENT PEOPLE SUFFER AND DIE. JUST LIKE HE DID WHEN HE WAS ALIVE.
"AND YOU PROVIDE THE ULTIMATE COVER, MYERS."
CONGRATULATIONS, DREDD. YOU AND ANDERSON ARE THE ONLY JUDGES WHO KNOW I'M STILL ALIVE.
BUT NOT FOR LONG...
GNUHHHHH

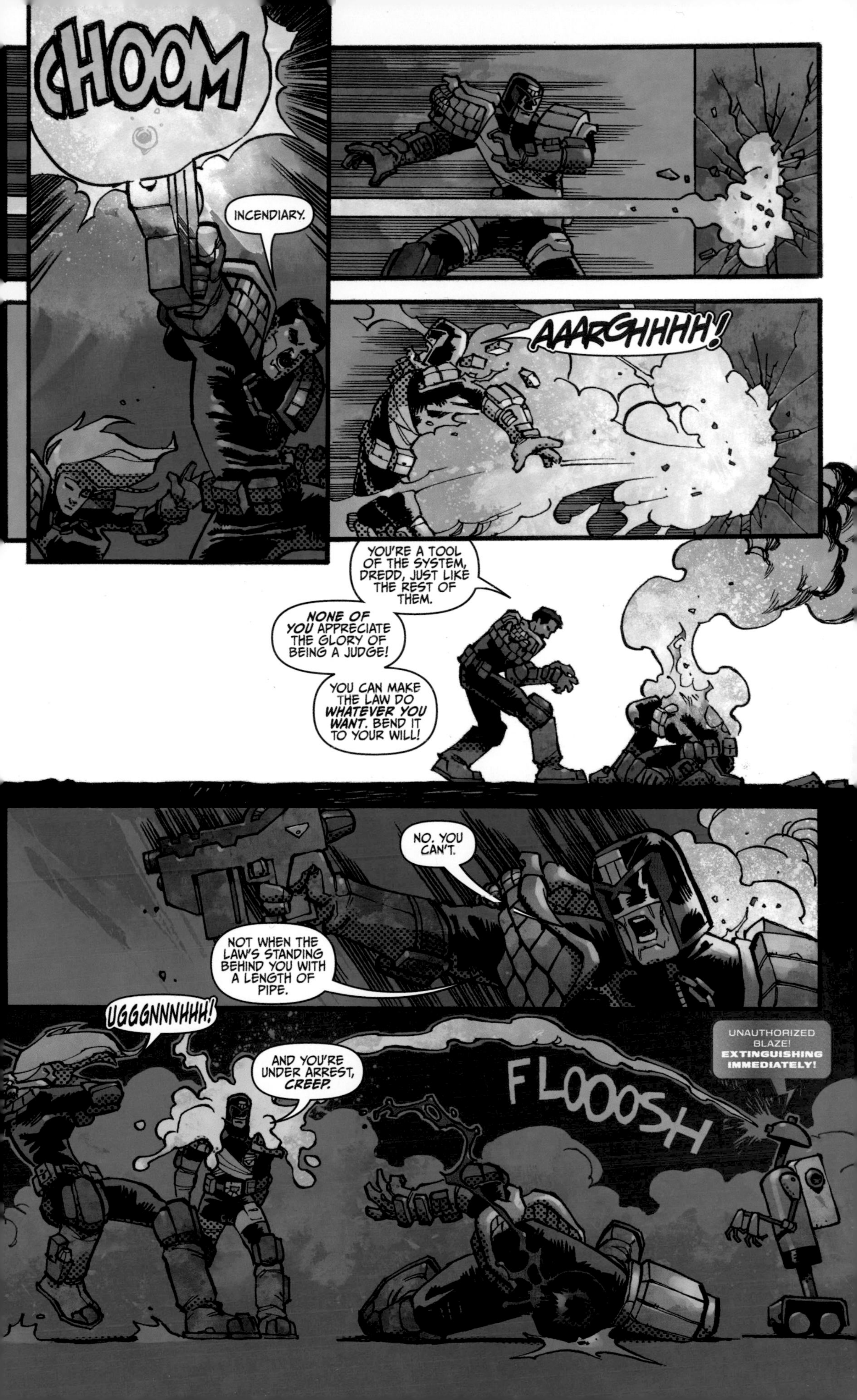
CHOOM
INCENDIARY.
AAARGHHHH!
YOU'RE A TOOL OF THE SYSTEM, DREDD, JUST LIKE THE REST OF THEM.
NONE OF YOU APPRECIATE THE GLORY OF BEING A JUDGE!
YOU CAN MAKE THE LAW DO WHATEVER YOU WANT. BEND IT TO YOUR WILL!
NO. YOU CAN'T.
NOT WHEN THE LAW'S STANDING BEHIND YOU WITH A LENGTH OF PIPE.
UGGGNNNHHH!
AND YOU'RE UNDER ARREST, CREEP.
FLOOOSH
UNAUTHORIZED BLAZE! EXTINGUISHING IMMEDIATELY!

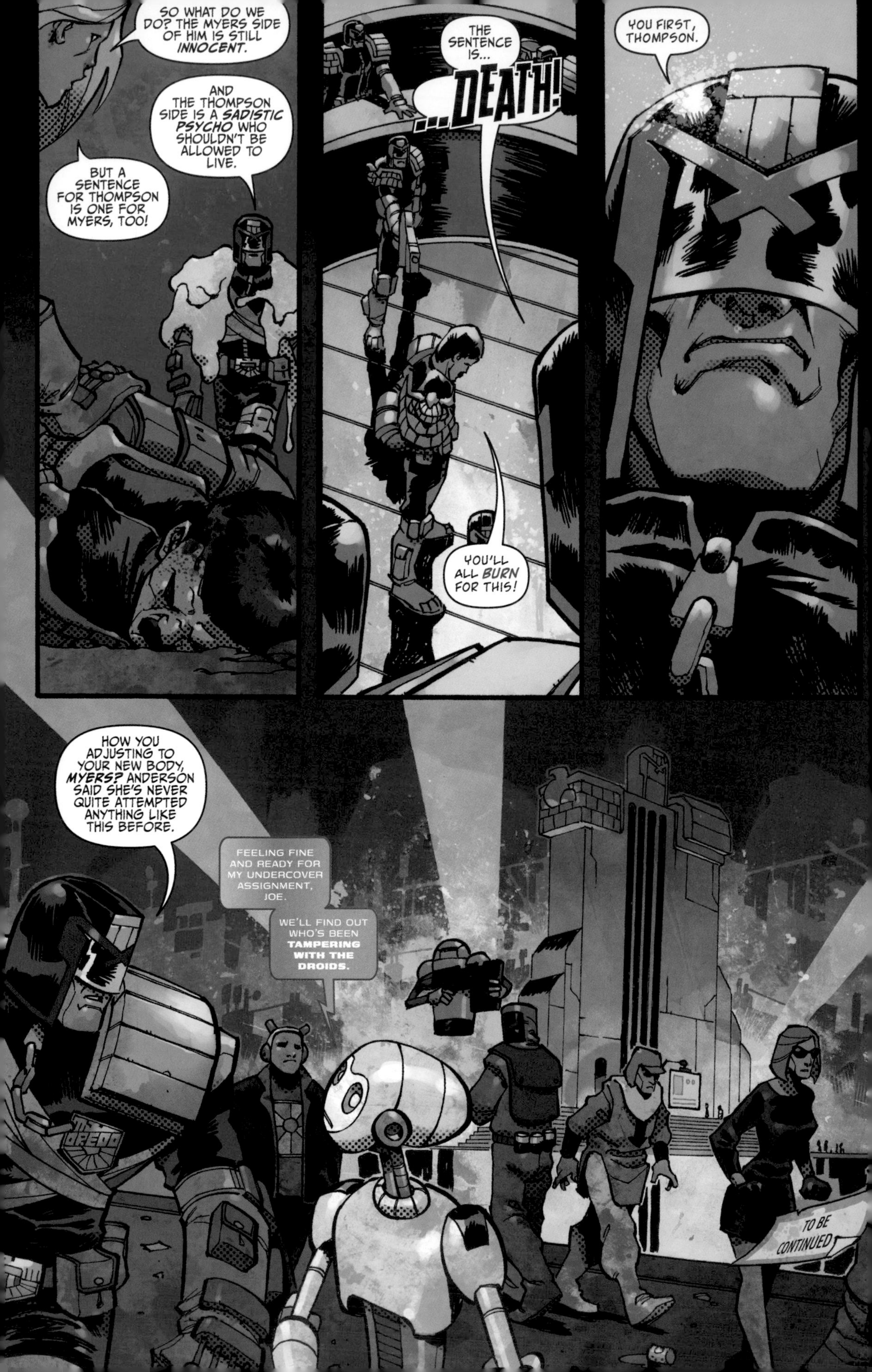

SO WHAT DO WE DO? THE MYERS SIDE OF HIM IS STILL INNOCENT.
AND THE THOMPSON SIDE IS A SADISTIC PSYCHO WHO SHOULDN'T BE ALLOWED TO LIVE.
BUT A SENTENCE FOR THOMPSON IS ONE FOR MYERS, TOO!
THE SENTENCE IS...
...DEATH!
YOU'LL ALL BURN FOR THIS!
YOU FIRST, THOMPSON.
HOW YOU ADJUSTING TO YOUR NEW BODY, MYERS? ANDERSON SAID SHE'S NEVER QUITE ATTEMPTED ANYTHING LIKE THIS BEFORE.
FEELING FINE AND READY FOR MY UNDERCOVER ASSIGNMENT, JOE.
WE'LL FIND OUT WHO'S BEEN TAMPERING WITH THE DROIDS.
TO BE CONTINUED

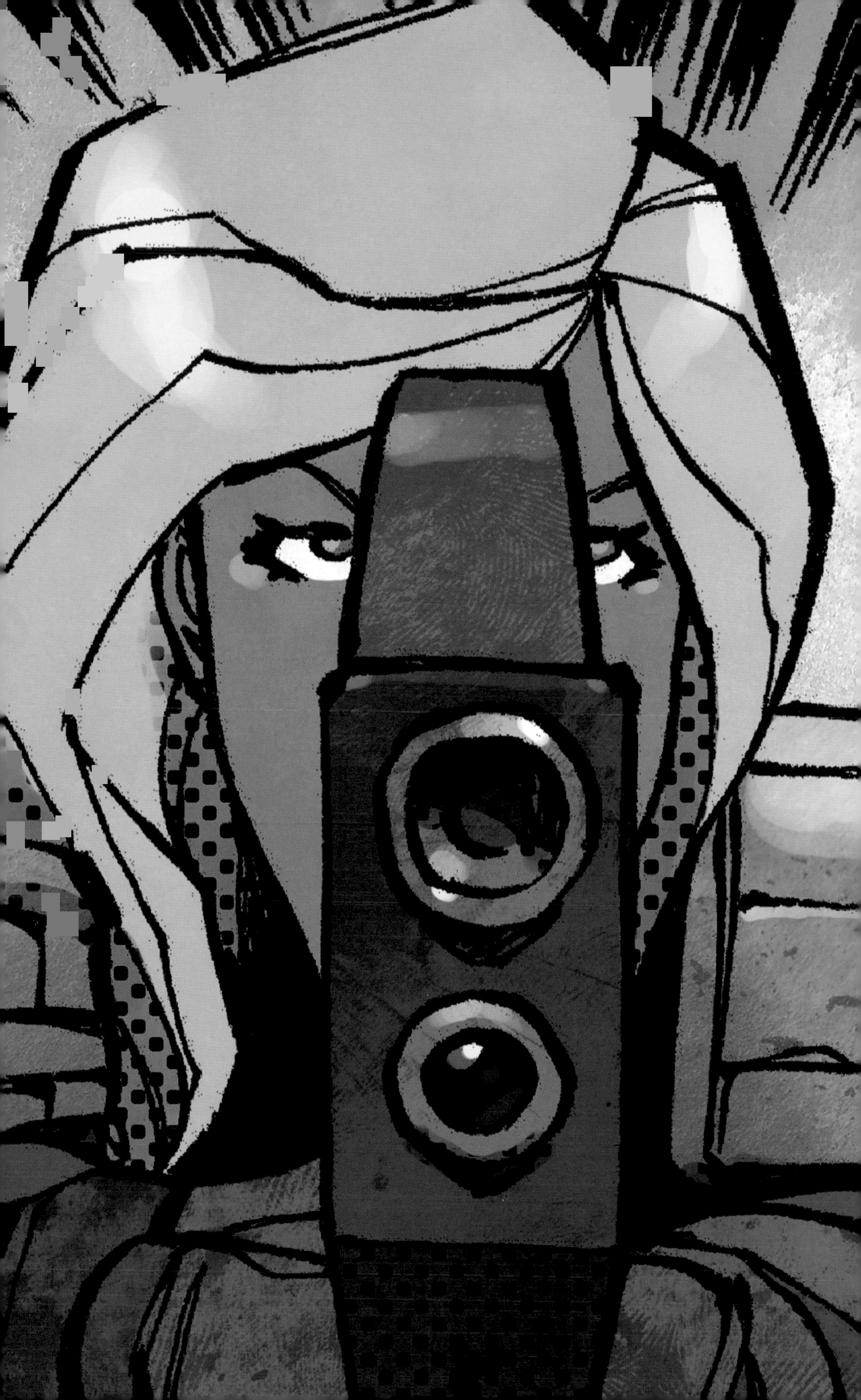

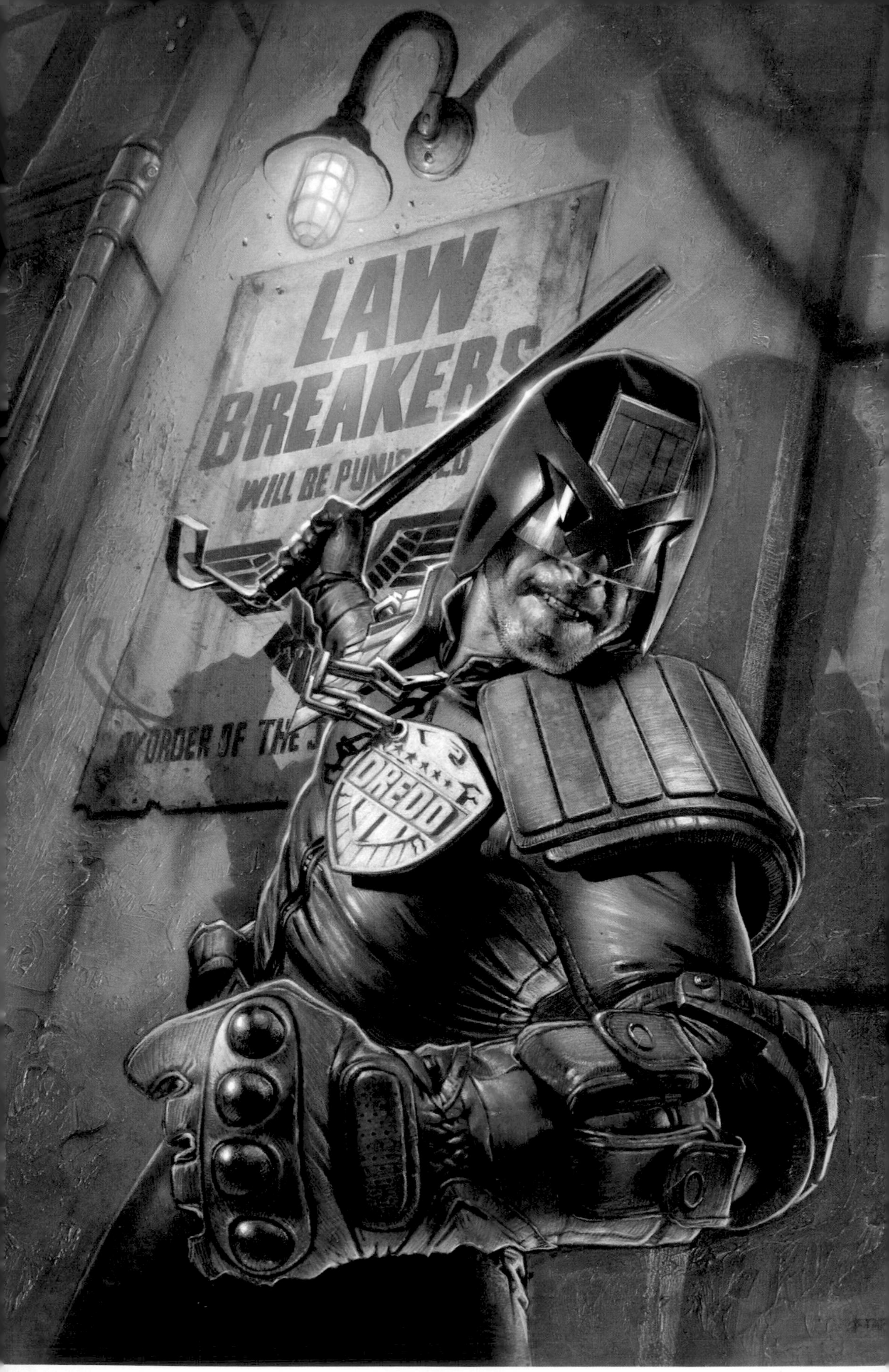
LAW
BREAKERS
DREDD

ART BY **GREG STAPLES**

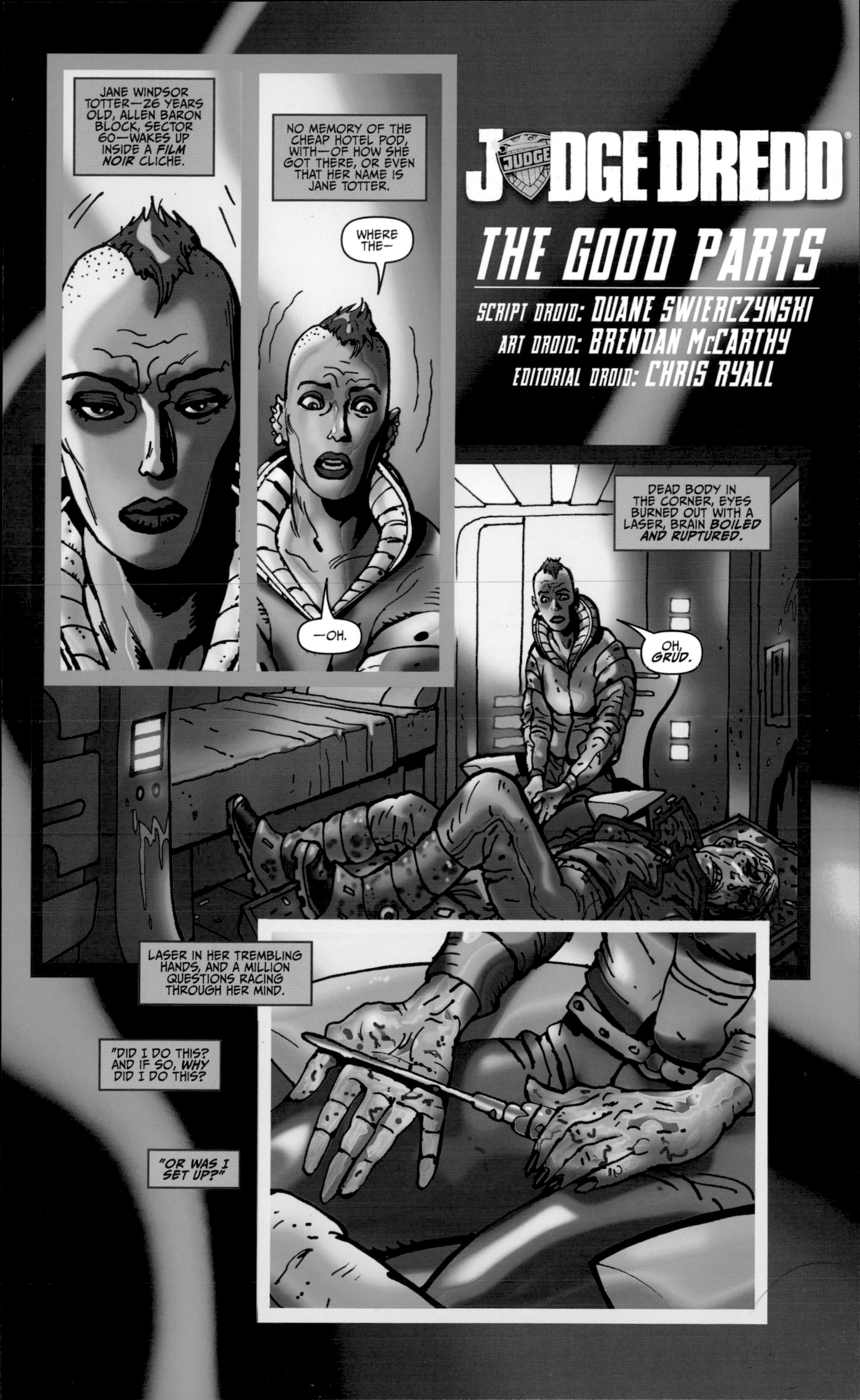

JANE WINDSOR TOTTER—26 YEARS OLD, ALLEN BARON BLOCK, SECTOR 60—WAKES UP INSIDE A FILM NOIR CLICHE.
NO MEMORY OF THE CHEAP HOTEL POD, WITH—OF HOW SHE GOT THERE, OR EVEN THAT HER NAME IS JANE TOTTER.
WHERE THE—
—OH.
JUDGE DREDD
THE GOOD PARTS
SCRIPT DROID: DUANE SWIERCZYNSKI
ART DROID: BRENDAN McCARTHY
EDITORIAL DROID: CHRIS RYALL
DEAD BODY IN THE CORNER, EYES BURNED OUT WITH A LASER, BRAIN BOILED AND RUPTURED.
OH, GRUD.
LASER IN HER TREMBLING HANDS, AND A MILLION QUESTIONS RACING THROUGH HER MIND.
"DID I DO THIS? AND IF SO, WHY DID I DO THIS?
"OR WAS I SET UP?"

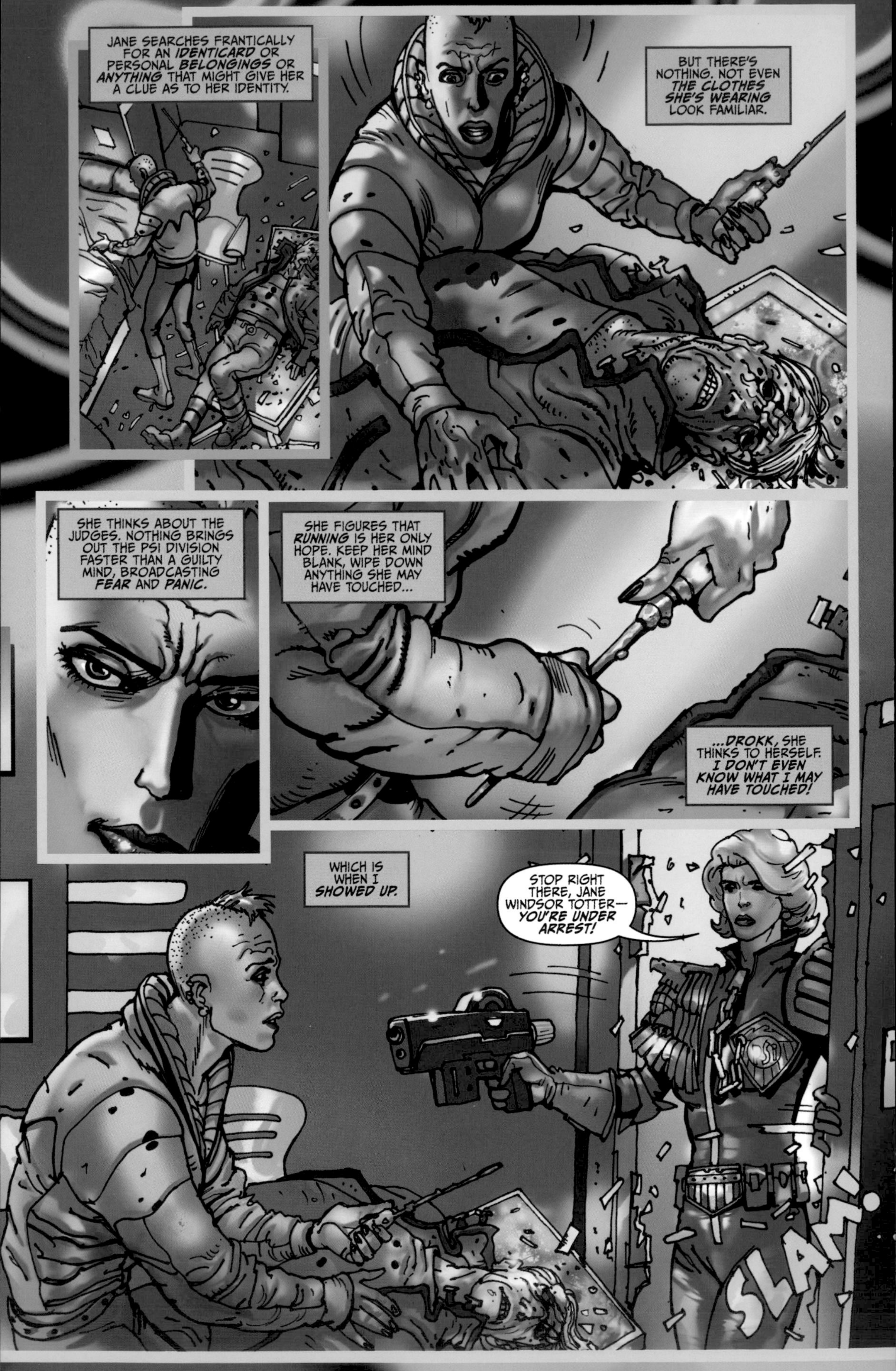
JANE SEARCHES FRANTICALLY FOR AN IDENTICARD OR PERSONAL BELONGINGS OR ANYTHING THAT MIGHT GIVE HER A CLUE AS TO HER IDENTITY.
BUT THERE'S NOTHING. NOT EVEN THE CLOTHES SHE'S WEARING LOOK FAMILIAR.
SHE THINKS ABOUT THE JUDGES. NOTHING BRINGS OUT THE PSI DIVISION FASTER THAN A GUILTY MIND, BROADCASTING FEAR AND PANIC.
SHE FIGURES THAT RUNNING IS HER ONLY HOPE. KEEP HER MIND BLANK, WIPE DOWN ANYTHING SHE MAY HAVE TOUCHED...
...DROKK, SHE THINKS TO HERSELF. I DON'T EVEN KNOW WHAT I MAY HAVE TOUCHED!
WHICH IS WHEN I SHOWED UP.
STOP RIGHT THERE, JANE WINDSOR TOTTER—YOU'RE UNDER ARREST!
SLAM!

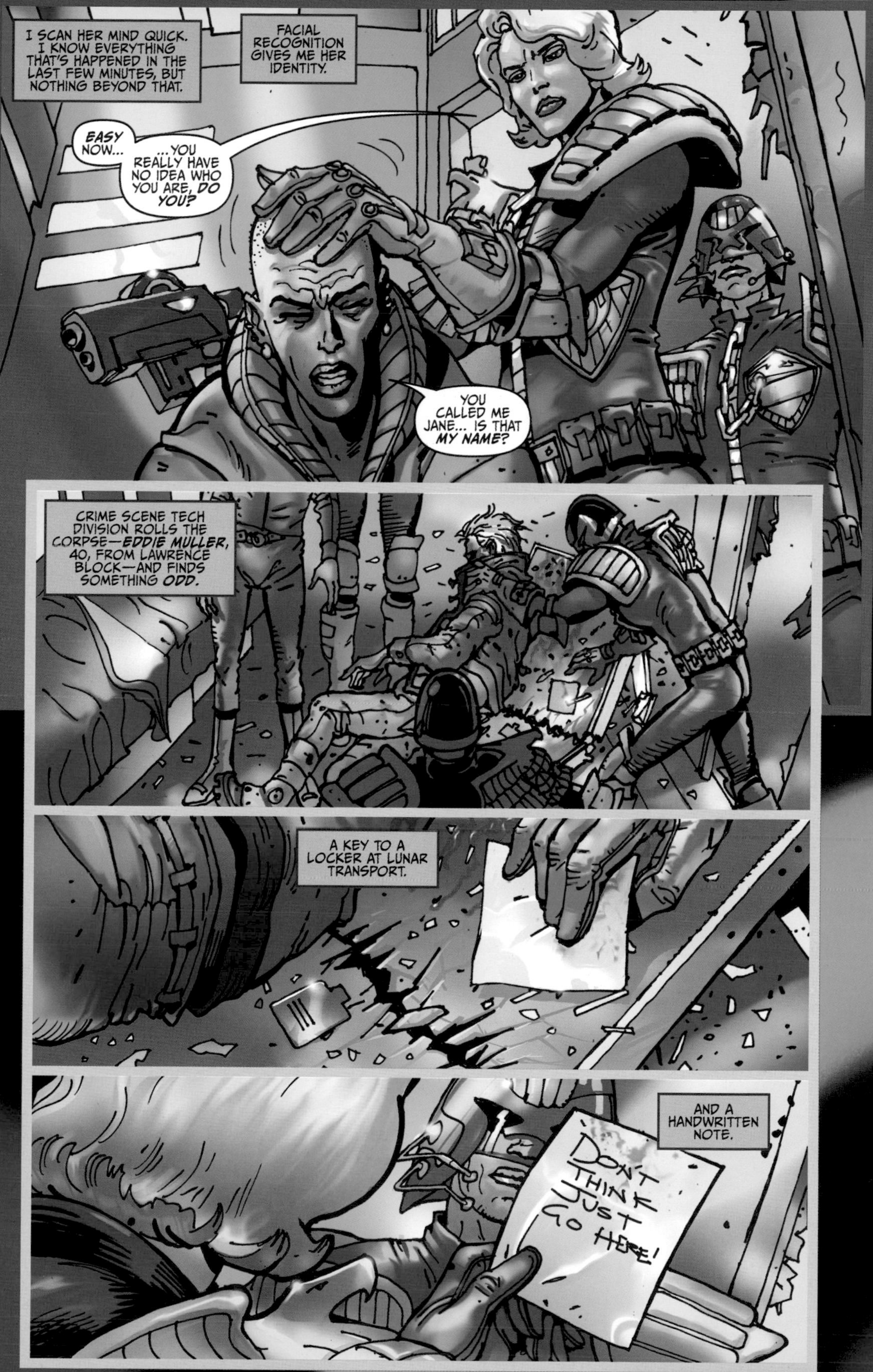
I SCAN HER MIND QUICK. I KNOW EVERYTHING THAT'S HAPPENED IN THE LAST FEW MINUTES, BUT NOTHING BEYOND THAT.
FACIAL RECOGNITION GIVES ME HER IDENTITY.
EASY NOW...
...YOU REALLY HAVE NO IDEA WHO YOU ARE, DO YOU?
YOU CALLED ME JANE... IS THAT MY NAME?
CRIME SCENE TECH DIVISION ROLLS THE CORPSE—EDDIE MULLER, 40, FROM LAWRENCE BLOCK—AND FINDS SOMETHING ODD.
A KEY TO A LOCKER AT LUNAR TRANSPORT.
AND A HANDWRITTEN NOTE.
DON'T THINK JUST GO HERE!

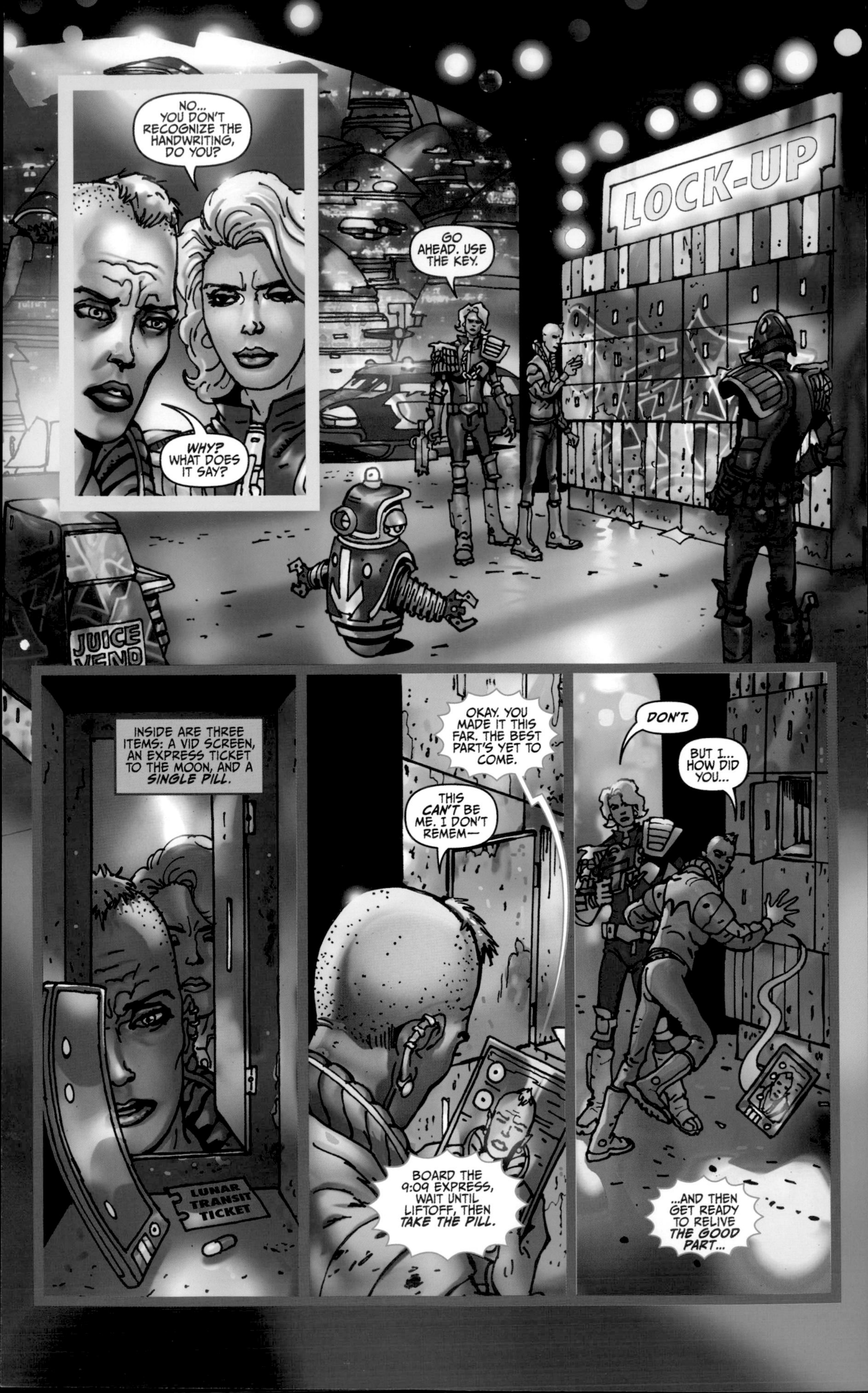
NO... YOU DON'T RECOGNIZE THE HANDWRITING, DO YOU?
WHY? WHAT DOES IT SAY?
GO AHEAD. USE THE KEY.
LOCK-UP
JUICE VEND
INSIDE ARE THREE ITEMS: A VID SCREEN, AN EXPRESS TICKET TO THE MOON, AND A SINGLE PILL.
LUNAR TRANSIT TICKET
OKAY. YOU MADE IT THIS FAR. THE BEST PART'S YET TO COME.
THIS CAN'T BE ME. I DON'T REMEM—
BOARD THE 9:09 EXPRESS, WAIT UNTIL LIFTOFF, THEN TAKE THE PILL.
DON'T.
BUT I... HOW DID YOU...
...AND THEN GET READY TO RELIVE THE GOOD PART...

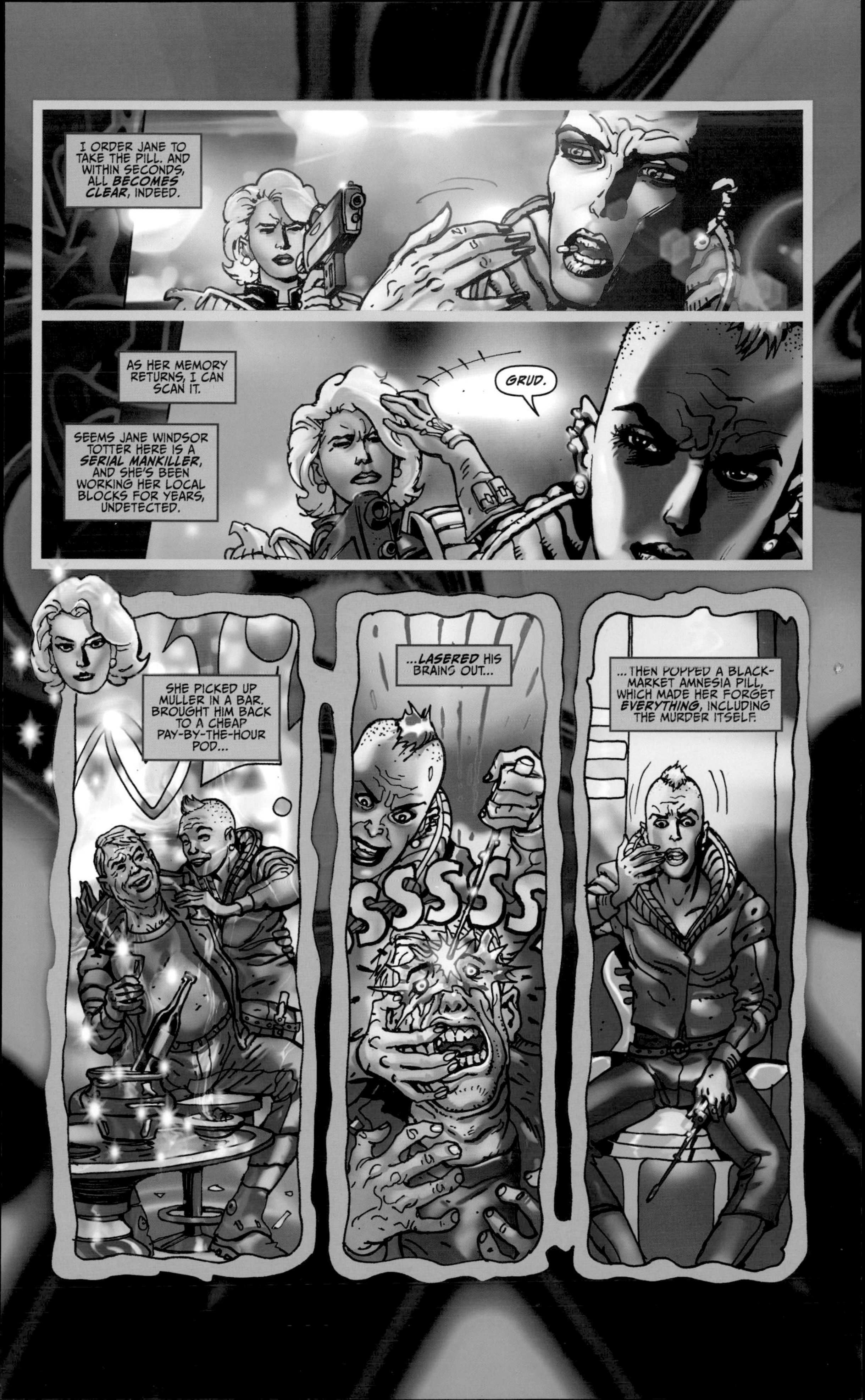

I ORDER JANE TO TAKE THE PILL. AND WITHIN SECONDS, ALL BECOMES CLEAR, INDEED.
AS HER MEMORY RETURNS, I CAN SCAN IT.
GRUD.
SEEMS JANE WINDSOR TOTTER HERE IS A SERIAL MANKILLER, AND SHE'S BEEN WORKING HER LOCAL BLOCKS FOR YEARS, UNDETECTED.
SHE PICKED UP MULLER IN A BAR. BROUGHT HIM BACK TO A CHEAP PAY-BY-THE-HOUR POD...
...LASERED HIS BRAINS OUT...
SSSSSS
...THEN POPPED A BLACK-MARKET AMNESIA PILL, WHICH MADE HER FORGET EVERYTHING, INCLUDING THE MURDER ITSELF.

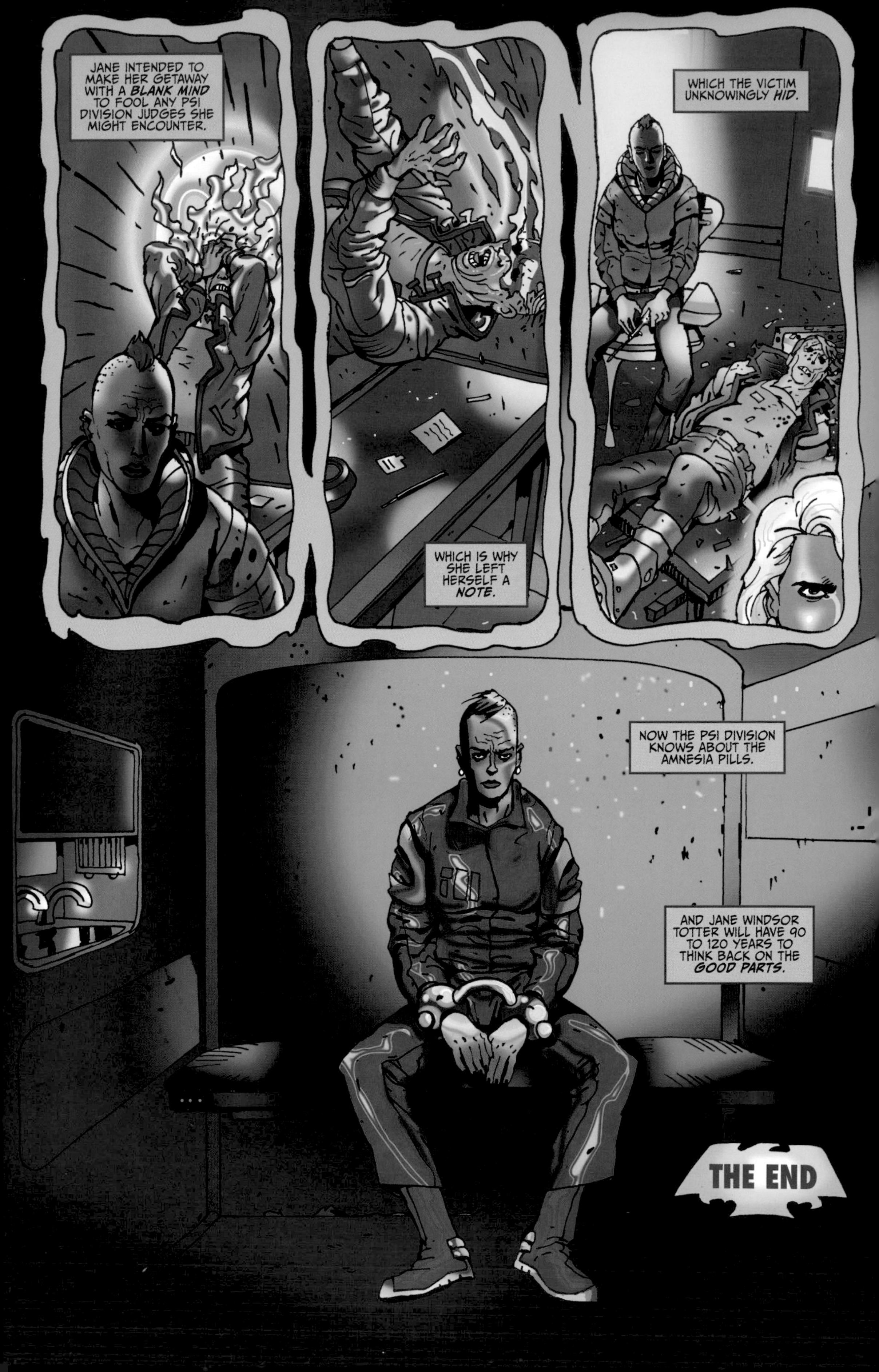
JANE INTENDED TO MAKE HER GETAWAY WITH A BLANK MIND TO FOOL ANY PSI DIVISION JUDGES SHE MIGHT ENCOUNTER.
WHICH IS WHY SHE LEFT HERSELF A NOTE.
WHICH THE VICTIM UNKNOWINGLY HID.
NOW THE PSI DIVISION KNOWS ABOUT THE AMNESIA PILLS.
AND JANE WINDSOR TOTTER WILL HAVE 90 TO 120 YEARS TO THINK BACK ON THE GOOD PARTS.
THE END

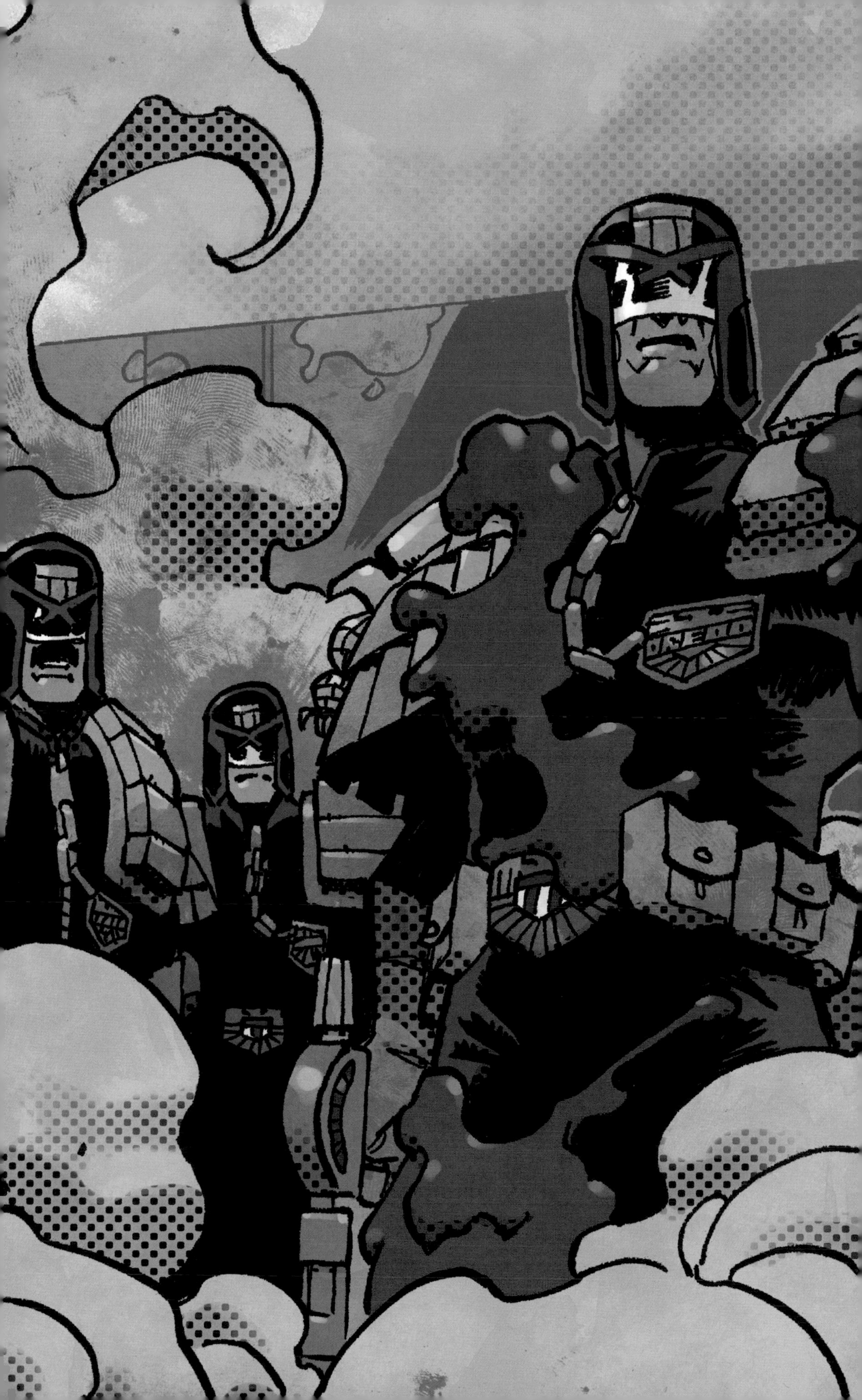

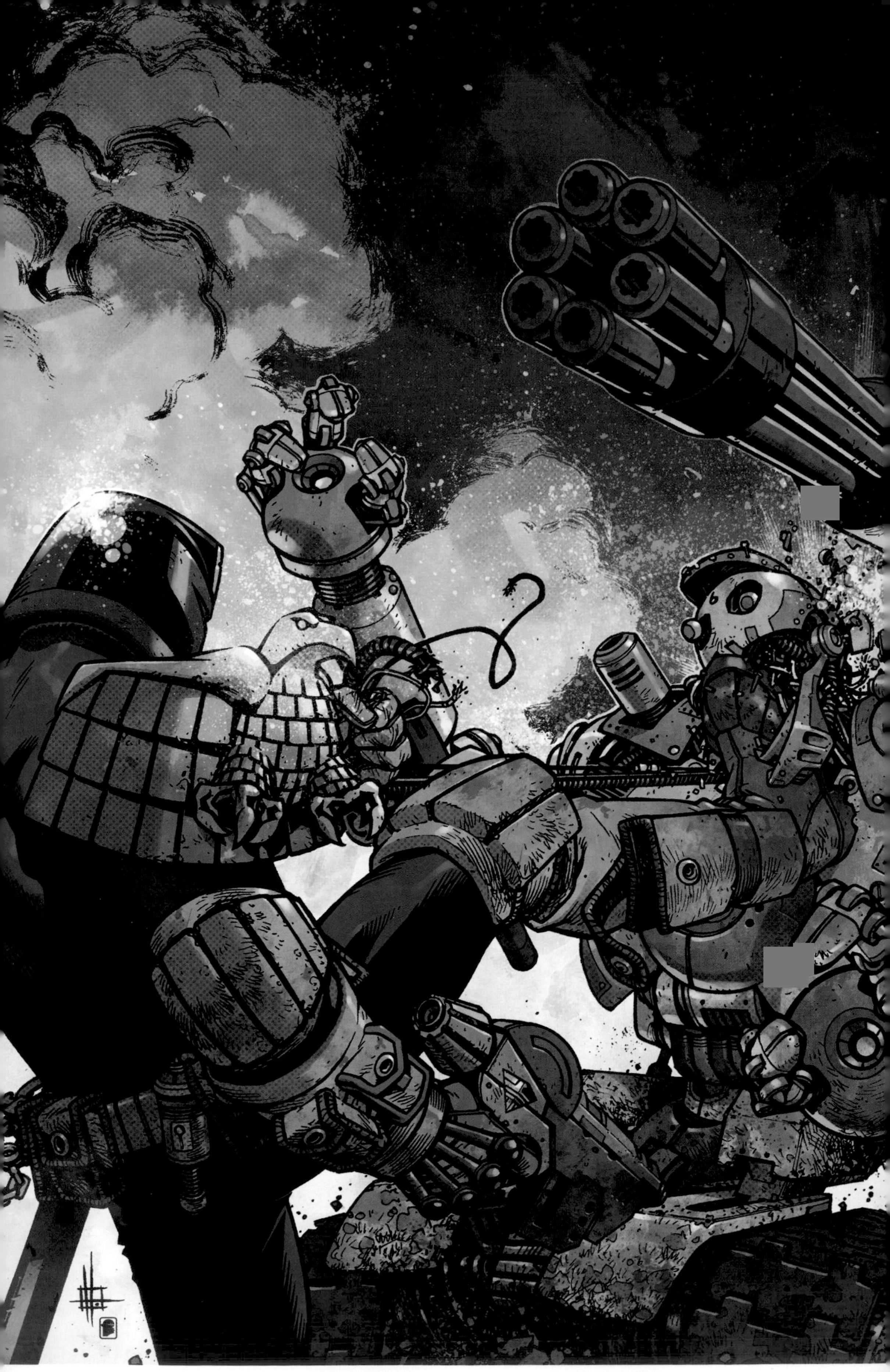

ART BY **ZACH HOWARD** ★ COLORS BY **NELSON DANIEL**

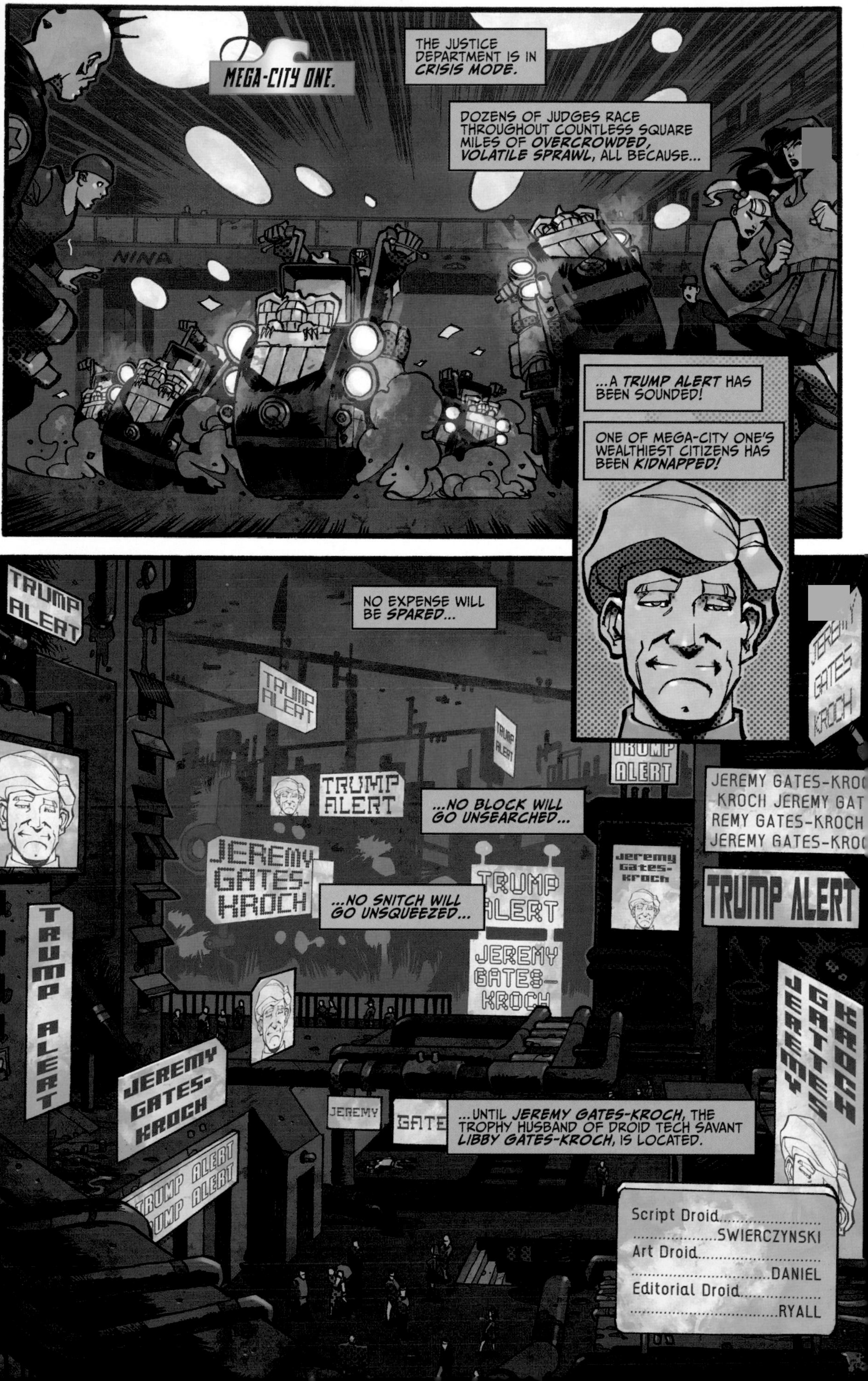
MEGA-CITY ONE.
THE JUSTICE DEPARTMENT IS IN CRISIS MODE.
DOZENS OF JUDGES RACE THROUGHOUT COUNTLESS SQUARE MILES OF OVERCROWDED, VOLATILE SPRAWL, ALL BECAUSE...
NINA
...A TRUMP ALERT HAS BEEN SOUNDED!
ONE OF MEGA-CITY ONE'S WEALTHIEST CITIZENS HAS BEEN KIDNAPPED!
TRUMP ALERT
NO EXPENSE WILL BE SPARED...
TRUMP ALERT
TRUMP ALERT
JEREMY GATES-KROCH
TRUMP ALERT
TRUMP ALERT
...NO BLOCK WILL GO UNSEARCHED...
JEREMY GATES-KROCH JEREMY GATES-KROCH JEREMY GATES-KROCH JEREMY GATES-KROCH
JEREMY GATES-KROCH
...NO SNITCH WILL GO UNSQUEEZED...
TRUMP ALERT
Jeremy Gates-Kroch
TRUMP ALERT
TRUMP ALERT
JEREMY GATES-KROCH
JEREMY GATES-KROCH
JEREMY GATES-KROCH
TRUMP ALERT
JEREMY
GATE
...UNTIL JEREMY GATES-KROCH, THE TROPHY HUSBAND OF DROID TECH SAVANT LIBBY GATES-KROCH, IS LOCATED.
TRUMP ALERT TRUMP ALERT
Script Droid........SWIERCZYNSKI
Art Droid........DANIEL
Editorial Droid........RYALL

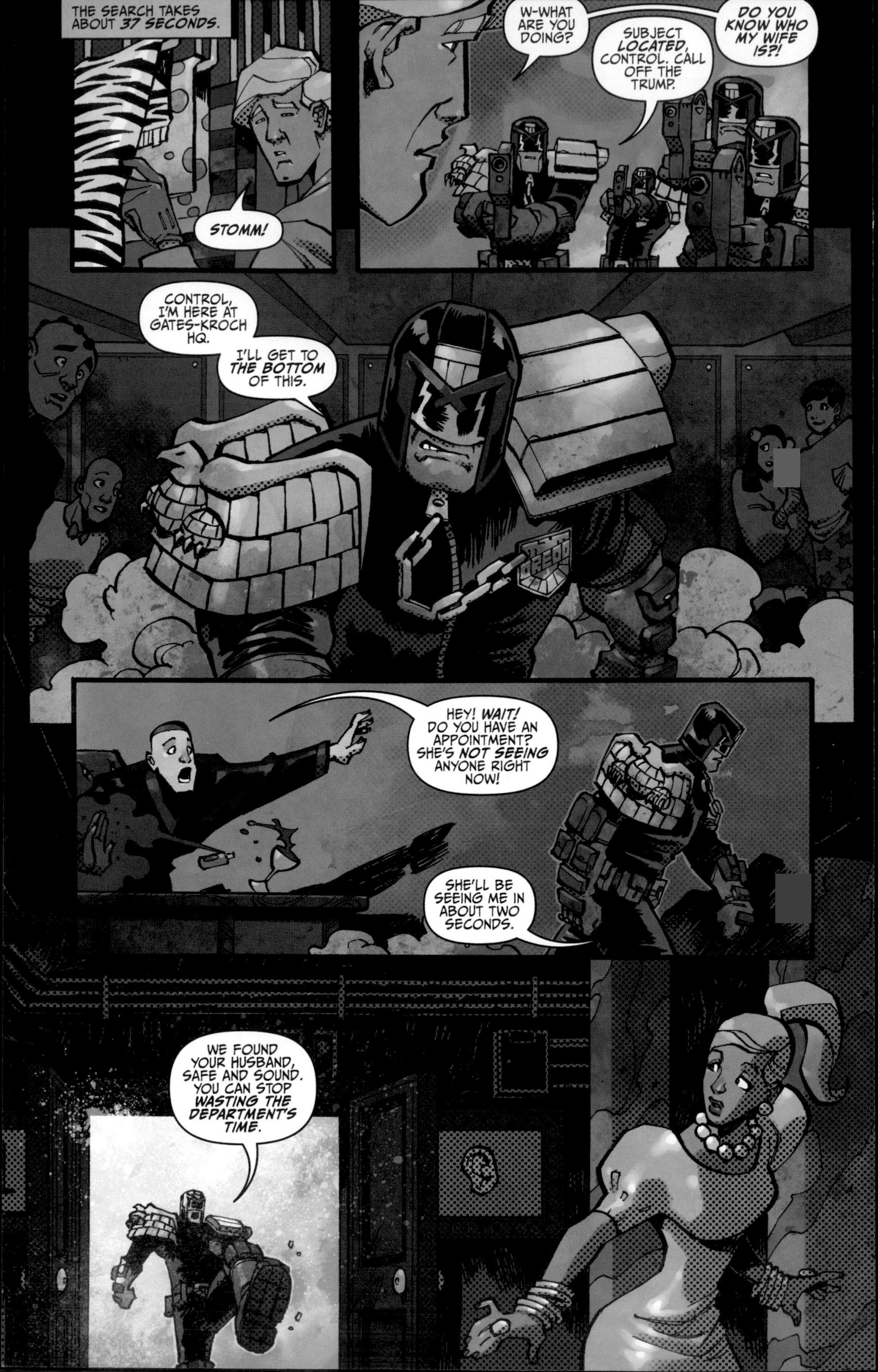
THE SEARCH TAKES ABOUT 37 SECONDS.
STOMM!
W-WHAT ARE YOU DOING?
SUBJECT LOCATED, CONTROL. CALL OFF THE TRUMP.
DO YOU KNOW WHO MY WIFE IS?!
CONTROL, I'M HERE AT GATES-KROCH HQ.
I'LL GET TO THE BOTTOM OF THIS.
HEY! WAIT! DO YOU HAVE AN APPOINTMENT? SHE'S NOT SEEING ANYONE RIGHT NOW!
SHE'LL BE SEEING ME IN ABOUT TWO SECONDS.
WE FOUND YOUR HUSBAND, SAFE AND SOUND. YOU CAN STOP WASTING THE DEPARTMENT'S TIME.

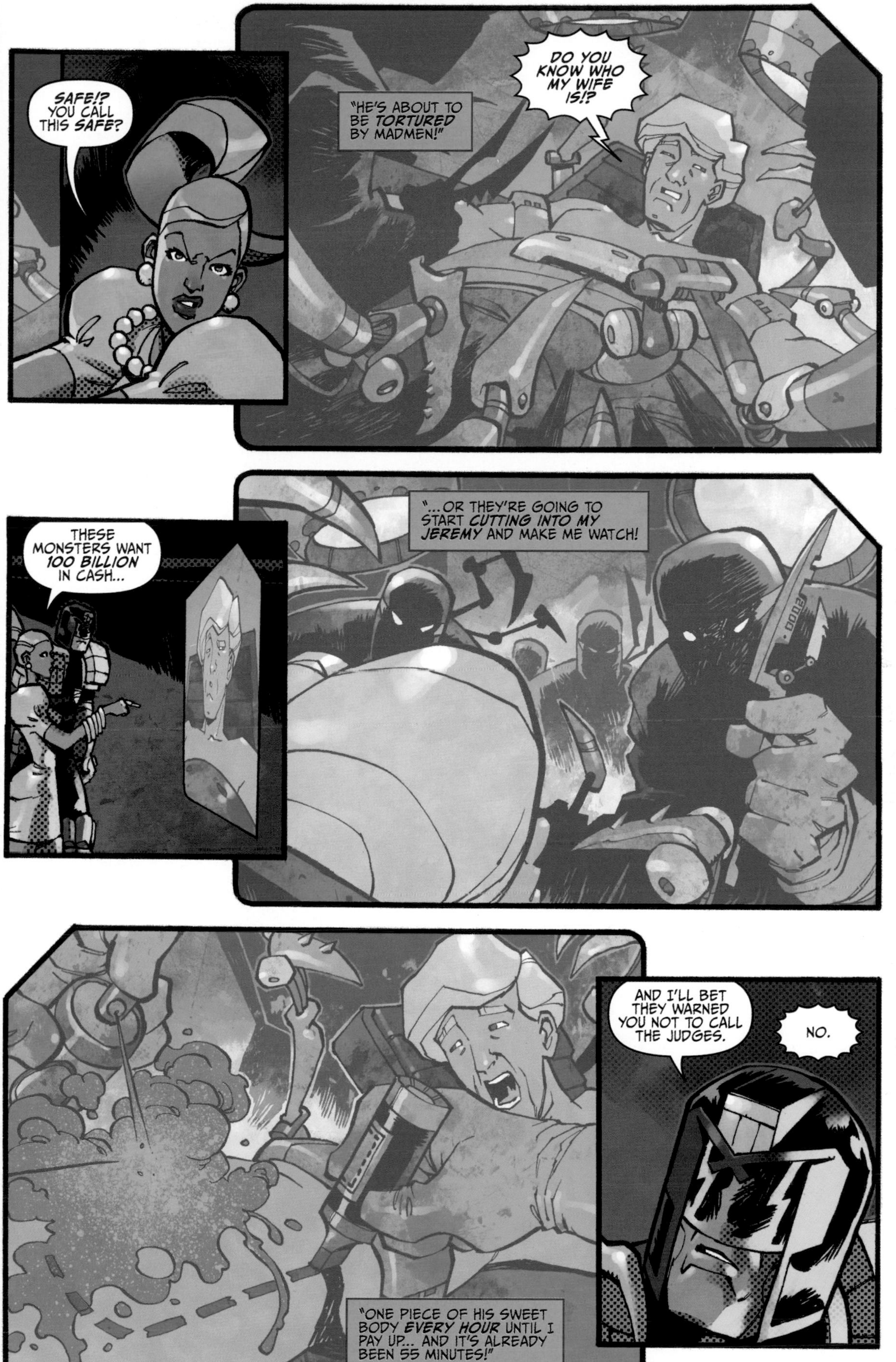
SAFE!? YOU CALL THIS SAFE?
"HE'S ABOUT TO BE TORTURED BY MADMEN!"
DO YOU KNOW WHO MY WIFE IS!?
THESE MONSTERS WANT 100 BILLION IN CASH...
"...OR THEY'RE GOING TO START CUTTING INTO MY JEREMY AND MAKE ME WATCH!
"ONE PIECE OF HIS SWEET BODY EVERY HOUR UNTIL I PAY UP... AND IT'S ALREADY BEEN 55 MINUTES!"
AND I'LL BET THEY WARNED YOU NOT TO CALL THE JUDGES.
NO.

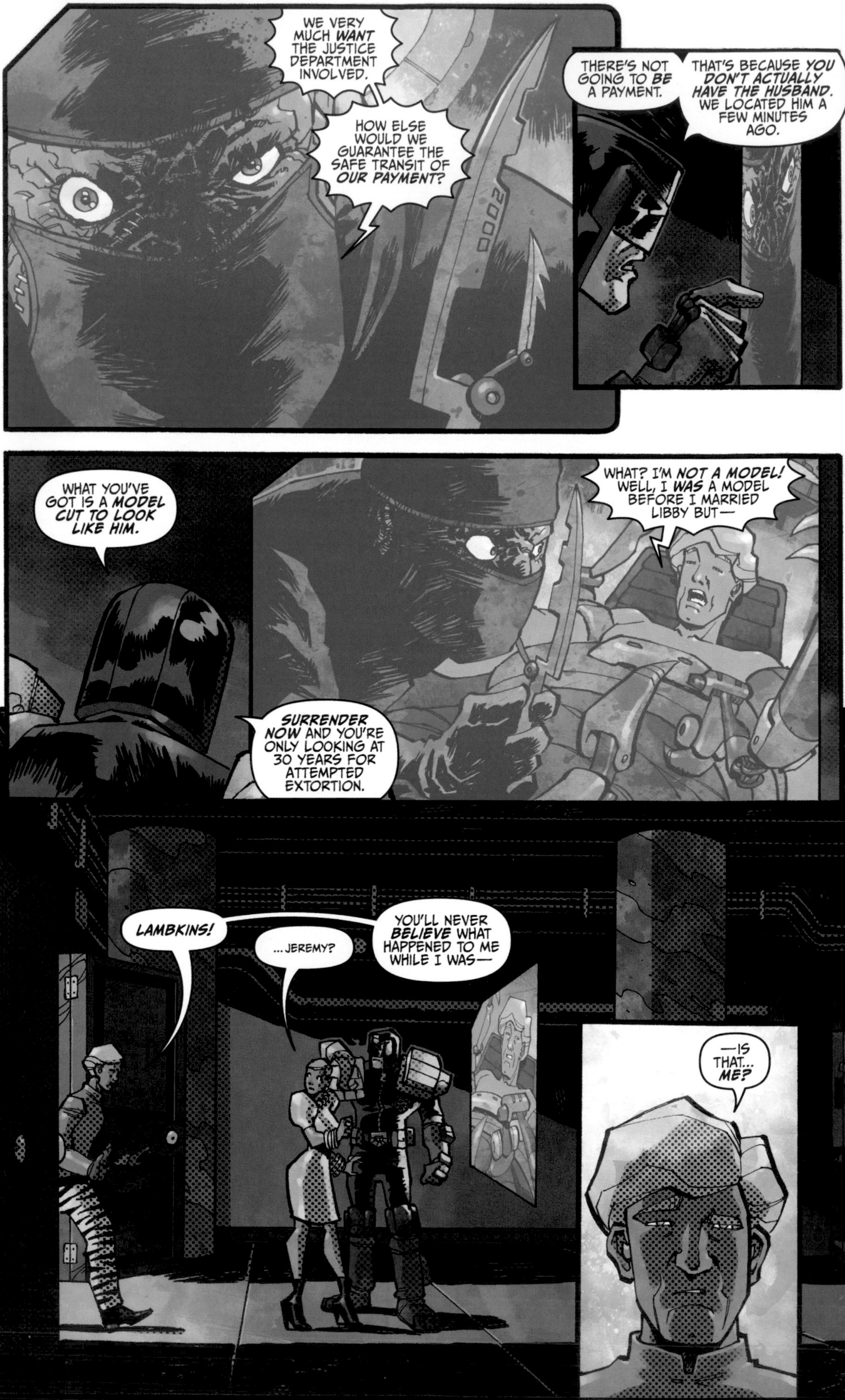
WE VERY MUCH WANT THE JUSTICE DEPARTMENT INVOLVED.
HOW ELSE WOULD WE GUARANTEE THE SAFE TRANSIT OF OUR PAYMENT?
THERE'S NOT GOING TO BE A PAYMENT.
THAT'S BECAUSE YOU DON'T ACTUALLY HAVE THE HUSBAND. WE LOCATED HIM A FEW MINUTES AGO.
2000
WHAT YOU'VE GOT IS A MODEL CUT TO LOOK LIKE HIM.
WHAT? I'M NOT A MODEL! WELL, I WAS A MODEL BEFORE I MARRIED LIBBY BUT—
SURRENDER NOW AND YOU'RE ONLY LOOKING AT 30 YEARS FOR ATTEMPTED EXTORTION.
LAMBKINS!
...JEREMY?
YOU'LL NEVER BELIEVE WHAT HAPPENED TO ME WHILE I WAS—
—IS THAT... ME?

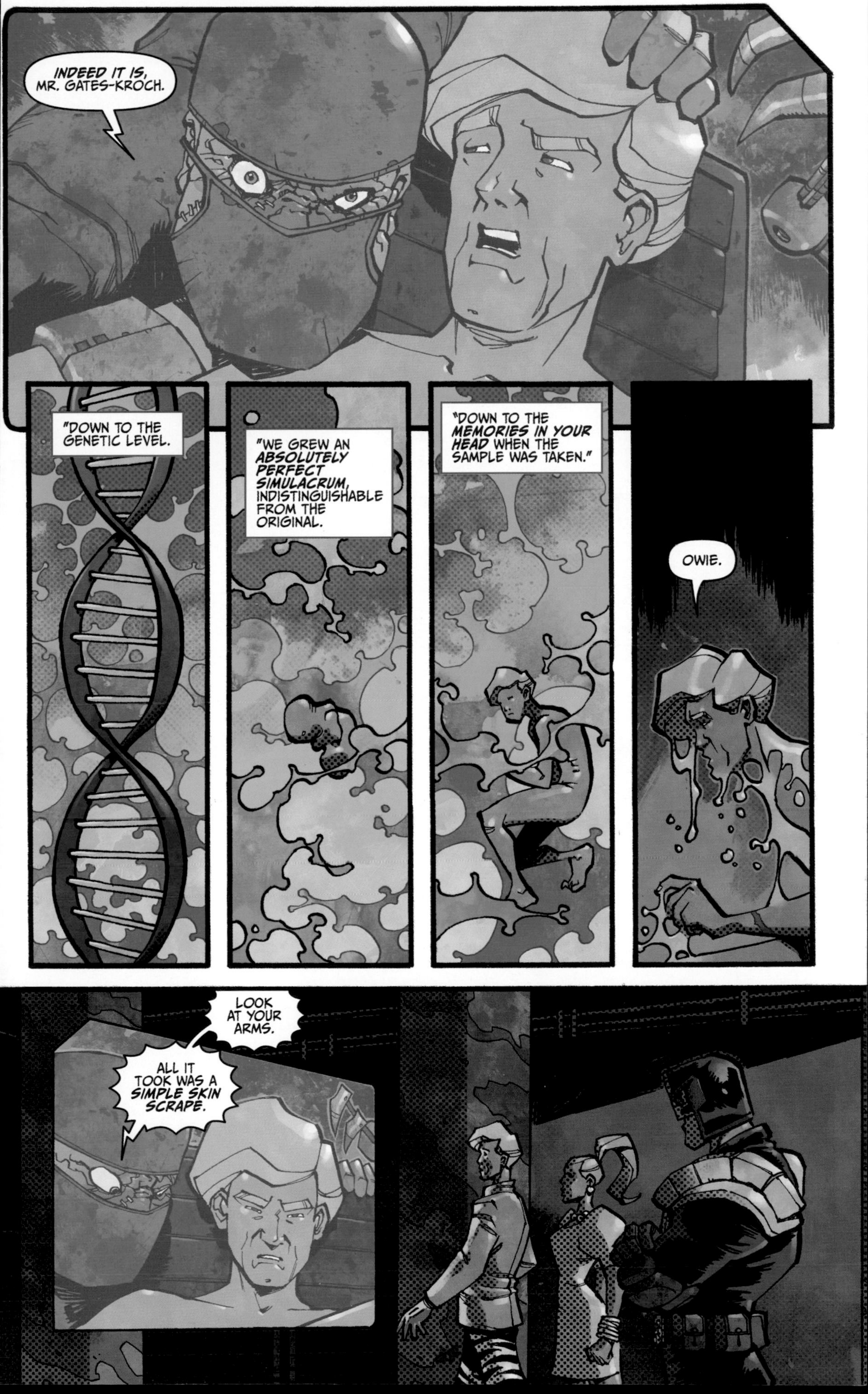
INDEED IT IS, MR. GATES-KROCH.
"DOWN TO THE GENETIC LEVEL.
"WE GREW AN ABSOLUTELY PERFECT SIMULACRUM, INDISTINGUISHABLE FROM THE ORIGINAL.
"DOWN TO THE MEMORIES IN YOUR HEAD WHEN THE SAMPLE WAS TAKEN."
OWIE.
ALL IT TOOK WAS A SIMPLE SKIN SCRAPE.
LOOK AT YOUR ARMS.

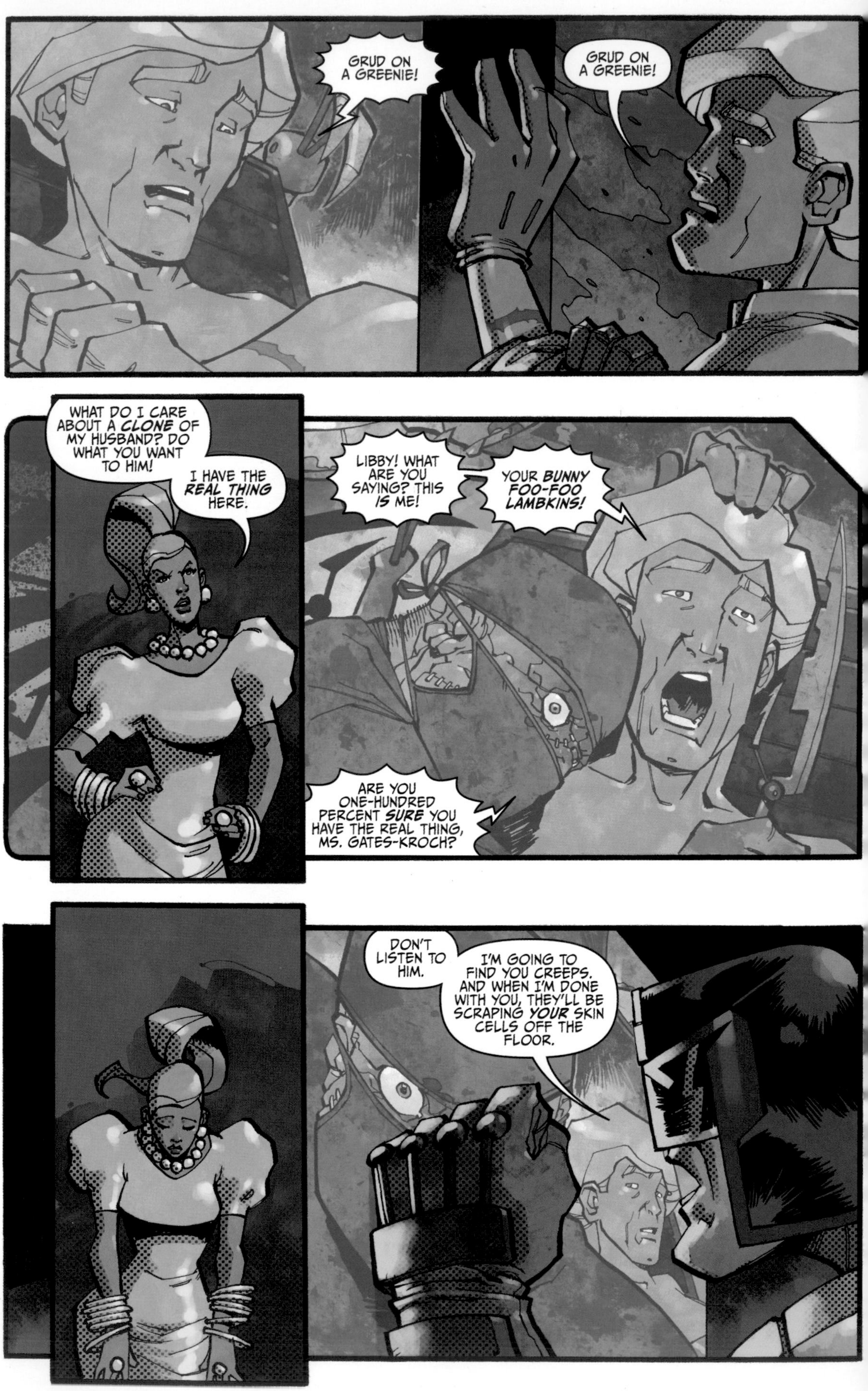
GRUD ON A GREENIE!
GRUD ON A GREENIE!
WHAT DO I CARE ABOUT A *CLONE* OF MY HUSBAND? DO WHAT YOU WANT TO HIM!
I HAVE THE *REAL THING* HERE.
LIBBY! WHAT ARE YOU SAYING? THIS *IS* ME!
YOUR *BUNNY FOO-FOO LAMBKINS!*
ARE YOU ONE-HUNDRED PERCENT *SURE* YOU HAVE THE REAL THING, MS. GATES-KROCH?
DON'T LISTEN TO HIM.
I'M GOING TO FIND YOU CREEPS. AND WHEN I'M DONE WITH YOU, THEY'LL BE SCRAPING *YOUR* SKIN CELLS OFF THE FLOOR.

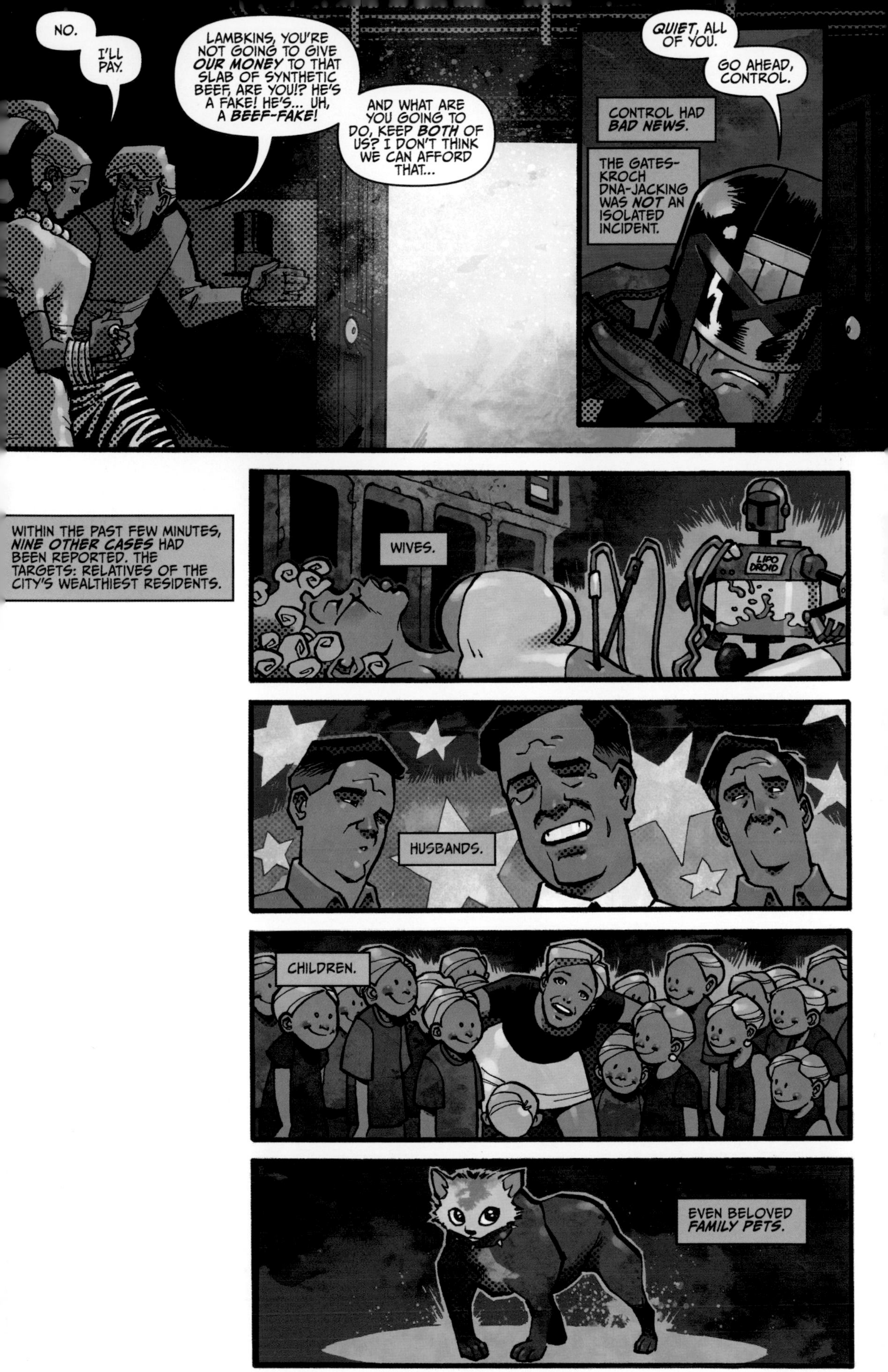
NO.
I'LL PAY.
LAMBKINS, YOU'RE NOT GOING TO GIVE OUR MONEY TO THAT SLAB OF SYNTHETIC BEEF, ARE YOU!? HE'S A FAKE! HE'S... UH, A BEEF-FAKE!
AND WHAT ARE YOU GOING TO DO, KEEP BOTH OF US? I DON'T THINK WE CAN AFFORD THAT...
QUIET, ALL OF YOU.
GO AHEAD, CONTROL.
CONTROL HAD BAD NEWS.
THE GATES-KROCH DNA-JACKING WAS NOT AN ISOLATED INCIDENT.
WITHIN THE PAST FEW MINUTES, NINE OTHER CASES HAD BEEN REPORTED. THE TARGETS: RELATIVES OF THE CITY'S WEALTHIEST RESIDENTS.
WIVES.
LIPO DROID
HUSBANDS.
CHILDREN.
EVEN BELOVED FAMILY PETS.

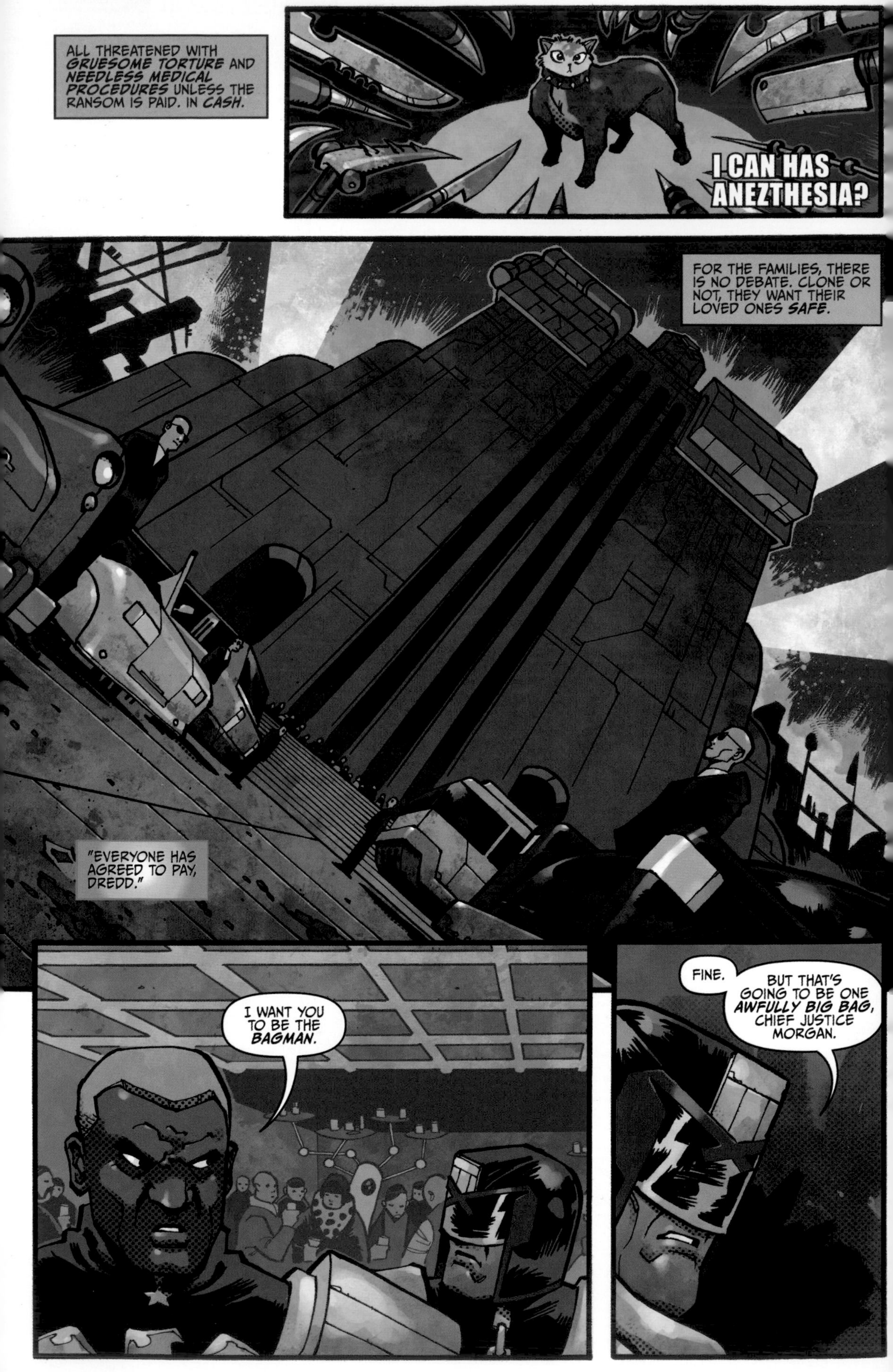
ALL THREATENED WITH GRUESOME TORTURE AND NEEDLESS MEDICAL PROCEDURES UNLESS THE RANSOM IS PAID. IN CASH.
I CAN HAS ANEZTHESIA?
FOR THE FAMILIES, THERE IS NO DEBATE. CLONE OR NOT, THEY WANT THEIR LOVED ONES SAFE.
"EVERYONE HAS AGREED TO PAY, DREDD."
I WANT YOU TO BE THE BAGMAN.
FINE.
BUT THAT'S GOING TO BE ONE AWFULLY BIG BAG, CHIEF JUSTICE MORGAN.

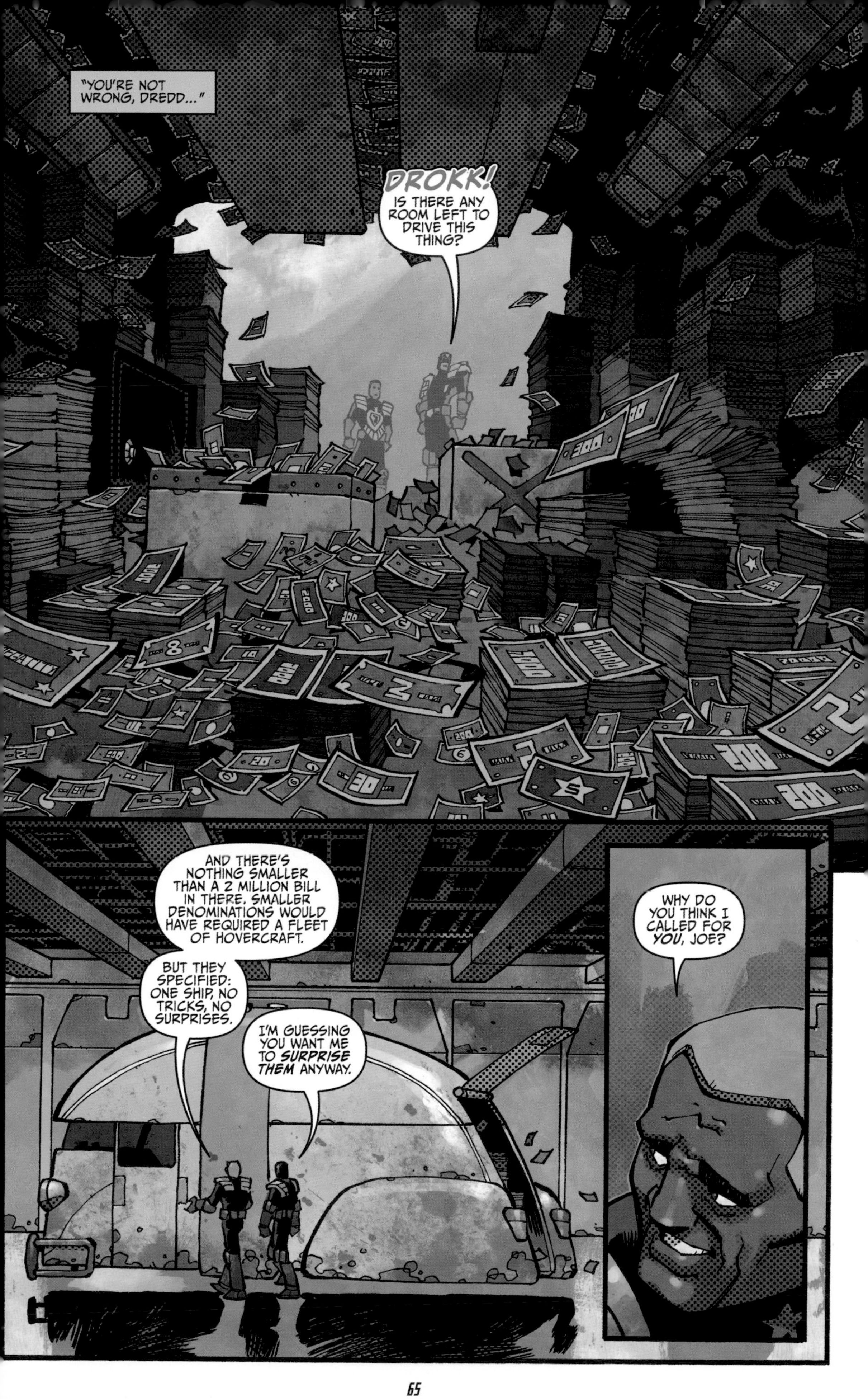
"YOU'RE NOT WRONG, DREDD..."
DROKK!
IS THERE ANY ROOM LEFT TO DRIVE THIS THING?
AND THERE'S NOTHING SMALLER THAN A 2 MILLION BILL IN THERE. SMALLER DENOMINATIONS WOULD HAVE REQUIRED A FLEET OF HOVERCRAFT.
BUT THEY SPECIFIED: ONE SHIP, NO TRICKS, NO SURPRISES.
I'M GUESSING YOU WANT ME TO *SURPRISE THEM* ANYWAY.
WHY DO YOU THINK I CALLED FOR *YOU*, JOE?

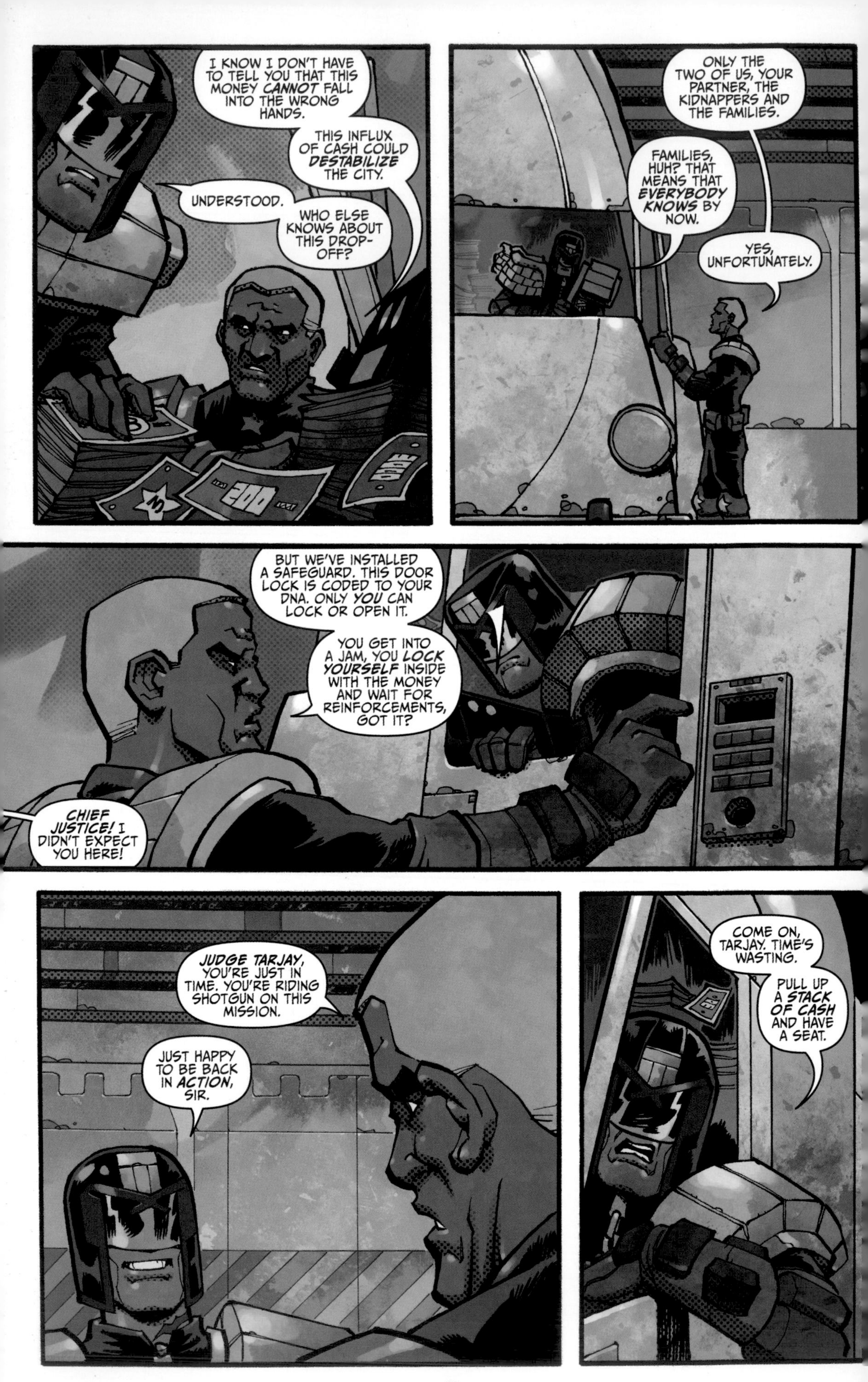
I KNOW I DON'T HAVE TO TELL YOU THAT THIS MONEY CANNOT FALL INTO THE WRONG HANDS.
THIS INFLUX OF CASH COULD DESTABILIZE THE CITY.
UNDERSTOOD.
WHO ELSE KNOWS ABOUT THIS DROP-OFF?
ONLY THE TWO OF US, YOUR PARTNER, THE KIDNAPPERS AND THE FAMILIES.
FAMILIES, HUH? THAT MEANS THAT EVERYBODY KNOWS BY NOW.
YES, UNFORTUNATELY.
BUT WE'VE INSTALLED A SAFEGUARD. THIS DOOR LOCK IS CODED TO YOUR DNA. ONLY YOU CAN LOCK OR OPEN IT.
YOU GET INTO A JAM, YOU LOCK YOURSELF INSIDE WITH THE MONEY AND WAIT FOR REINFORCEMENTS, GOT IT?
CHIEF JUSTICE! I DIDN'T EXPECT YOU HERE!
JUDGE TARJAY, YOU'RE JUST IN TIME. YOU'RE RIDING SHOTGUN ON THIS MISSION.
JUST HAPPY TO BE BACK IN ACTION, SIR.
COME ON, TARJAY. TIME'S WASTING.
PULL UP A STACK OF CASH AND HAVE A SEAT.

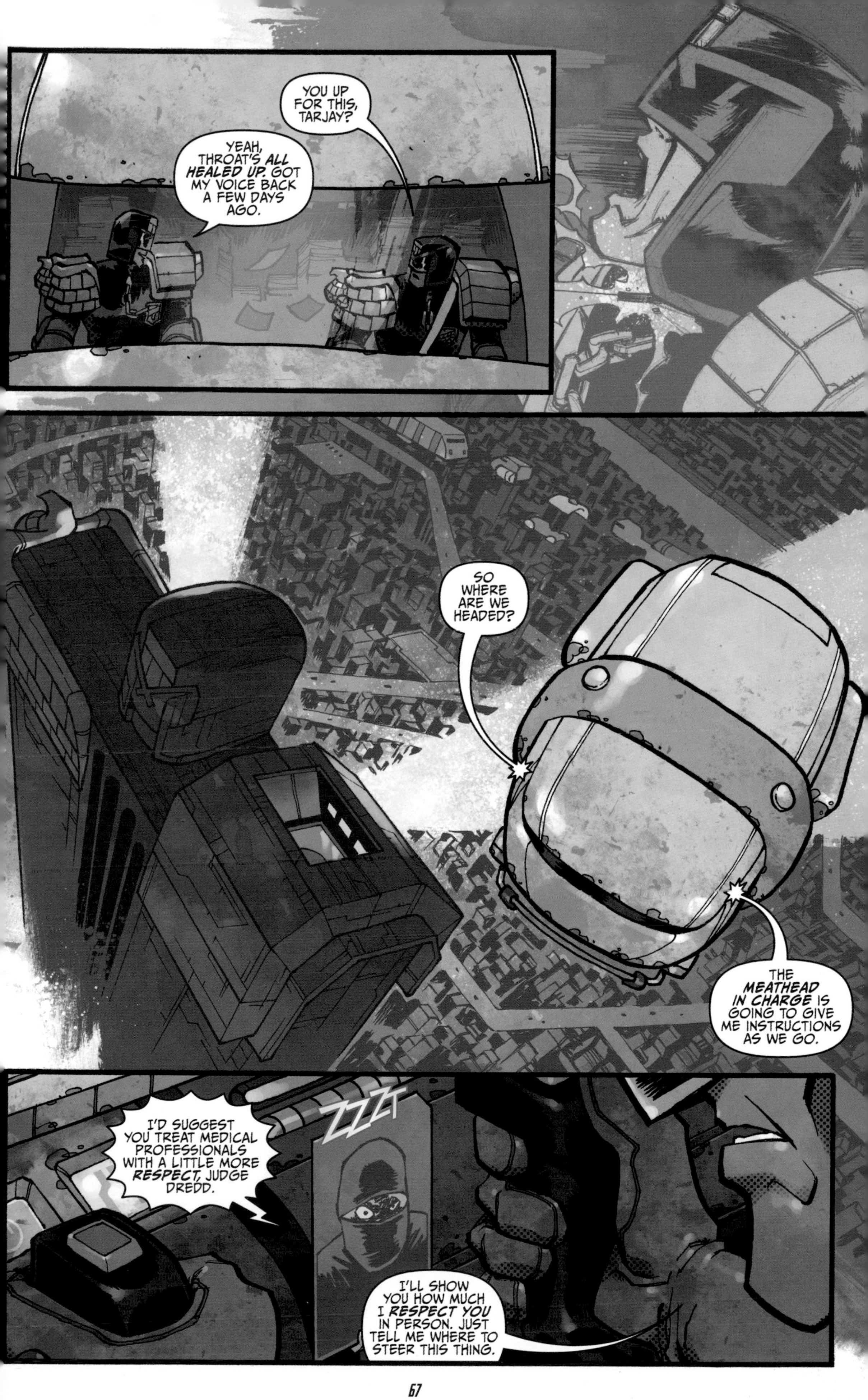
YOU UP FOR THIS, TARJAY?
YEAH, THROAT'S ALL HEALED UP. GOT MY VOICE BACK A FEW DAYS AGO.
SO WHERE ARE WE HEADED?
THE MEATHEAD IN CHARGE IS GOING TO GIVE ME INSTRUCTIONS AS WE GO.
ZZZT
I'D SUGGEST YOU TREAT MEDICAL PROFESSIONALS WITH A LITTLE MORE RESPECT, JUDGE DREDD.
I'LL SHOW YOU HOW MUCH I RESPECT YOU IN PERSON. JUST TELL ME WHERE TO STEER THIS THING.

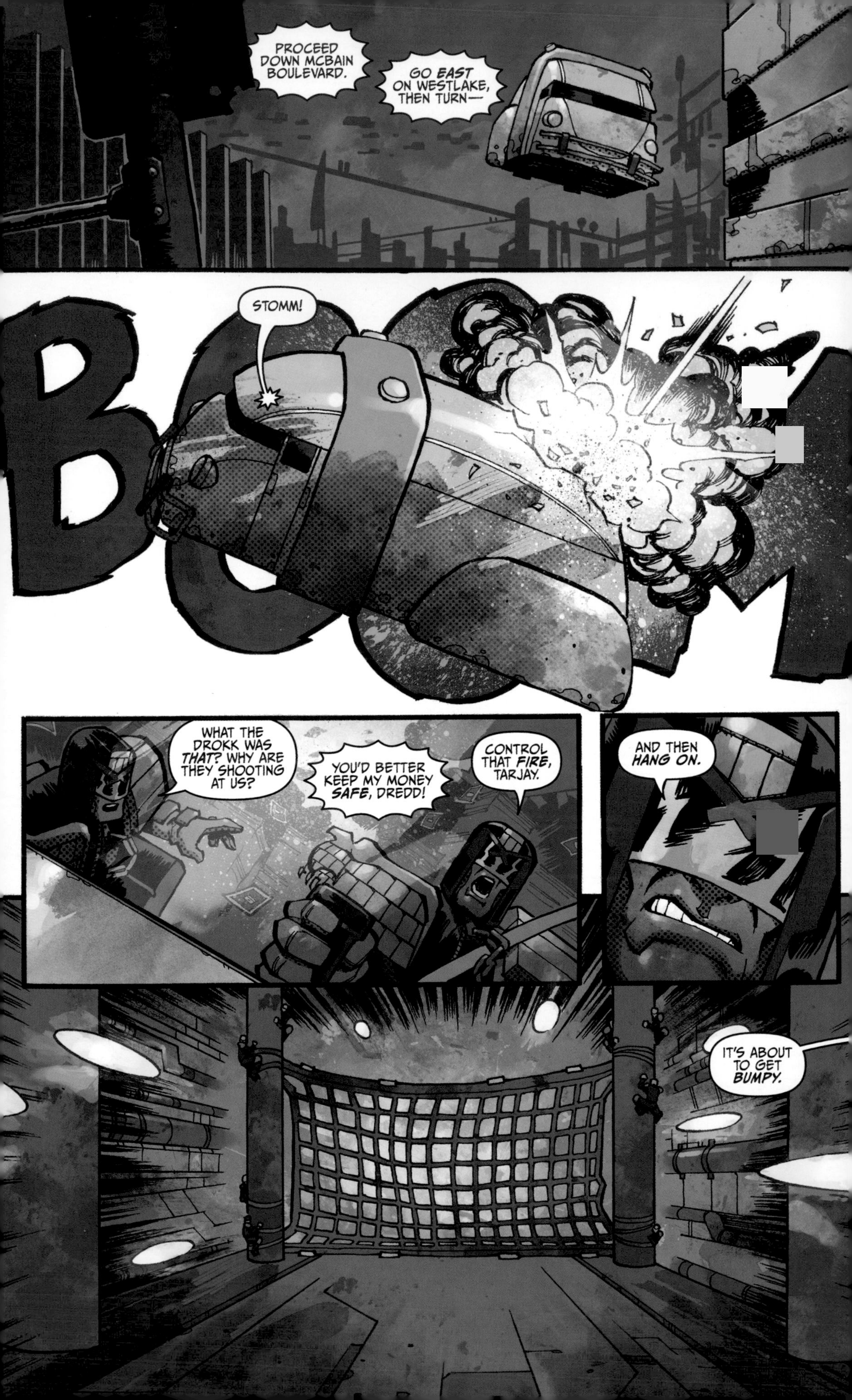
PROCEED DOWN MCBAIN BOULEVARD.
GO *EAST* ON WESTLAKE, THEN TURN—
STOMM!
BOOM
WHAT THE DROKK WAS *THAT*? WHY ARE THEY SHOOTING AT US?
YOU'D BETTER KEEP MY MONEY *SAFE*, DREDD!
CONTROL THAT *FIRE*, TARJAY.
AND THEN *HANG ON.*
IT'S ABOUT TO GET *BUMPY.*

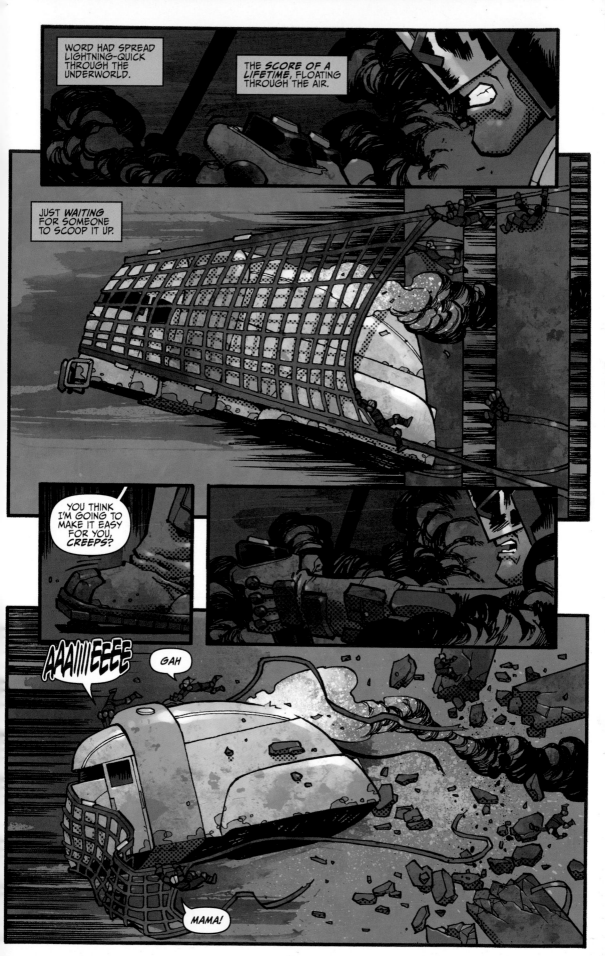

WORD HAD SPREAD LIGHTNING-QUICK THROUGH THE UNDERWORLD.

THE *SCORE OF A LIFETIME*, FLOATING THROUGH THE AIR.

JUST *WAITING* FOR SOMEONE TO SCOOP IT UP.

YOU THINK I'M GOING TO MAKE IT EASY FOR YOU, *CREEPS?*

AAAIIIIEEEE

GAH

MAMA!

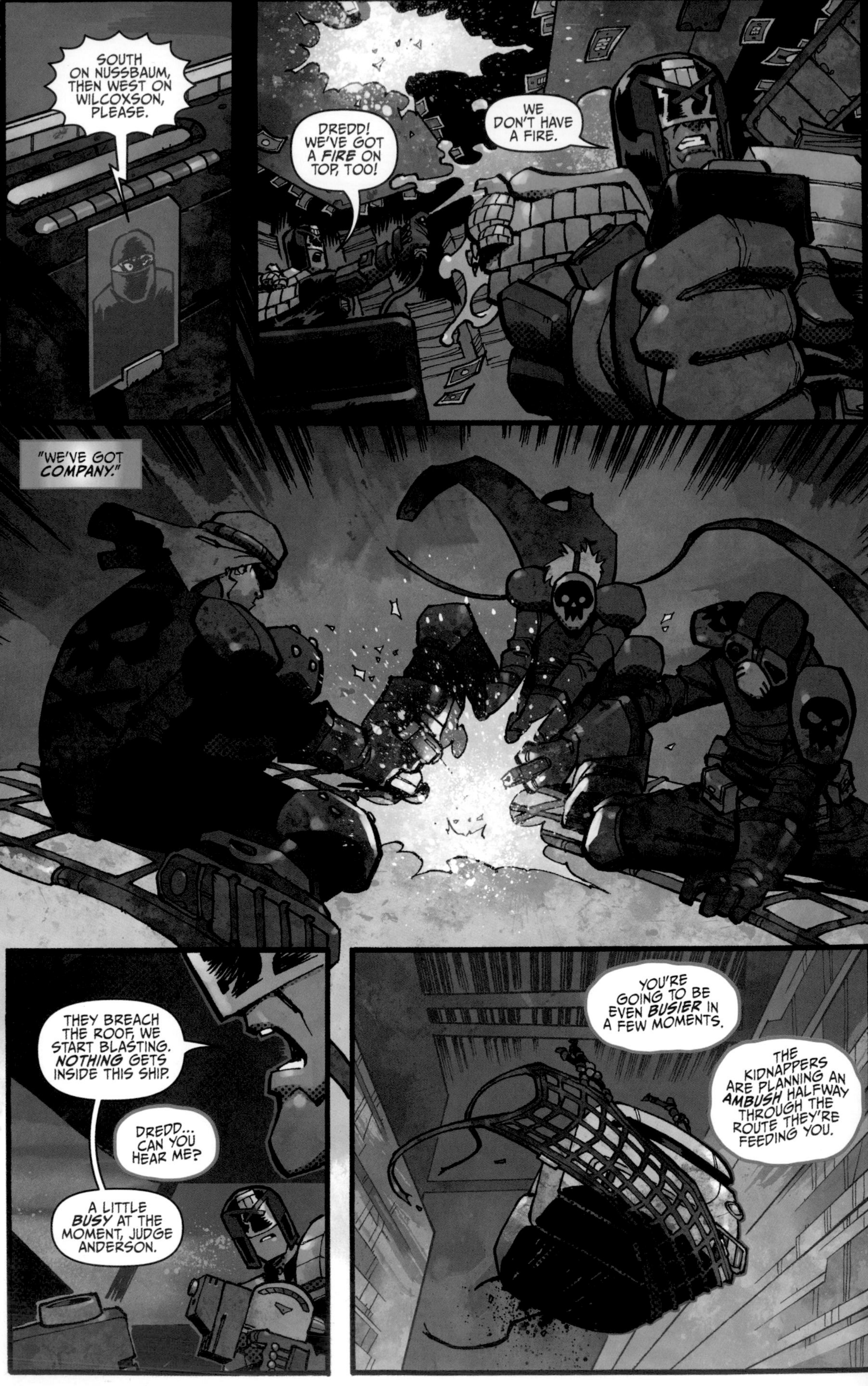

SOUTH ON NUSSBAUM, THEN WEST ON WILCOXSON, PLEASE.
DREDD! WE'VE GOT A FIRE ON TOP, TOO!
WE DON'T HAVE A FIRE.
"WE'VE GOT COMPANY."
THEY BREACH THE ROOF, WE START BLASTING. NOTHING GETS INSIDE THIS SHIP.
DREDD... CAN YOU HEAR ME?
A LITTLE BUSY AT THE MOMENT, JUDGE ANDERSON.
YOU'RE GOING TO BE EVEN BUSIER IN A FEW MOMENTS.
THE KIDNAPPERS ARE PLANNING AN AMBUSH HALFWAY THROUGH THE ROUTE THEY'RE FEEDING YOU.

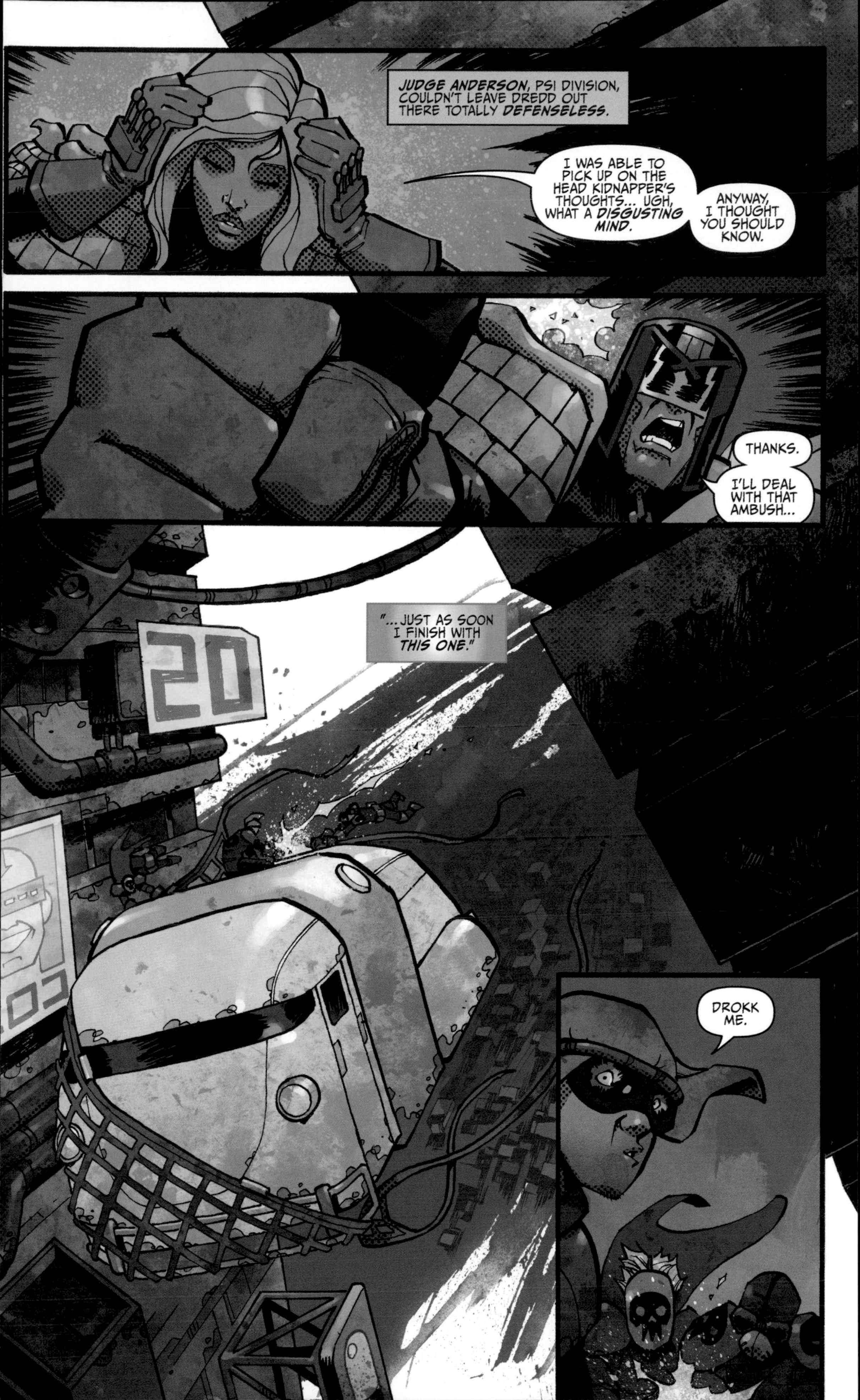
JUDGE ANDERSON, PSI DIVISION, COULDN'T LEAVE DREDD OUT THERE TOTALLY DEFENSELESS.
I WAS ABLE TO PICK UP ON THE HEAD KIDNAPPER'S THOUGHTS... UGH, WHAT A DISGUSTING MIND.
ANYWAY, I THOUGHT YOU SHOULD KNOW.
THANKS.
I'LL DEAL WITH THAT AMBUSH...
"...JUST AS SOON I FINISH WITH THIS ONE."
20
DROKK ME.

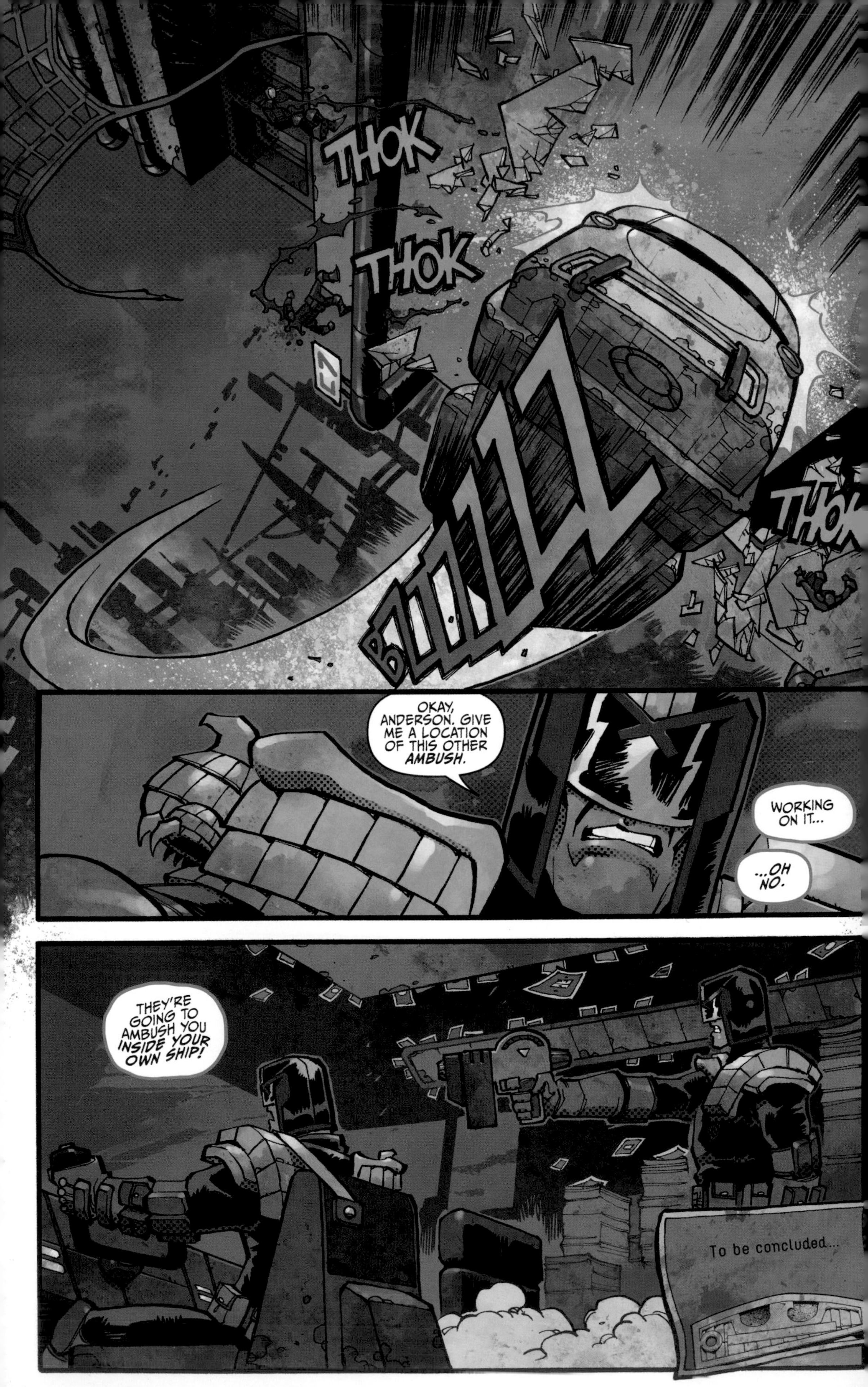
THOK
THOK
BZZZZZ
THOK
OKAY, ANDERSON. GIVE ME A LOCATION OF THIS OTHER AMBUSH.
WORKING ON IT...
...OH NO.
THEY'RE GOING TO AMBUSH YOU INSIDE YOUR OWN SHIP!
To be concluded...

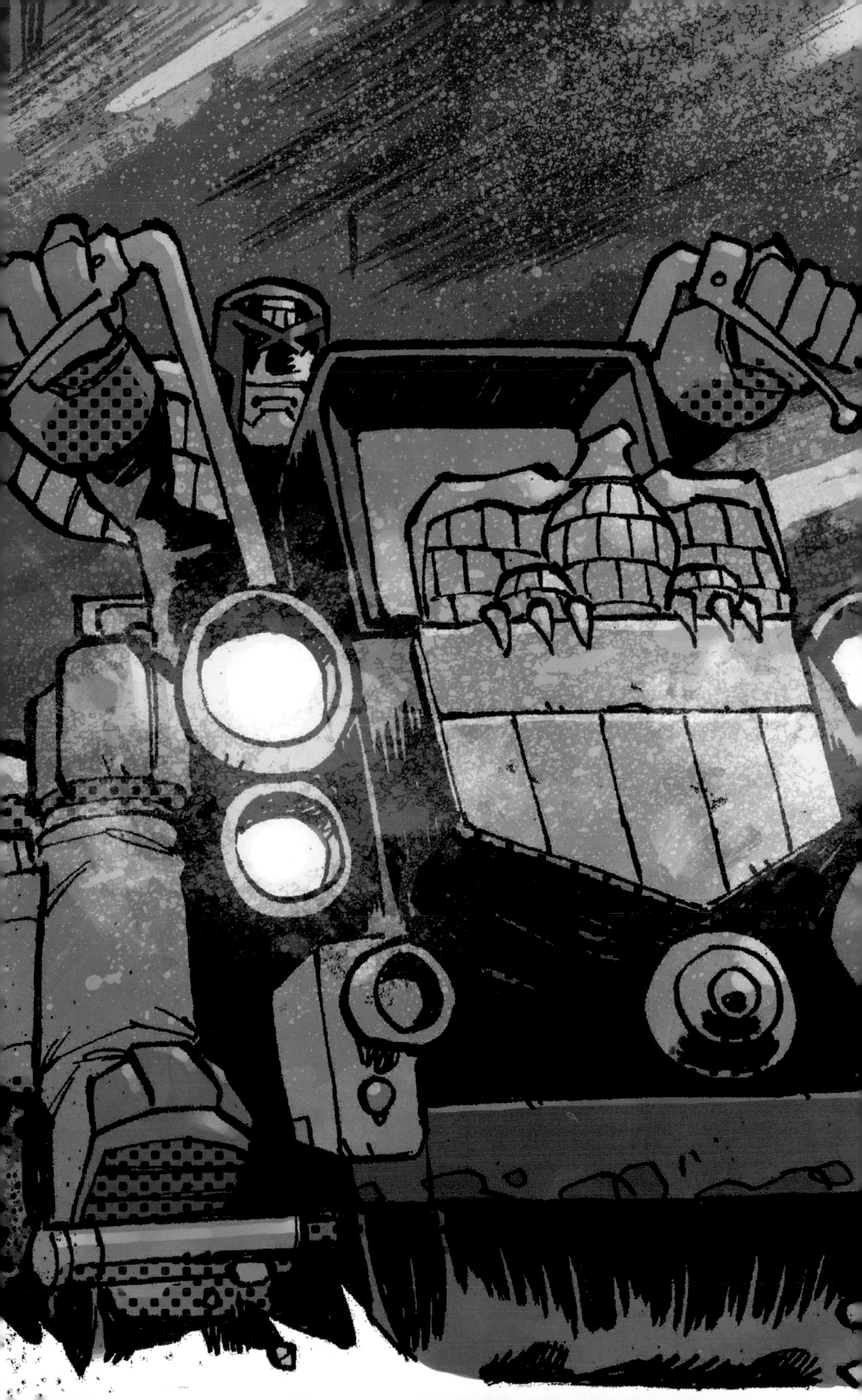

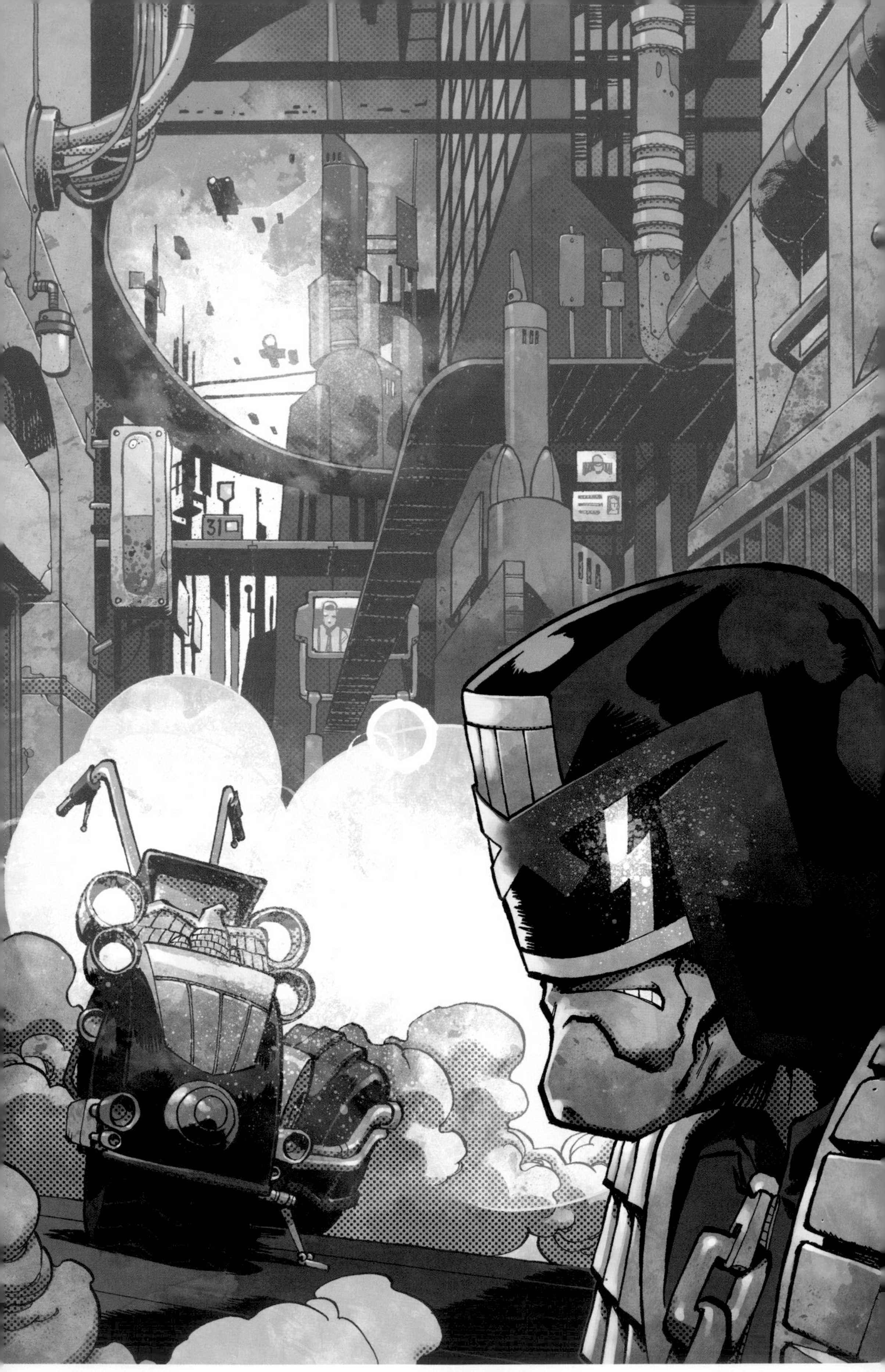
31

ART BY ***NELSON DANIEL***

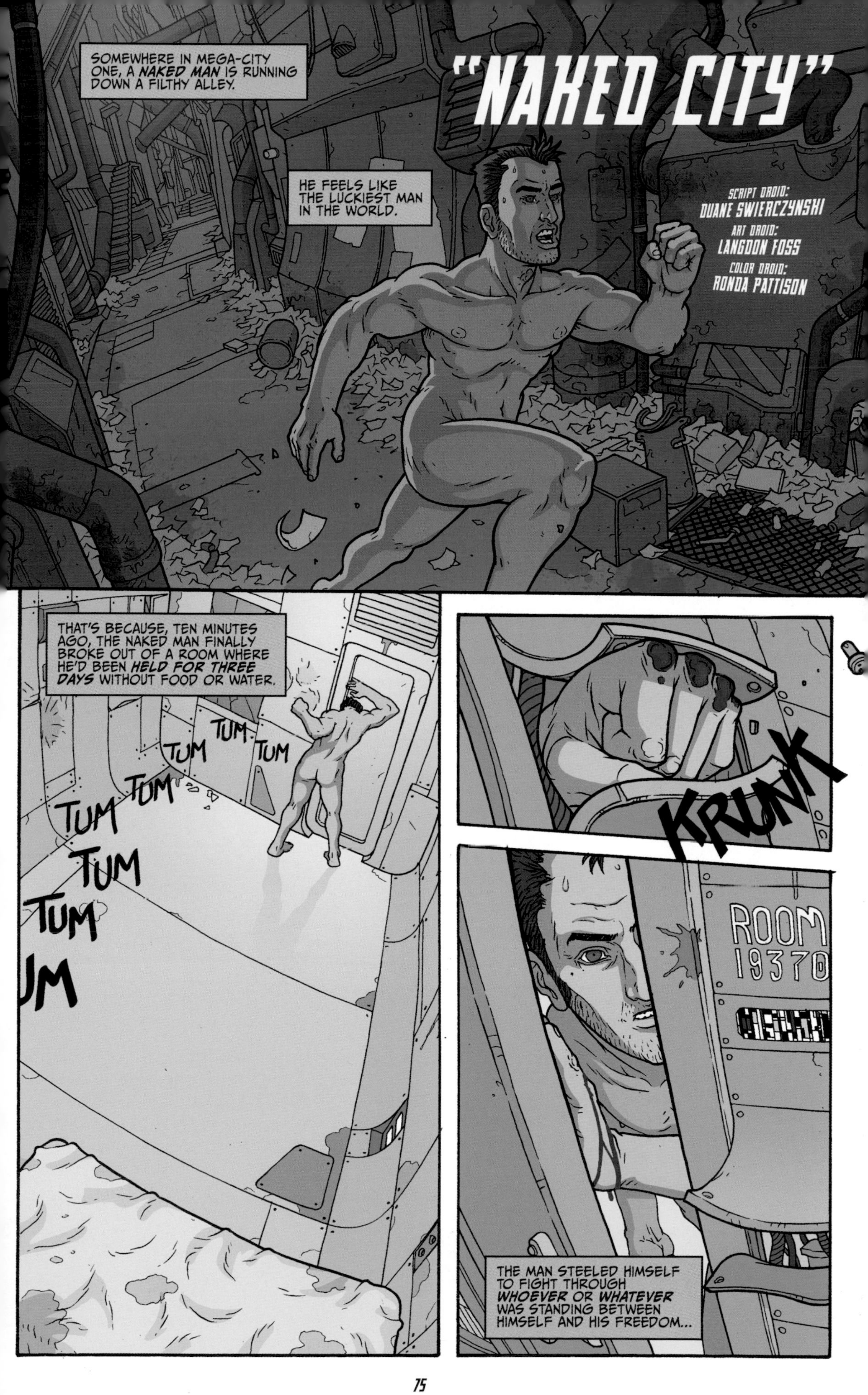

SOMEWHERE IN MEGA-CITY ONE, A NAKED MAN IS RUNNING DOWN A FILTHY ALLEY.
"NAKED CITY"
HE FEELS LIKE THE LUCKIEST MAN IN THE WORLD.
SCRIPT DROID: DUANE SWIERCZYNSKI
ART DROID: LANGDON FOSS
COLOR DROID: RONDA PATTISON
THAT'S BECAUSE, TEN MINUTES AGO, THE NAKED MAN FINALLY BROKE OUT OF A ROOM WHERE HE'D BEEN HELD FOR THREE DAYS WITHOUT FOOD OR WATER.
TUM TUM TUM TUM TUM TUM TUM UM
KRUNK
ROOM 19370
THE MAN STEELED HIMSELF TO FIGHT THROUGH WHOEVER OR WHATEVER WAS STANDING BETWEEN HIMSELF AND HIS FREEDOM...

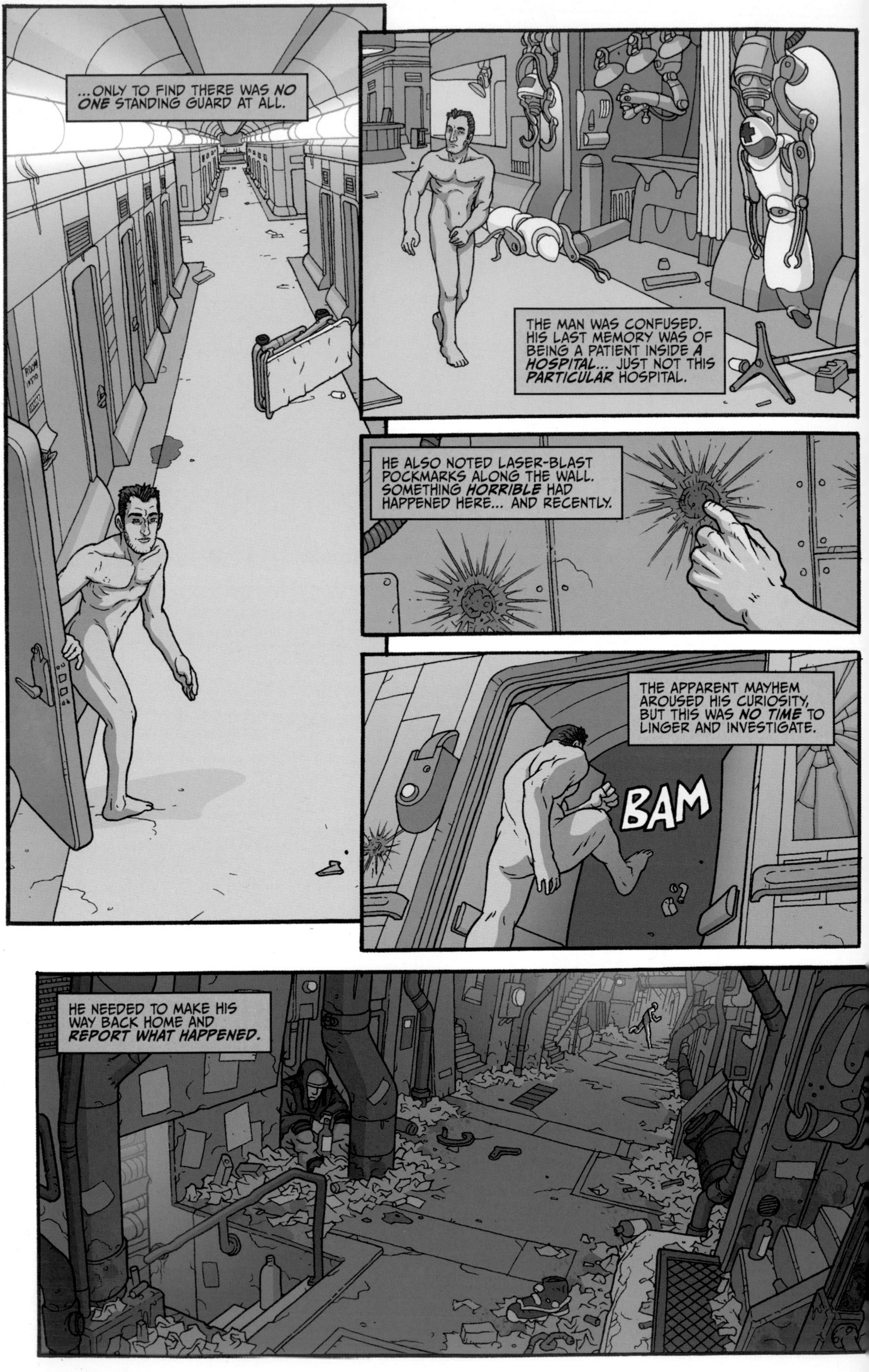
...ONLY TO FIND THERE WAS NO ONE STANDING GUARD AT ALL.
ROOM 1370
THE MAN WAS CONFUSED. HIS LAST MEMORY WAS OF BEING A PATIENT INSIDE A HOSPITAL... JUST NOT THIS PARTICULAR HOSPITAL.
HE ALSO NOTED LASER-BLAST POCKMARKS ALONG THE WALL. SOMETHING HORRIBLE HAD HAPPENED HERE... AND RECENTLY.
THE APPARENT MAYHEM AROUSED HIS CURIOSITY, BUT THIS WAS NO TIME TO LINGER AND INVESTIGATE.
BAM
HE NEEDED TO MAKE HIS WAY BACK HOME AND REPORT WHAT HAPPENED.

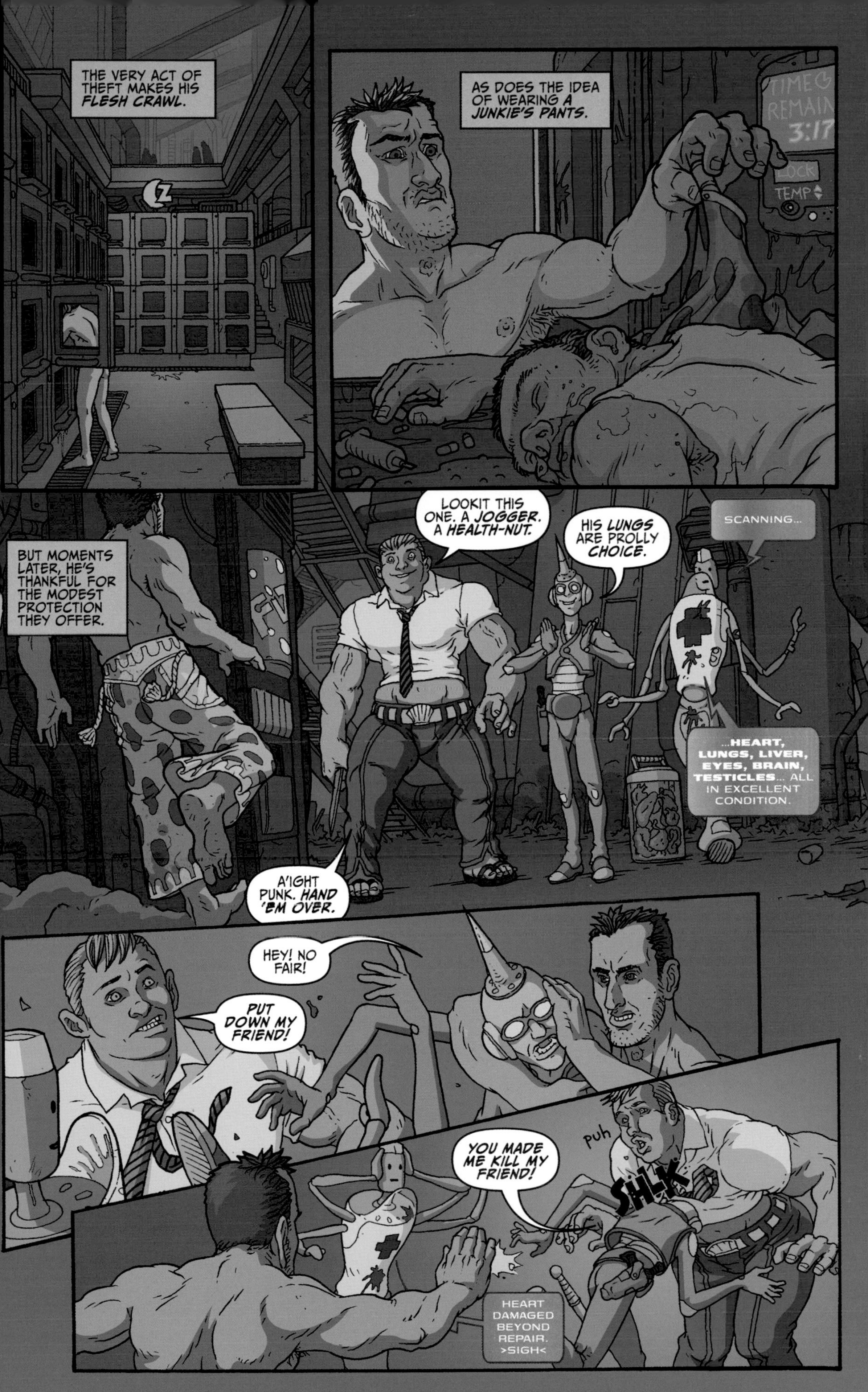

THE VERY ACT OF THEFT MAKES HIS *FLESH CRAWL.*
Z
AS DOES THE IDEA OF WEARING A *JUNKIE'S PANTS.*
TIME REMAIN 3:17
LOCK
TEMP
BUT MOMENTS LATER, HE'S THANKFUL FOR THE MODEST PROTECTION THEY OFFER.
LOOKIT THIS ONE. A *JOGGER.* A *HEALTH-NUT.*
HIS *LUNGS* ARE PROLLY *CHOICE.*
SCANNING...
...**HEART, LUNGS, LIVER, EYES, BRAIN, TESTICLES**... ALL IN EXCELLENT CONDITION.
A'IGHT PUNK. *HAND 'EM OVER.*
HEY! NO FAIR!
PUT DOWN MY FRIEND!
puh
YOU MADE ME KILL MY FRIEND!
SHLK
HEART DAMAGED BEYOND REPAIR. >SIGH<

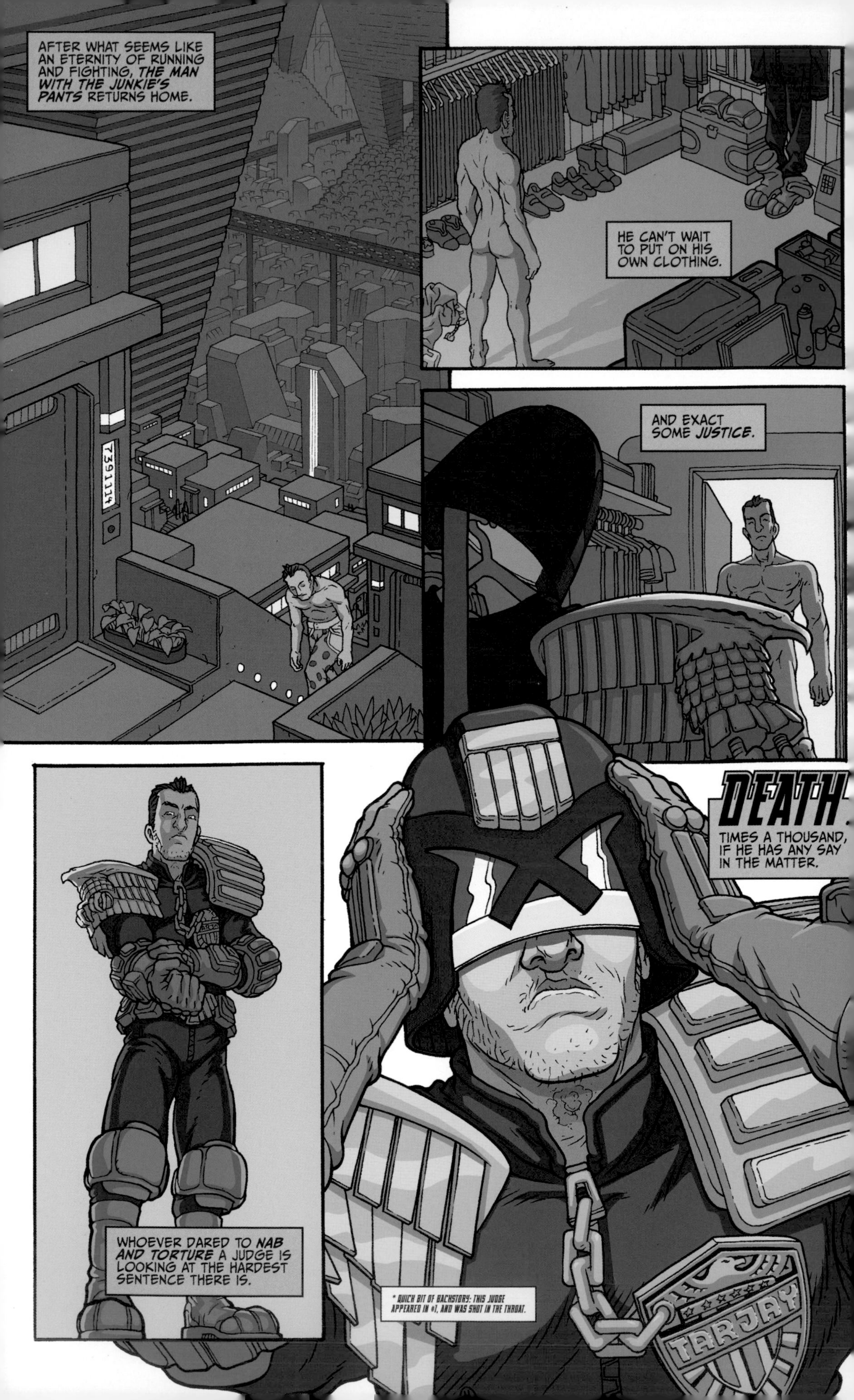
AFTER WHAT SEEMS LIKE AN ETERNITY OF RUNNING AND FIGHTING, THE MAN WITH THE JUNKIE'S PANTS RETURNS HOME.
7391114
HE CAN'T WAIT TO PUT ON HIS OWN CLOTHING.
AND EXACT SOME JUSTICE.
WHOEVER DARED TO NAB AND TORTURE A JUDGE IS LOOKING AT THE HARDEST SENTENCE THERE IS.
DEATH.
TIMES A THOUSAND, IF HE HAS ANY SAY IN THE MATTER.
* QUICK BIT OF BACKSTORY: THIS JUDGE APPEARED IN #1, AND WAS SHOT IN THE THROAT.
TARJAY

JUDGE TARJAY WAS NEVER SO HAPPY TO REPORT FOR DUTY AT THE *JUSTICE DEPARTMENT.*

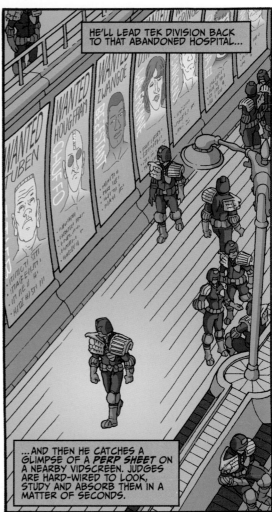

HE'LL LEAD TEK DIVISION BACK TO THAT ABANDONED HOSPITAL...

WANTED RUBEN

WANTED HOUGFRAM CHUFFO

WANTED ZWANGOF RE-ESTADT

...AND THEN HE CATCHES A GLIMPSE OF A *PERP SHEET* ON A NEARBY VIDSCREEN. JUDGES ARE HARD-WIRED TO LOOK, STUDY AND ABSORB THEM IN A MATTER OF SECONDS.

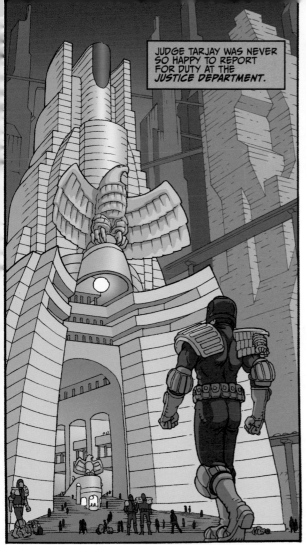

BUT THIS TIME, A *FAMILIAR FACE* STARES BACK AT HIM.

WANTED JUDGE MARTIN TARJAY

• CORRUPTION
• ATTEMPTED M
  OF A JUDGE
  HIJACKING
  LLEGAL CLONIN

AND NOW JUDGE TARJAY HAS SOME IDEA OF WHY SOMEONE WOULD WANT TO *LOCK HIM AWAY IN A ROOM* SOMEWHERE.

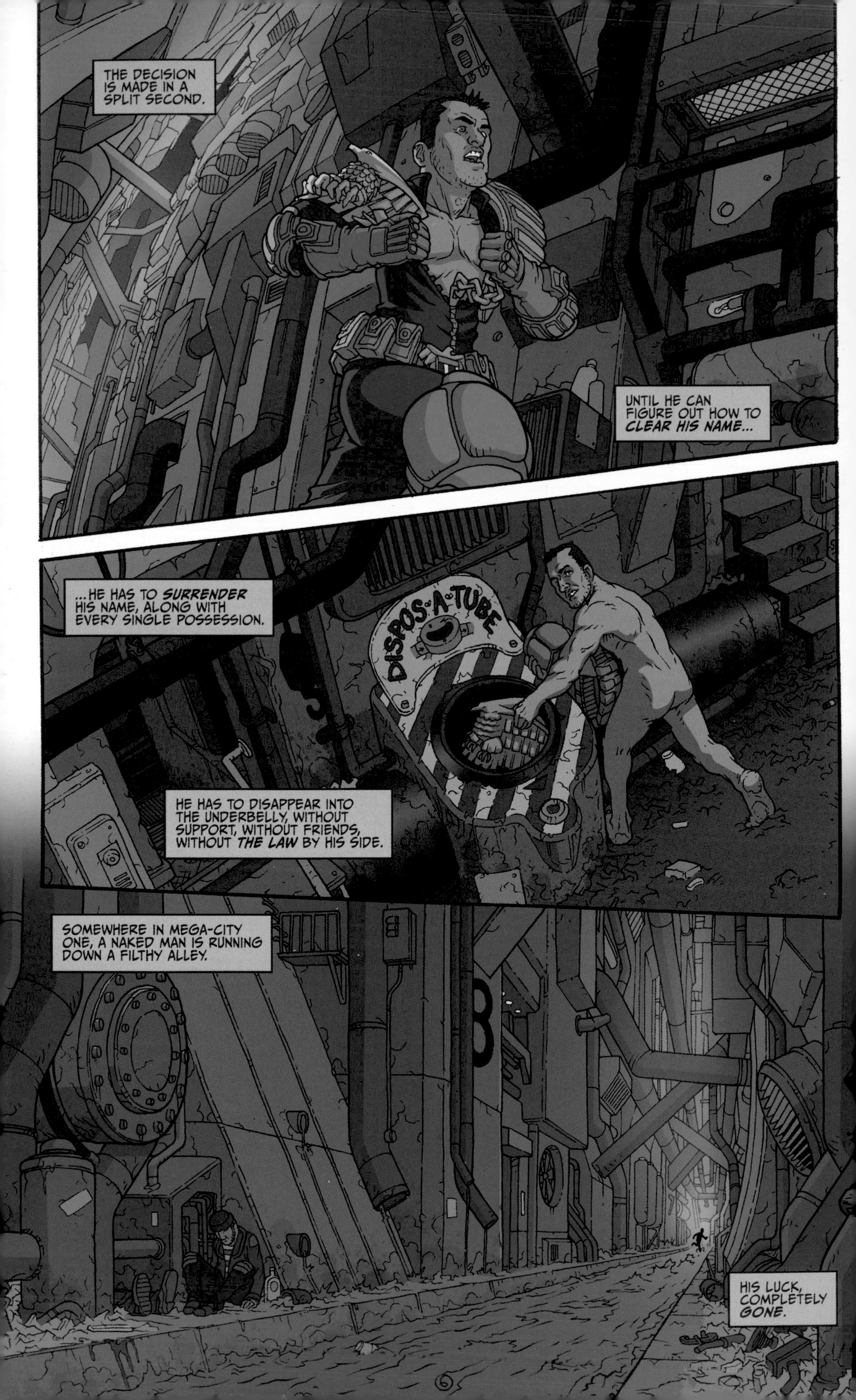
THE DECISION IS MADE IN A SPLIT SECOND.
UNTIL HE CAN FIGURE OUT HOW TO CLEAR HIS NAME...
...HE HAS TO SURRENDER HIS NAME, ALONG WITH EVERY SINGLE POSSESSION.
DISPOS-A-TUBE
HE HAS TO DISAPPEAR INTO THE UNDERBELLY, WITHOUT SUPPORT, WITHOUT FRIENDS, WITHOUT THE LAW BY HIS SIDE.
SOMEWHERE IN MEGA-CITY ONE, A NAKED MAN IS RUNNING DOWN A FILTHY ALLEY.
HIS LUCK, COMPLETELY GONE.
6

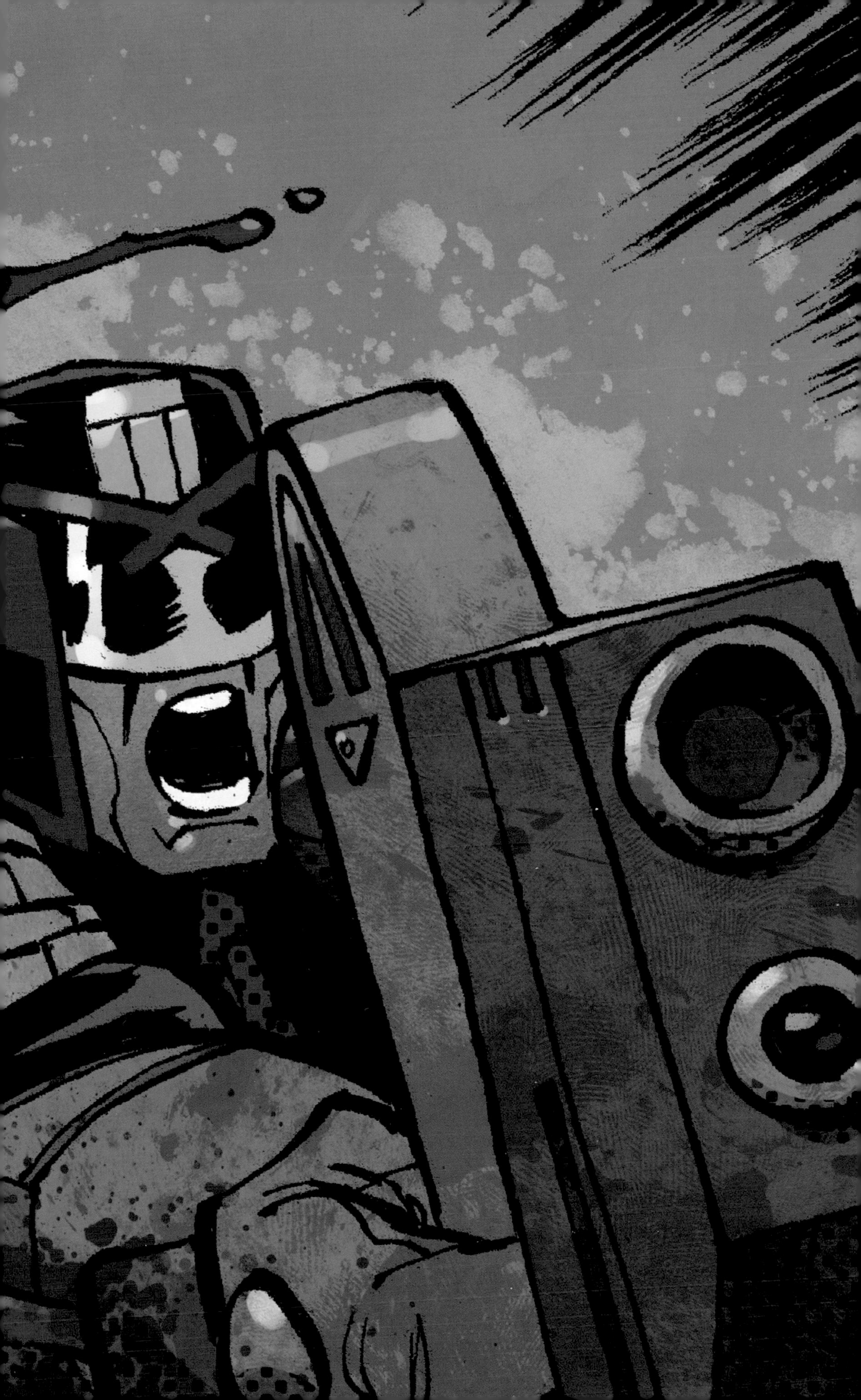

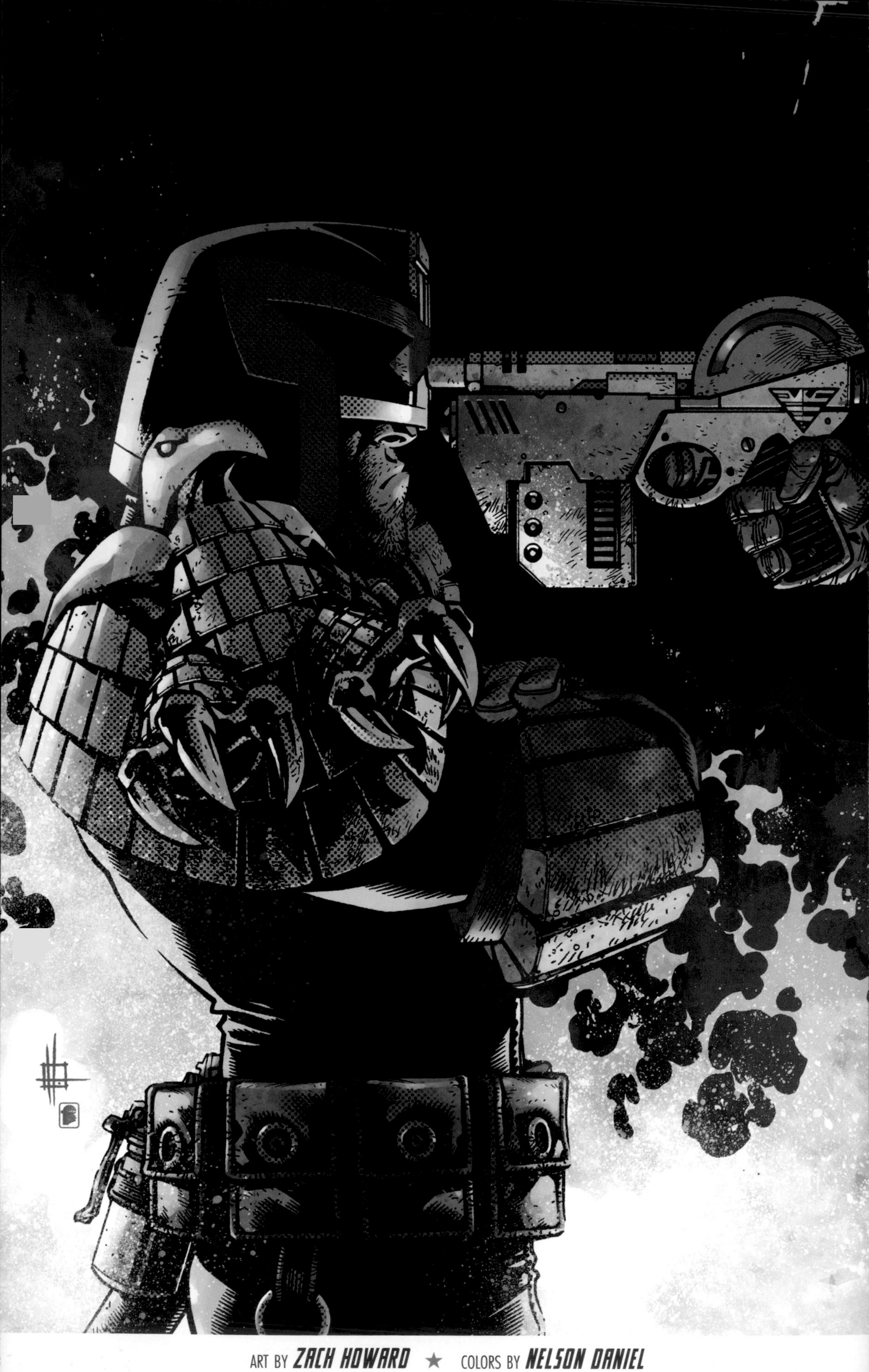

ART BY ZACH HOWARD ★ COLORS BY NELSON DANIEL

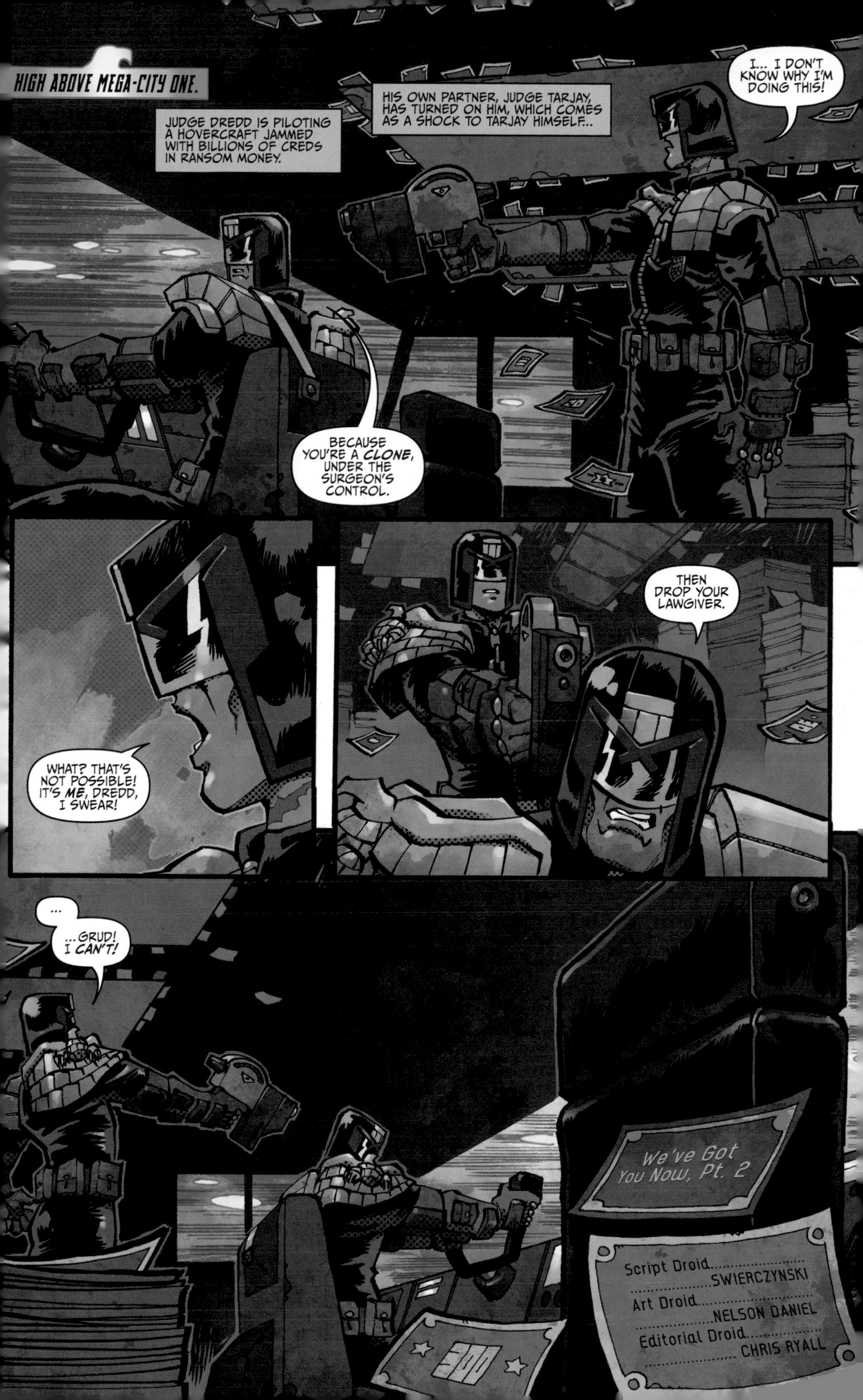
HIGH ABOVE MEGA-CITY ONE.
JUDGE DREDD IS PILOTING A HOVERCRAFT JAMMED WITH BILLIONS OF CREDS IN RANSOM MONEY.
HIS OWN PARTNER, JUDGE TARJAY, HAS TURNED ON HIM, WHICH COMES AS A SHOCK TO TARJAY HIMSELF...
I... I DON'T KNOW WHY I'M DOING THIS!
BECAUSE YOU'RE A CLONE, UNDER THE SURGEON'S CONTROL.
WHAT? THAT'S NOT POSSIBLE! IT'S ME, DREDD, I SWEAR!
THEN DROP YOUR LAWGIVER.
...
...GRUD! I CAN'T!
We've Got You Now, Pt. 2
Script Droid.......SWIERCZYNSKI
Art Droid.......NELSON DANIEL
Editorial Droid.......CHRIS RYALL

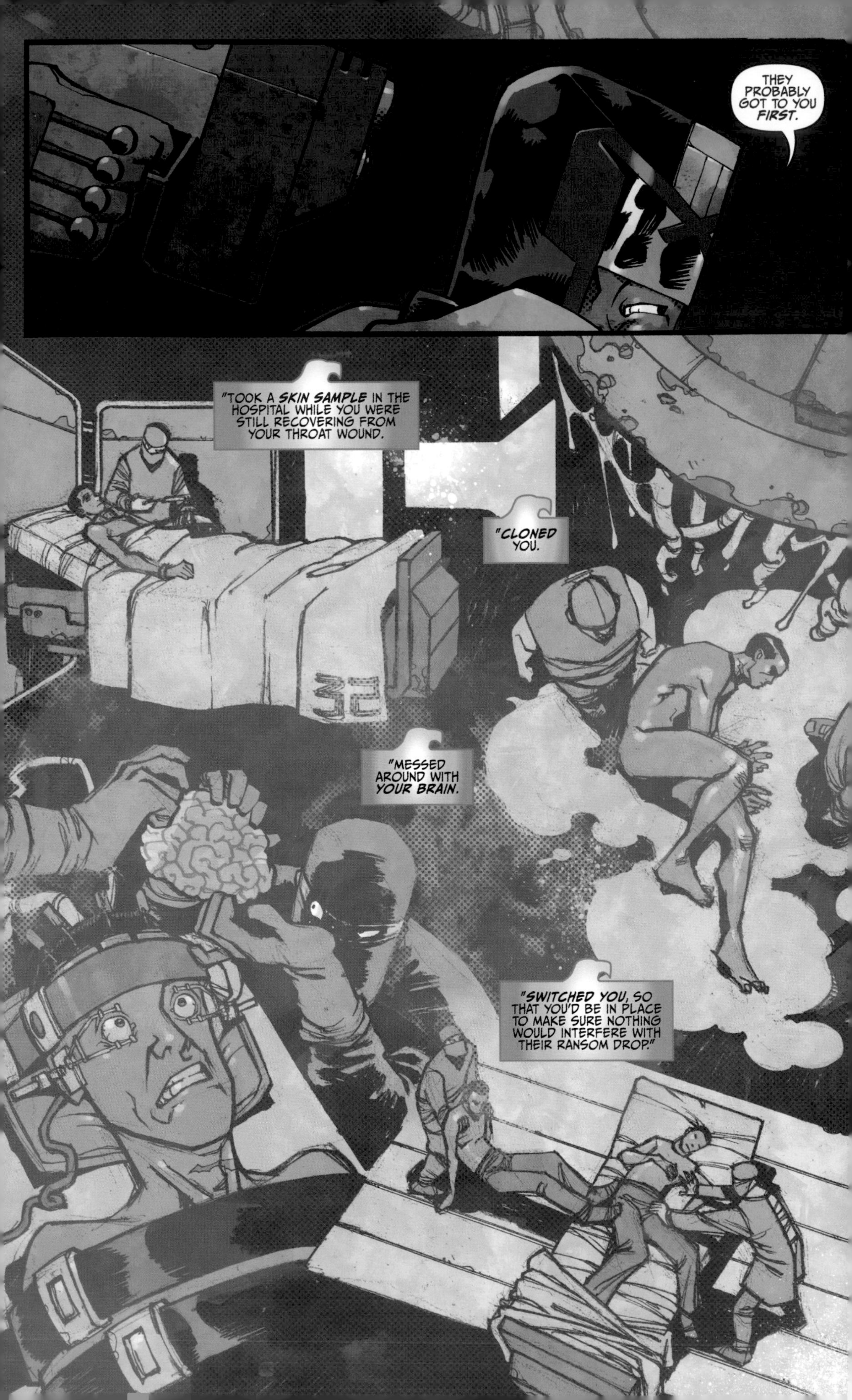
THEY PROBABLY GOT TO YOU *FIRST*.
"TOOK A *SKIN SAMPLE* IN THE HOSPITAL WHILE YOU WERE STILL RECOVERING FROM YOUR THROAT WOUND.
"*CLONED* YOU.
"MESSED AROUND WITH *YOUR BRAIN*.
"*SWITCHED YOU*, SO THAT YOU'D BE IN PLACE TO MAKE SURE NOTHING WOULD INTERFERE WITH THEIR RANSOM DROP."

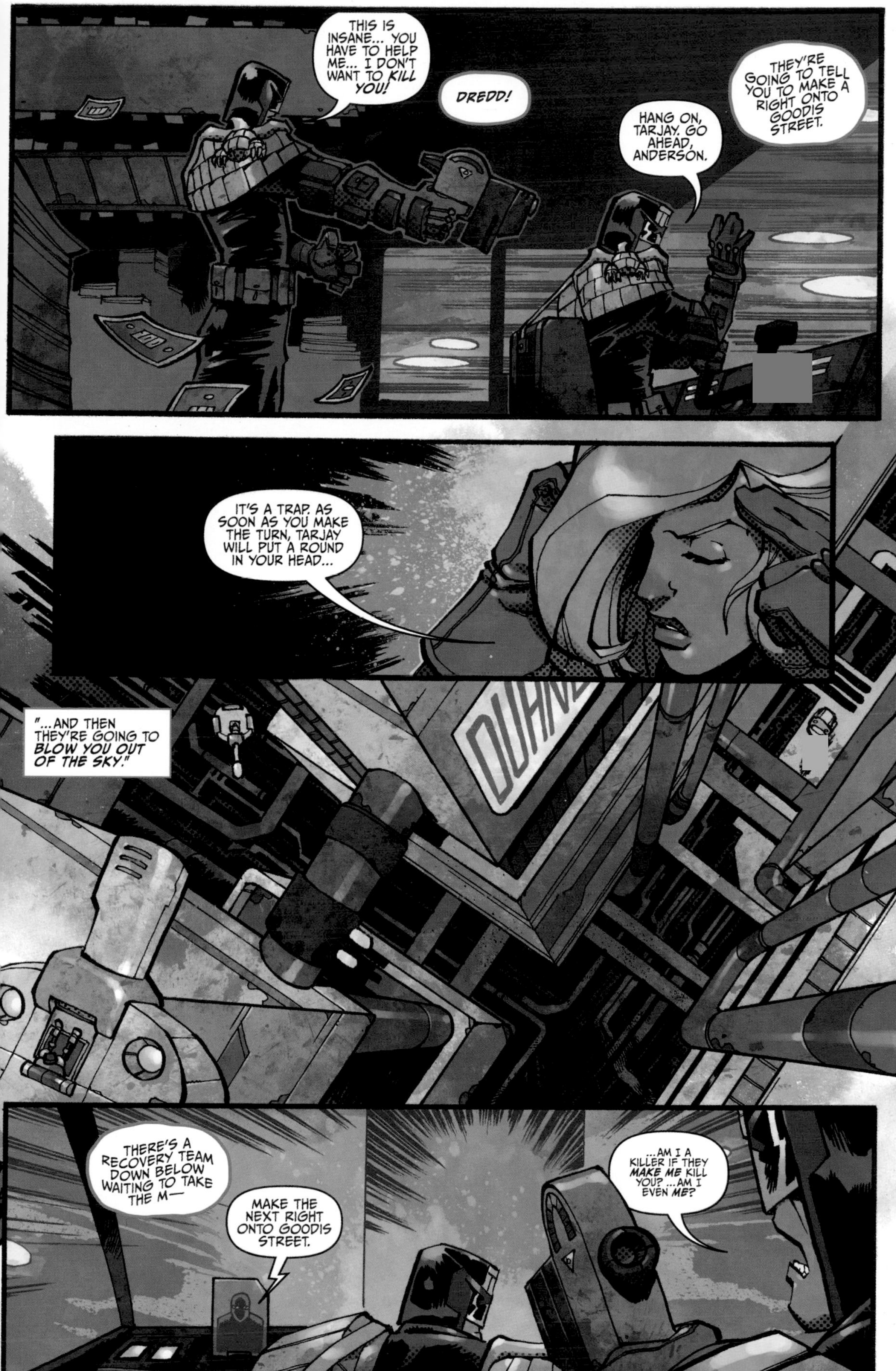
THIS IS INSANE... YOU HAVE TO HELP ME... I DON'T WANT TO *KILL YOU!*
DREDD!
HANG ON, TARJAY. GO AHEAD, ANDERSON.
THEY'RE GOING TO TELL YOU TO MAKE A RIGHT ONTO GOODIS STREET.
IT'S A TRAP. AS SOON AS YOU MAKE THE TURN, TARJAY WILL PUT A ROUND IN YOUR HEAD...
"...AND THEN THEY'RE GOING TO *BLOW YOU OUT OF THE SKY.*"
THERE'S A RECOVERY TEAM DOWN BELOW WAITING TO TAKE THE M—
MAKE THE NEXT RIGHT ONTO GOODIS STREET.
...AM I A KILLER IF THEY *MAKE ME* KILL YOU? ...AM I EVEN *ME?*

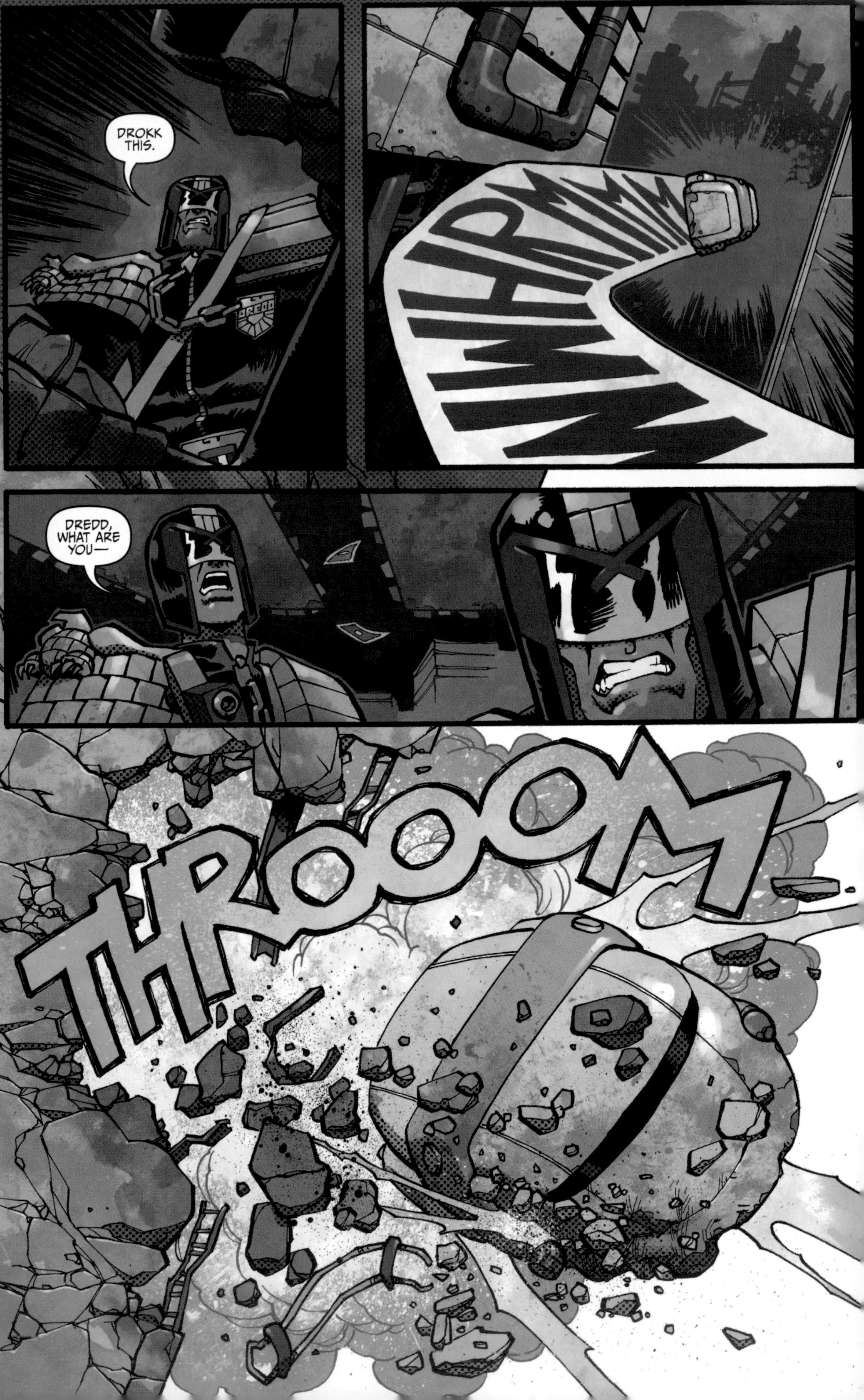
DROKK THIS.
WHIMMMMM
DREDD, WHAT ARE YOU—
THROOOM-

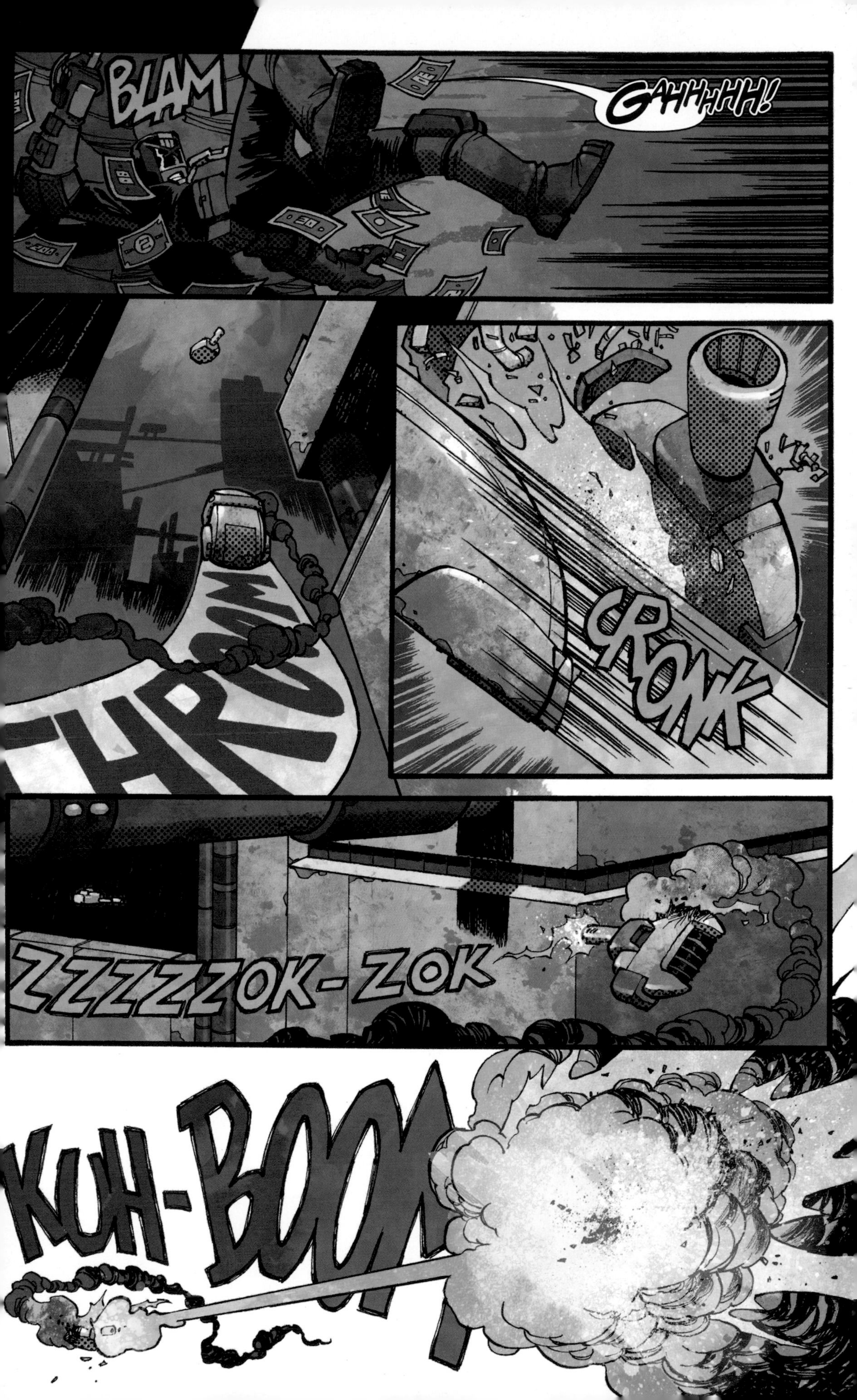
BLAM
GAHHHHH!
THROOM
CRONK
ZZZZZZOK-ZOK
KUH-BOOM

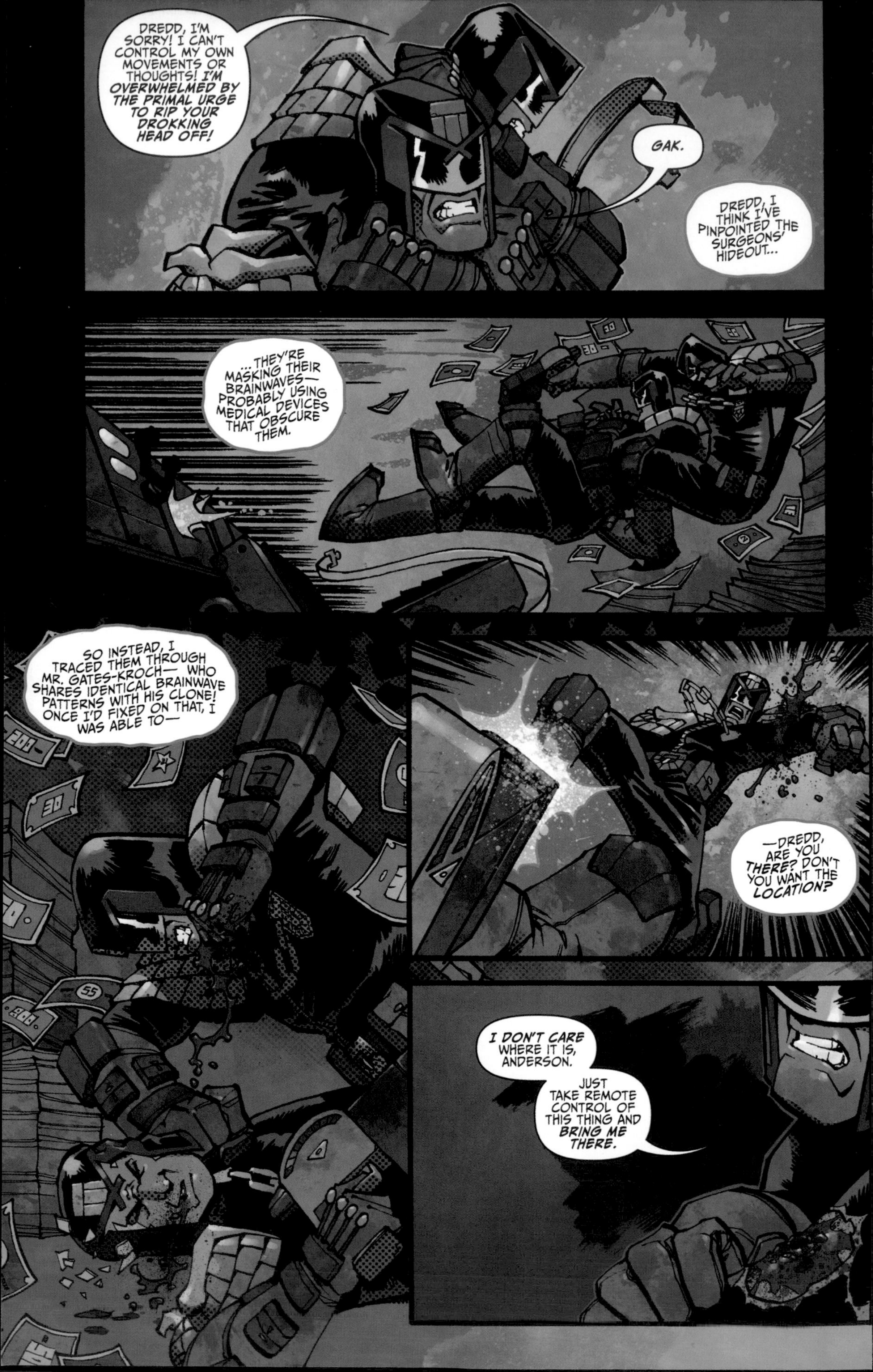
DREDD, I'M SORRY! I CAN'T CONTROL MY OWN MOVEMENTS OR THOUGHTS! I'M OVERWHELMED BY THE PRIMAL URGE TO RIP YOUR DROKKING HEAD OFF!
GAK.
DREDD, I THINK I'VE PINPOINTED THE SURGEONS' HIDEOUT...
...THEY'RE MASKING THEIR BRAINWAVES— PROBABLY USING MEDICAL DEVICES THAT OBSCURE THEM.
SO INSTEAD, I TRACED THEM THROUGH MR. GATES-KROCH— WHO SHARES IDENTICAL BRAINWAVE PATTERNS WITH HIS CLONE! ONCE I'D FIXED ON THAT, I WAS ABLE TO—
—DREDD, ARE YOU THERE? DON'T YOU WANT THE LOCATION?
I DON'T CARE WHERE IT IS, ANDERSON.
JUST TAKE REMOTE CONTROL OF THIS THING AND BRING ME THERE.

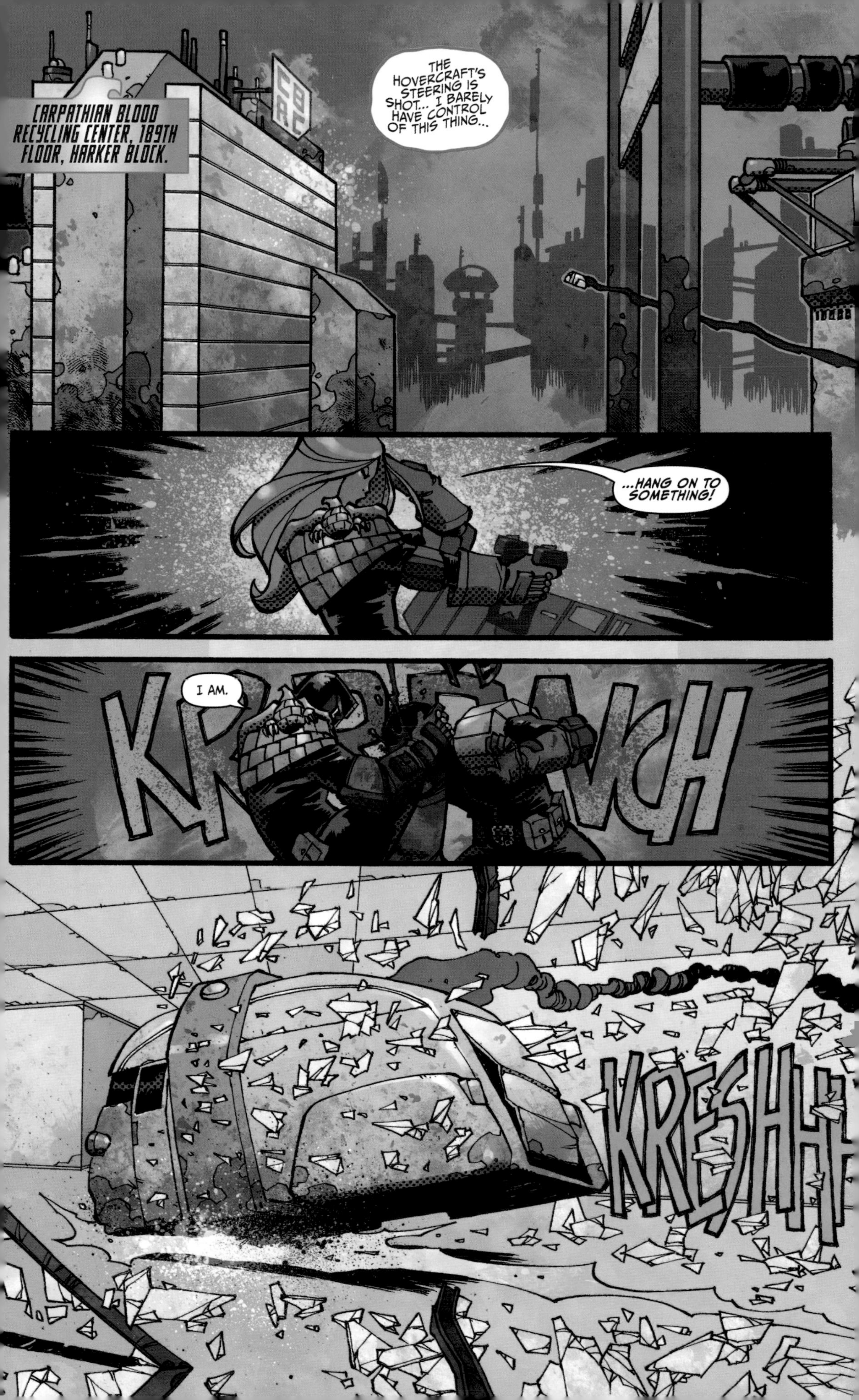
CARPATHIAN BLOOD RECYCLING CENTER, 189TH FLOOR, HARKER BLOCK.
CBRC
THE HOVERCRAFT'S STEERING IS SHOT... I BARELY HAVE CONTROL OF THIS THING...
...HANG ON TO SOMETHING!
I AM.
KRESHH

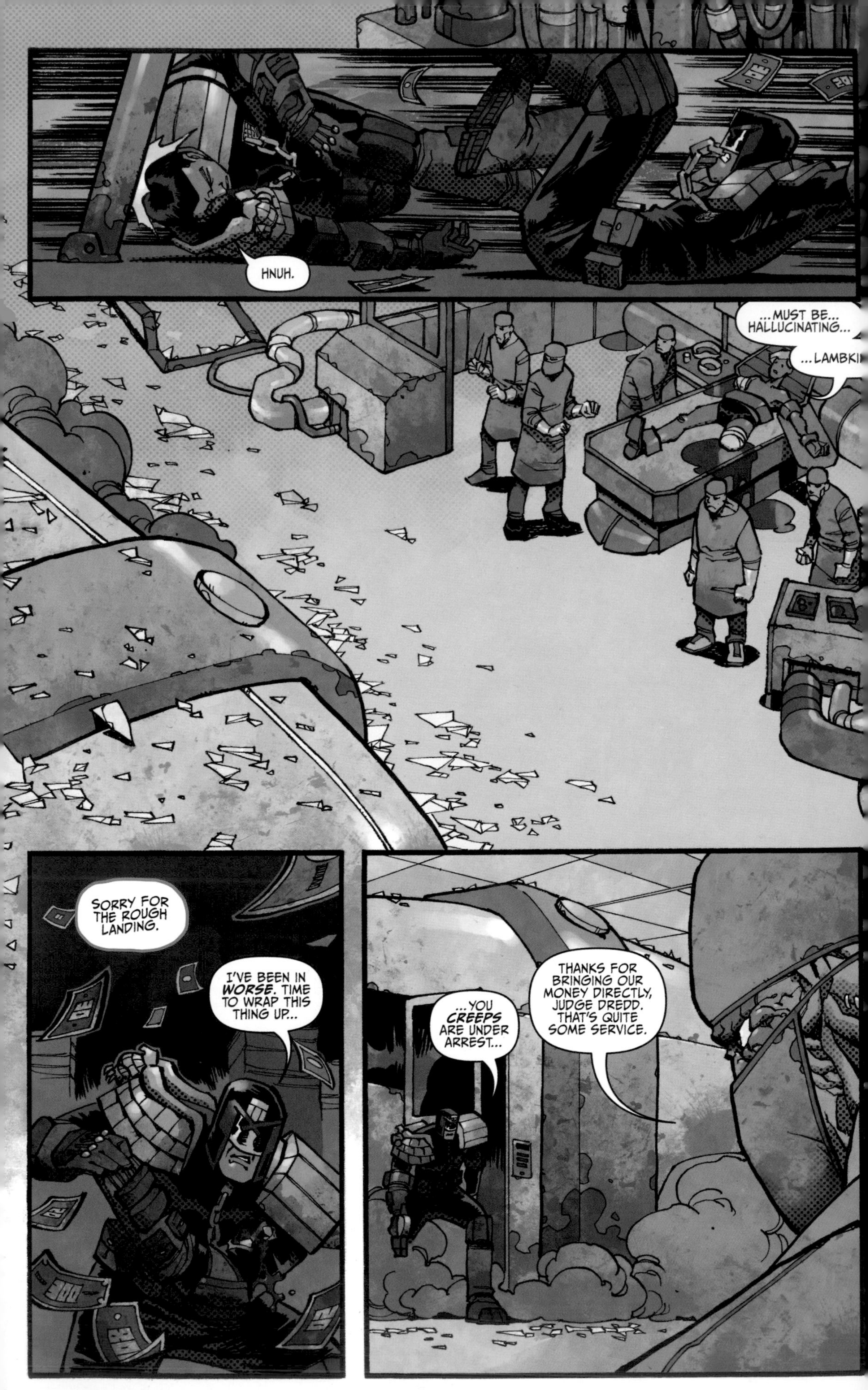
HNUH.
...MUST BE... HALLUCINATING...
...LAMBKI
SORRY FOR THE ROUGH LANDING.
I'VE BEEN IN WORSE. TIME TO WRAP THIS THING UP...
...YOU CREEPS ARE UNDER ARREST...
THANKS FOR BRINGING OUR MONEY DIRECTLY, JUDGE DREDD. THAT'S QUITE SOME SERVICE.

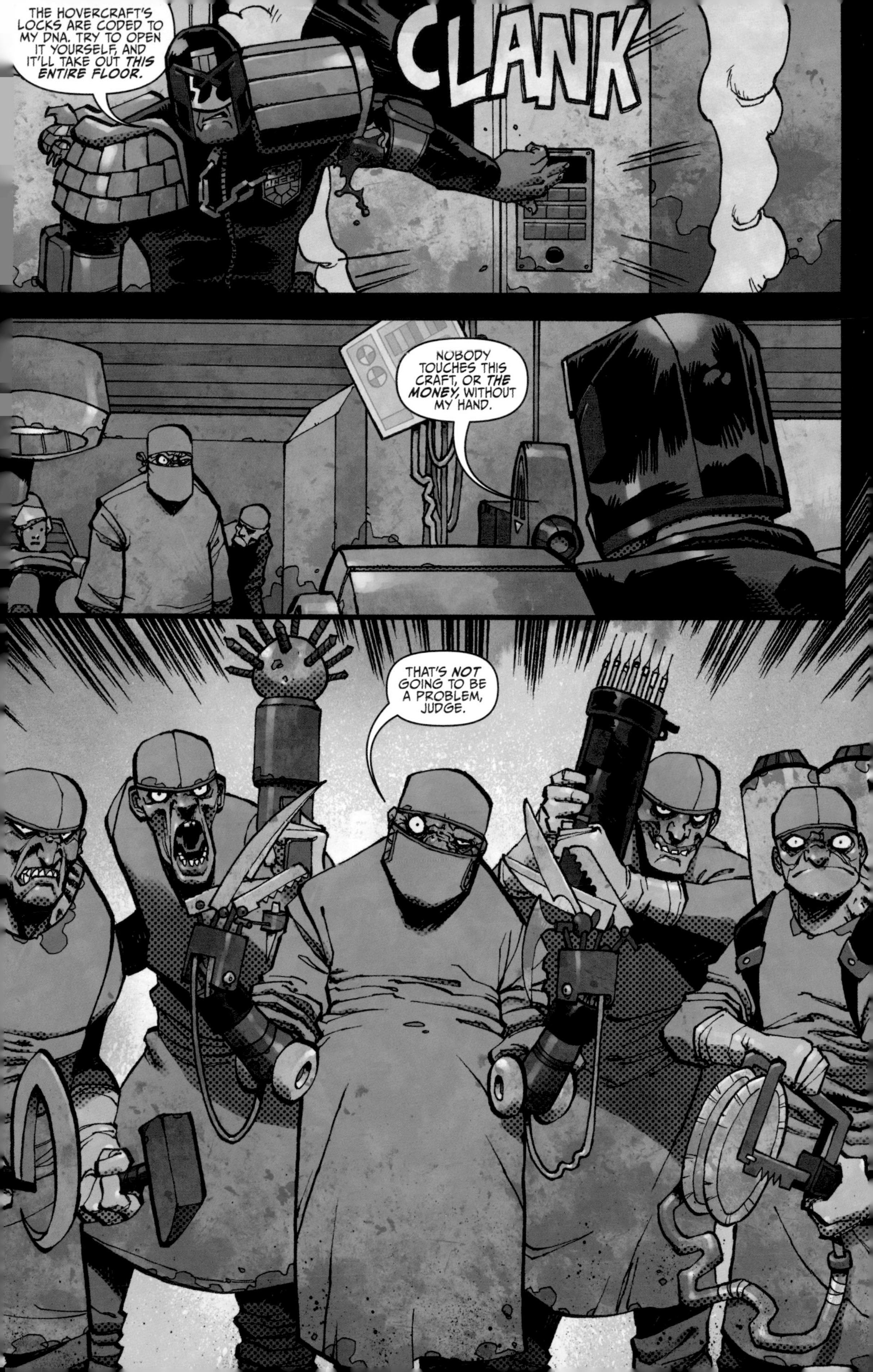
THE HOVERCRAFT'S LOCKS ARE CODED TO MY DNA. TRY TO OPEN IT YOURSELF, AND IT'LL TAKE OUT *THIS ENTIRE FLOOR.*
CLANK
NOBODY TOUCHES THIS CRAFT, OR *THE MONEY,* WITHOUT MY HAND.
THAT'S *NOT* GOING TO BE A PROBLEM, JUDGE.

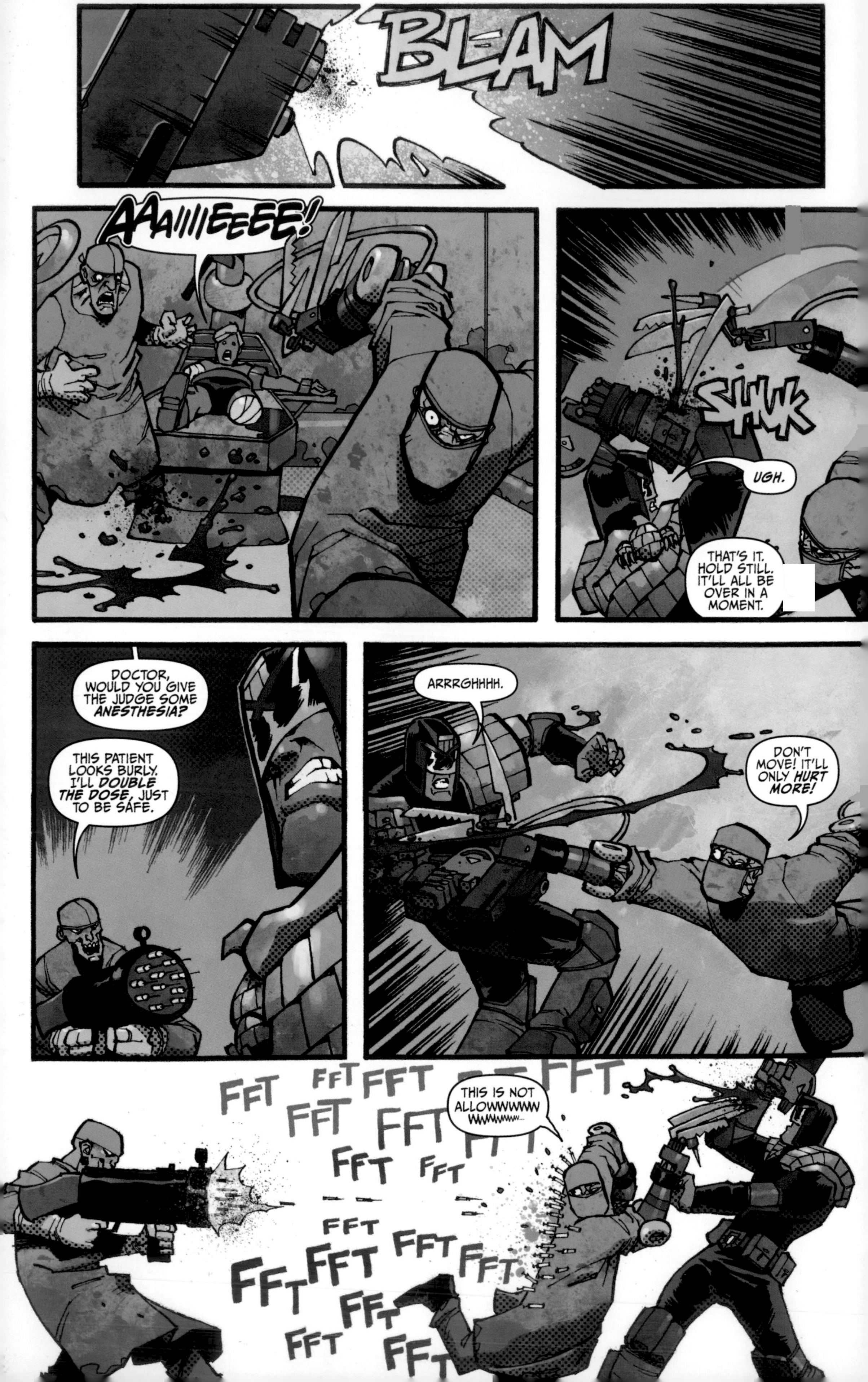
BLAM
AAAIIIIIEEEEE!
SHUK
UGH.
THAT'S IT. HOLD STILL. IT'LL ALL BE OVER IN A MOMENT.
DOCTOR, WOULD YOU GIVE THE JUDGE SOME *ANESTHESIA?*
THIS PATIENT LOOKS BURLY. I'LL *DOUBLE THE DOSE,* JUST TO BE SAFE.
ARRRGHHHH.
DON'T MOVE! IT'LL ONLY *HURT MORE!*
FFT FFT FFT FFT FFT FFT FFT FFT
THIS IS NOT ALLOWWWWW WWWWWWW...
FFT FFT FFT FFT FFT FFT FFT FFT

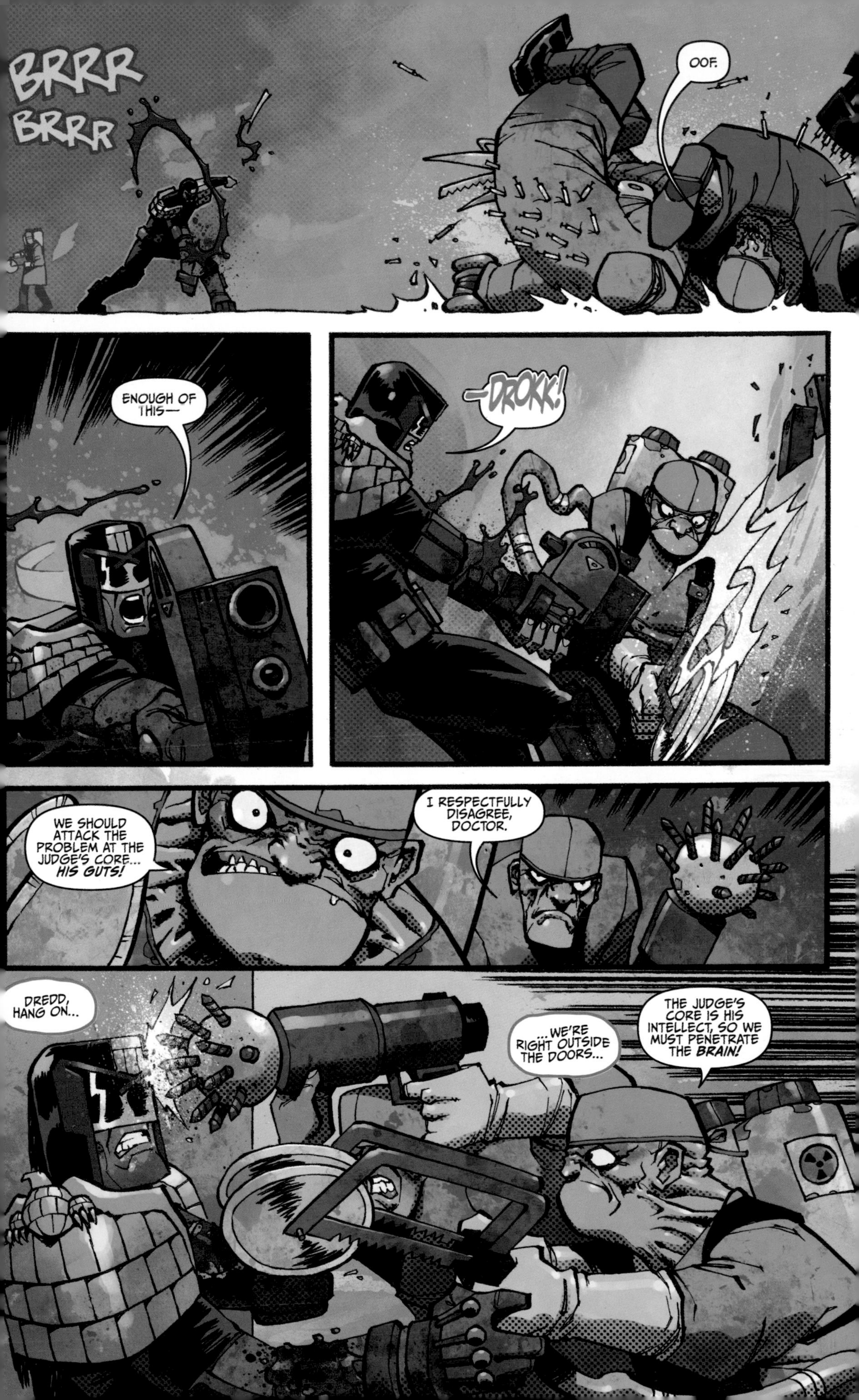
BRRR
BRRR
OOF.
ENOUGH OF THIS—
—DROKK!
WE SHOULD ATTACK THE PROBLEM AT THE JUDGE'S CORE... HIS GUTS!
I RESPECTFULLY DISAGREE, DOCTOR.
DREDD, HANG ON...
...WE'RE RIGHT OUTSIDE THE DOORS...
THE JUDGE'S CORE IS HIS INTELLECT, SO WE MUST PENETRATE THE BRAIN!

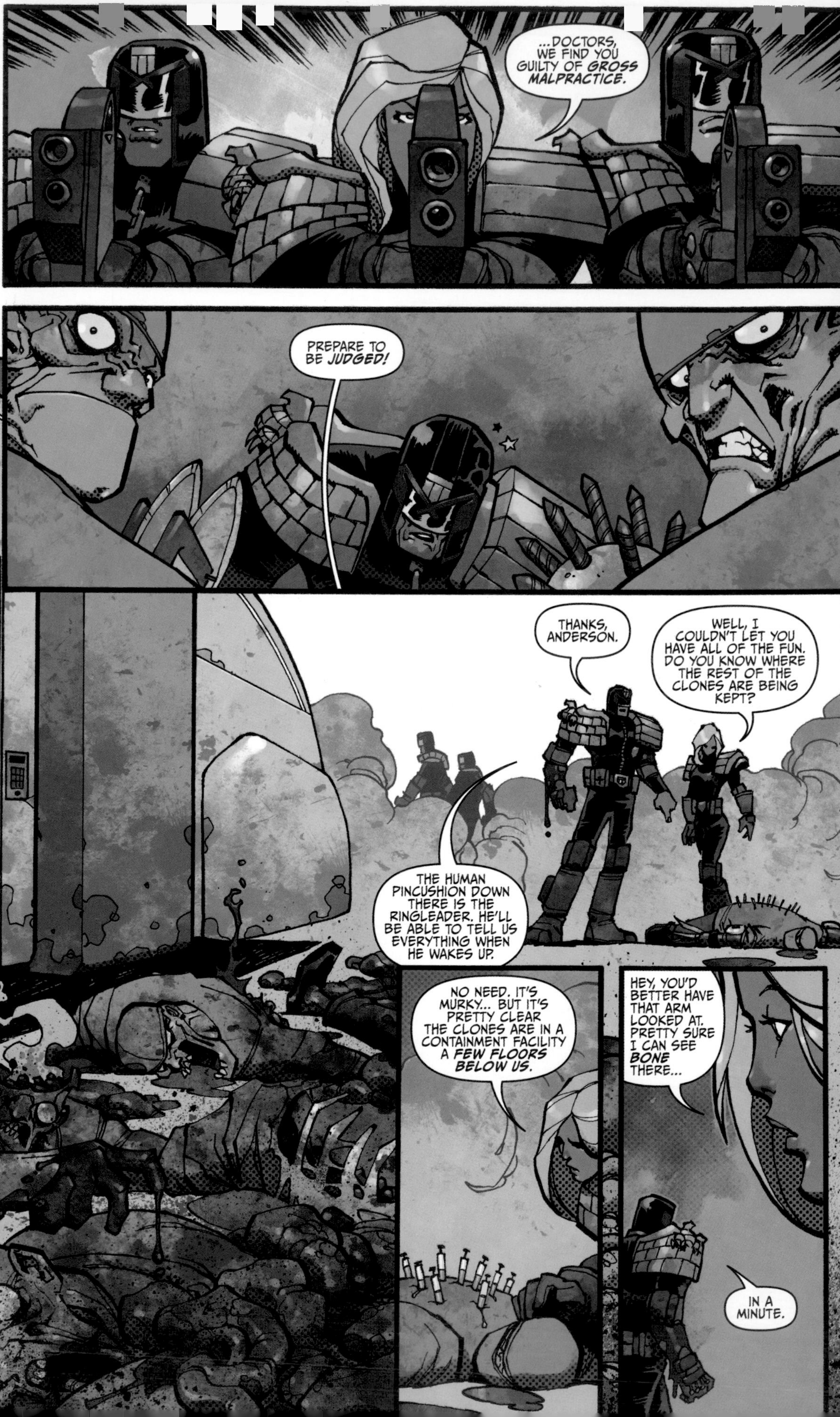
...DOCTORS, WE FIND YOU GUILTY OF GROSS MALPRACTICE.
PREPARE TO BE JUDGED!
THANKS, ANDERSON.
WELL, I COULDN'T LET YOU HAVE ALL OF THE FUN. DO YOU KNOW WHERE THE REST OF THE CLONES ARE BEING KEPT?
THE HUMAN PINCUSHION DOWN THERE IS THE RINGLEADER. HE'LL BE ABLE TO TELL US EVERYTHING WHEN HE WAKES UP.
NO NEED. IT'S MURKY... BUT IT'S PRETTY CLEAR THE CLONES ARE IN A CONTAINMENT FACILITY A FEW FLOORS BELOW US.
HEY, YOU'D BETTER HAVE THAT ARM LOOKED AT. PRETTY SURE I CAN SEE BONE THERE...
IN A MINUTE.

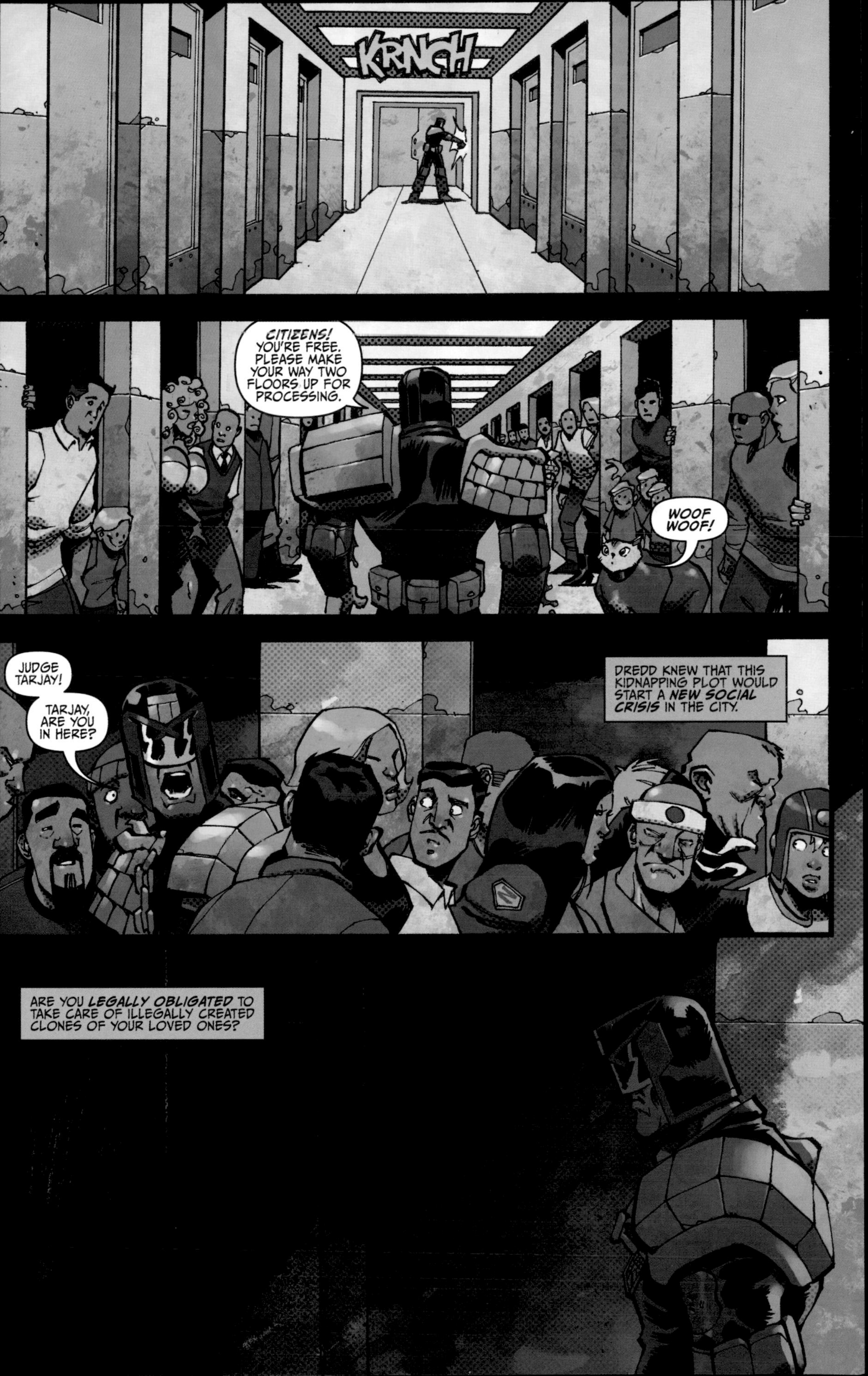
KRNCH
CITIZENS! YOU'RE FREE. PLEASE MAKE YOUR WAY TWO FLOORS UP FOR PROCESSING.
WOOF WOOF!
JUDGE TARJAY!
TARJAY, ARE YOU IN HERE?
DREDD KNEW THAT THIS KIDNAPPING PLOT WOULD START A NEW SOCIAL CRISIS IN THE CITY.
ARE YOU LEGALLY OBLIGATED TO TAKE CARE OF ILLEGALLY CREATED CLONES OF YOUR LOVED ONES?

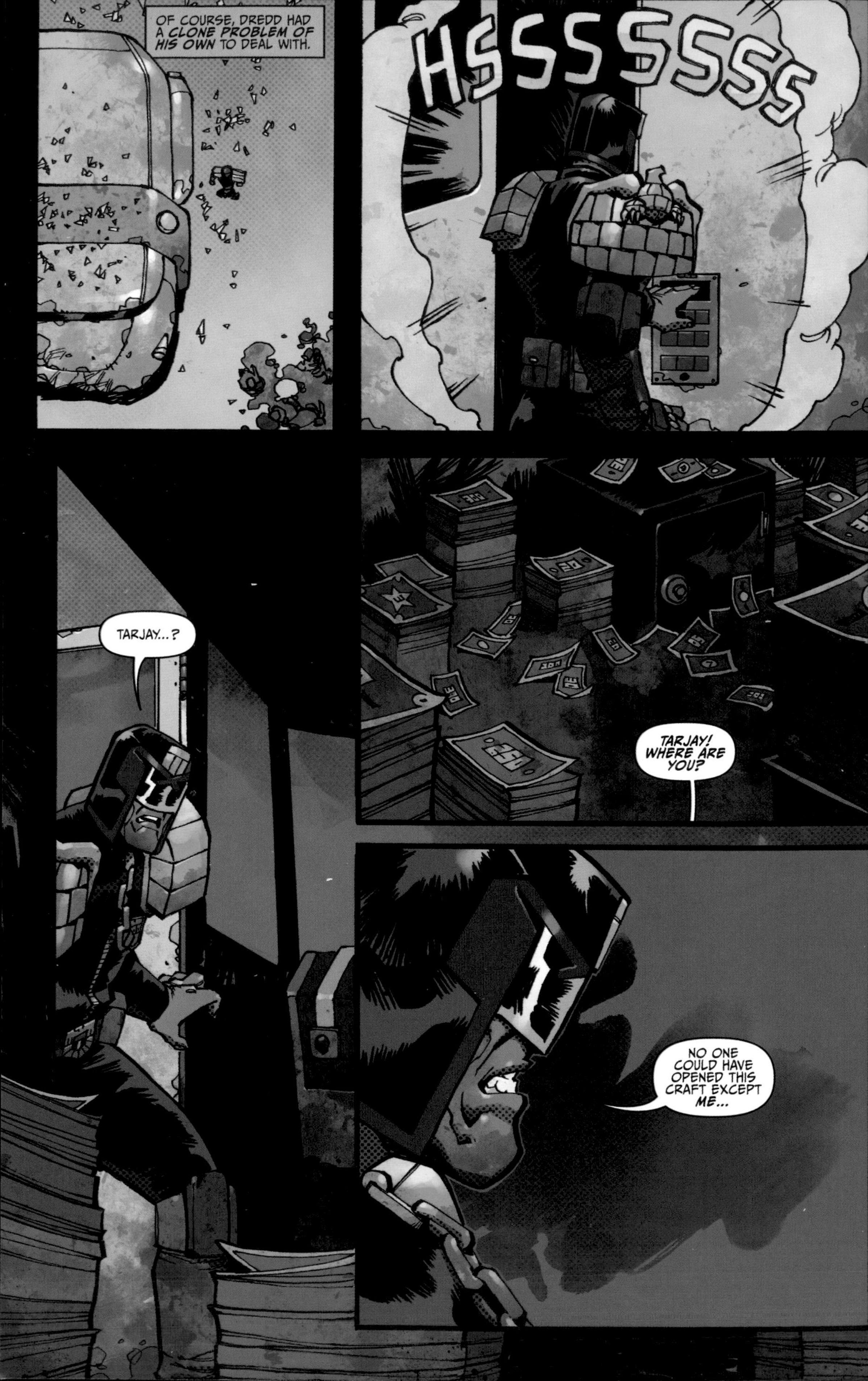

OF COURSE, DREDD HAD A CLONE PROBLEM OF HIS OWN TO DEAL WITH.
HSSSSSSS
TARJAY...?
TARJAY! WHERE ARE YOU?
NO ONE COULD HAVE OPENED THIS CRAFT EXCEPT ME...

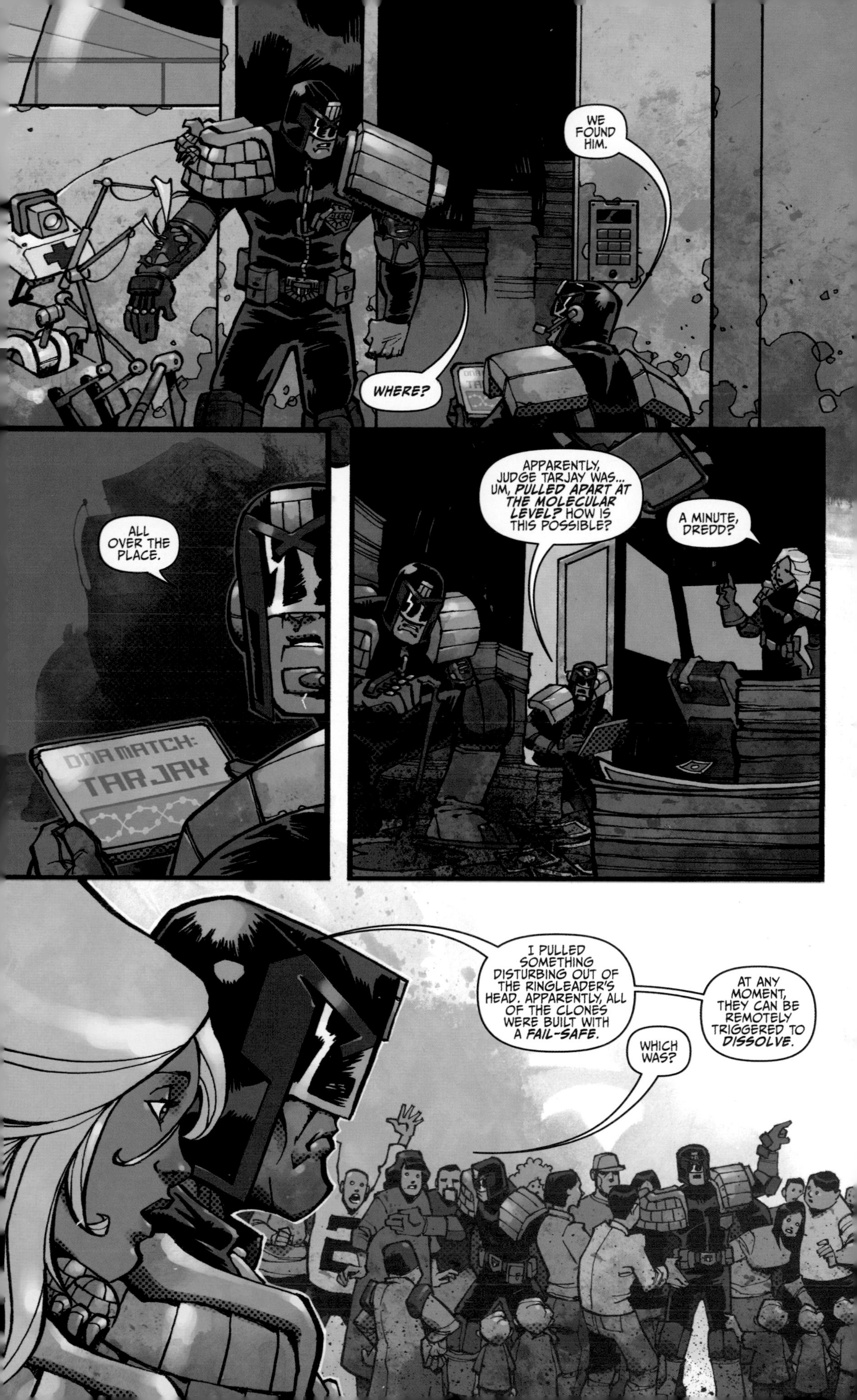

WE FOUND HIM.
WHERE?
ALL OVER THE PLACE.
DNA MATCH: TARJAY
APPARENTLY, JUDGE TARJAY WAS... UM, PULLED APART AT THE MOLECULAR LEVEL? HOW IS THIS POSSIBLE?
A MINUTE, DREDD?
I PULLED SOMETHING DISTURBING OUT OF THE RINGLEADER'S HEAD. APPARENTLY, ALL OF THE CLONES WERE BUILT WITH A FAIL-SAFE.
WHICH WAS?
AT ANY MOMENT, THEY CAN BE REMOTELY TRIGGERED TO DISSOLVE.

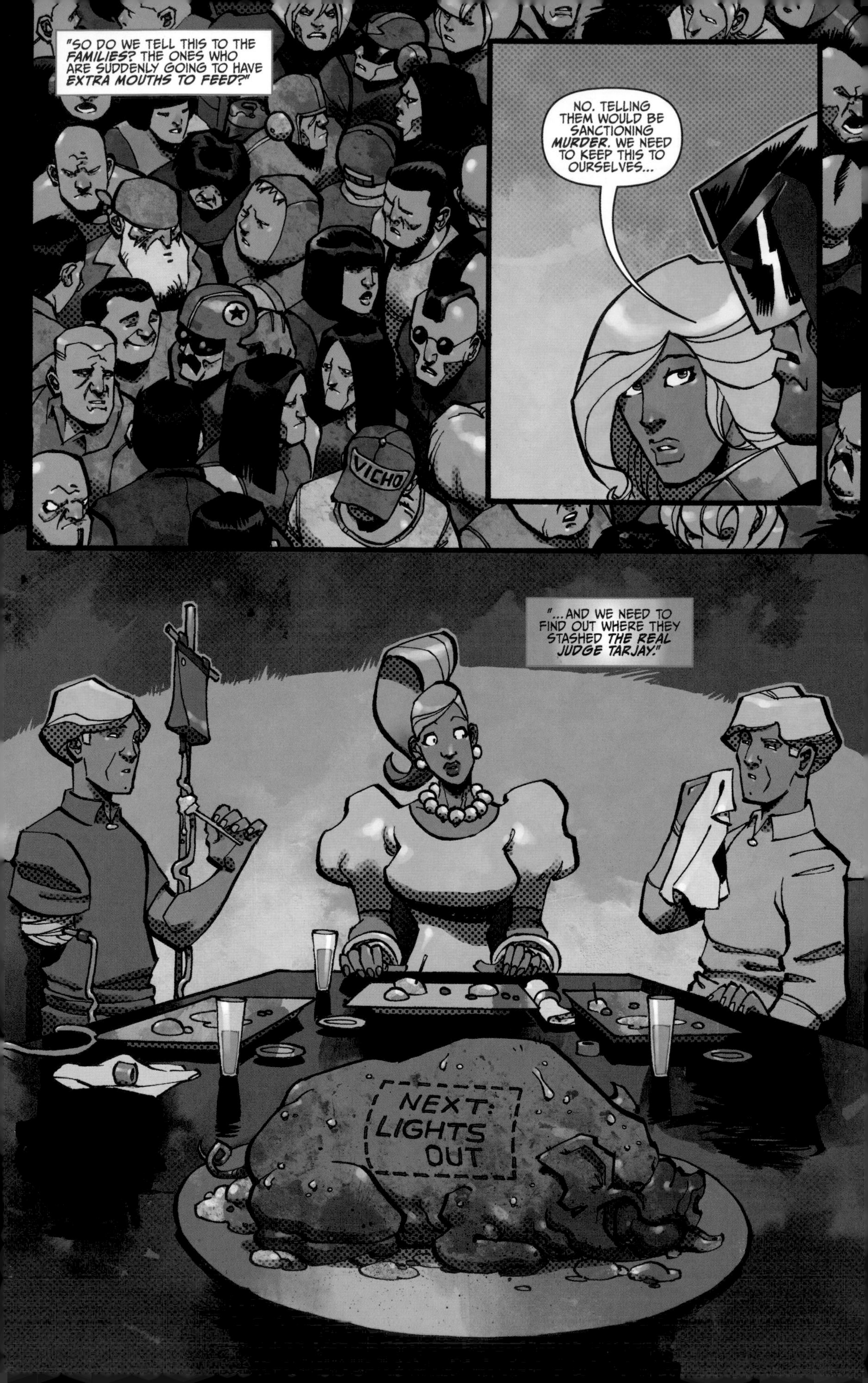
"SO DO WE TELL THIS TO THE FAMILIES? THE ONES WHO ARE SUDDENLY GOING TO HAVE EXTRA MOUTHS TO FEED?"
NO. TELLING THEM WOULD BE SANCTIONING MURDER. WE NEED TO KEEP THIS TO OURSELVES...
VICHO
"...AND WE NEED TO FIND OUT WHERE THEY STASHED THE REAL JUDGE TARJAY."
NEXT: LIGHTS OUT

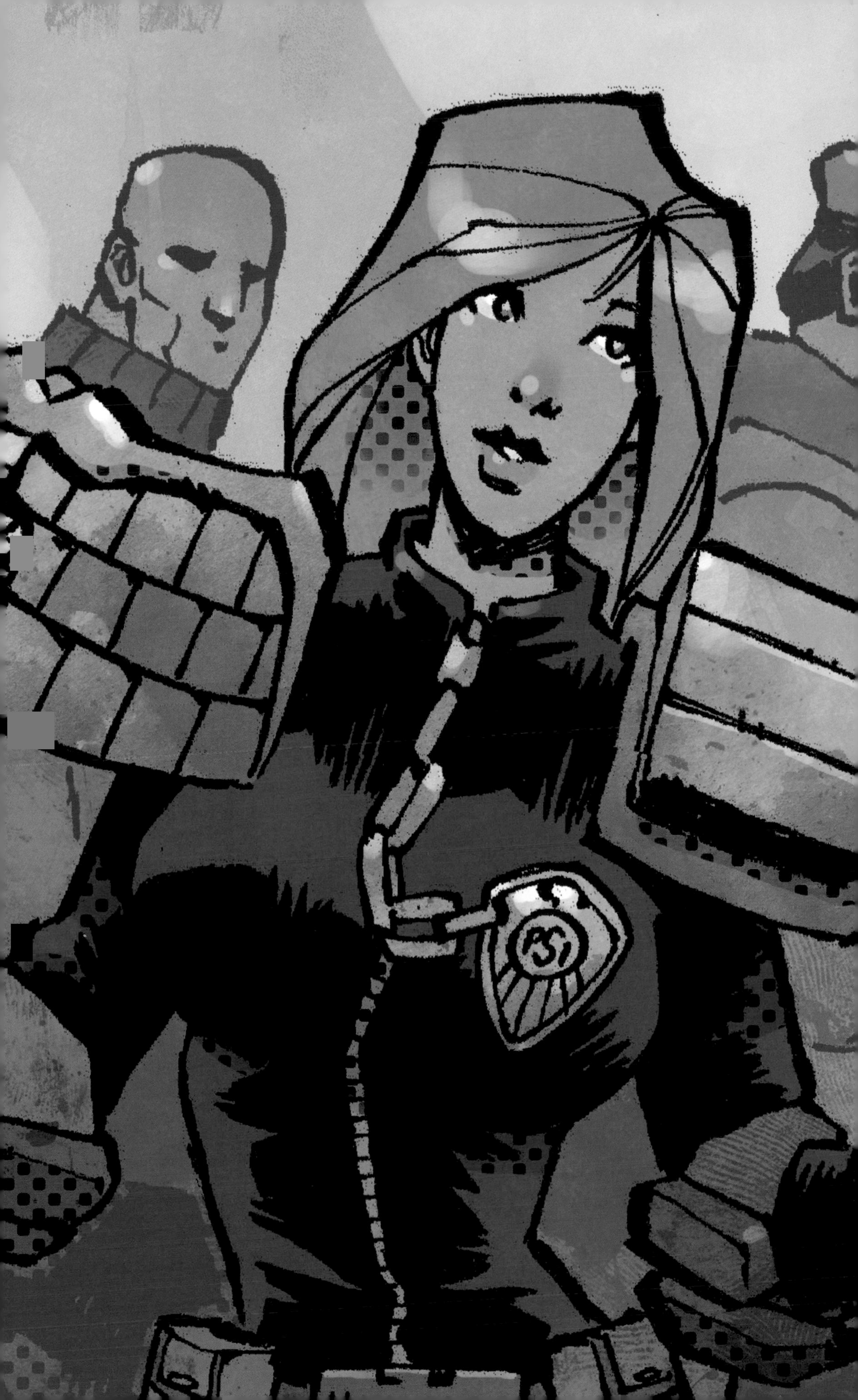

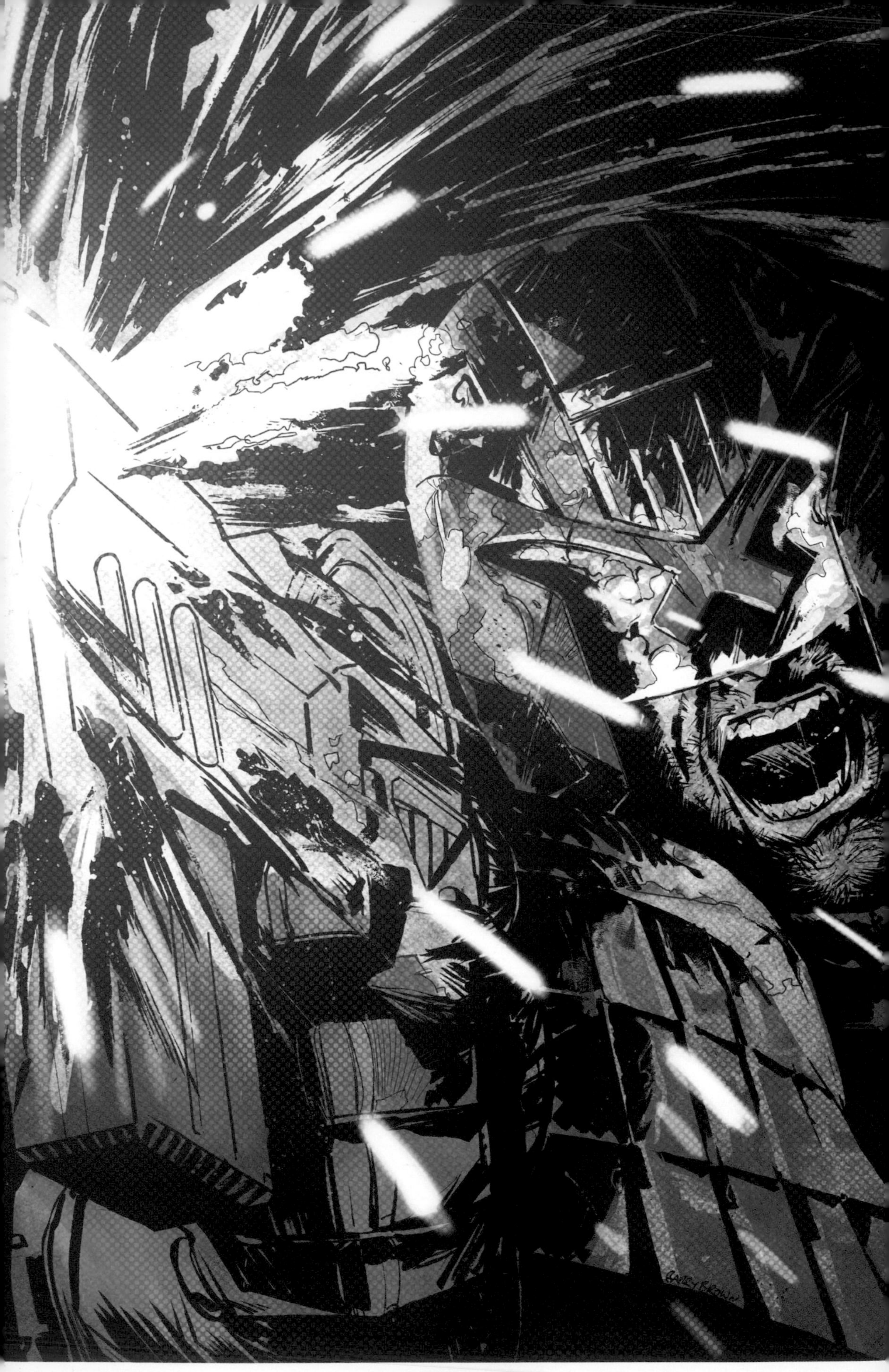
GARRY BROWN

ART BY **GARRY BROWN**

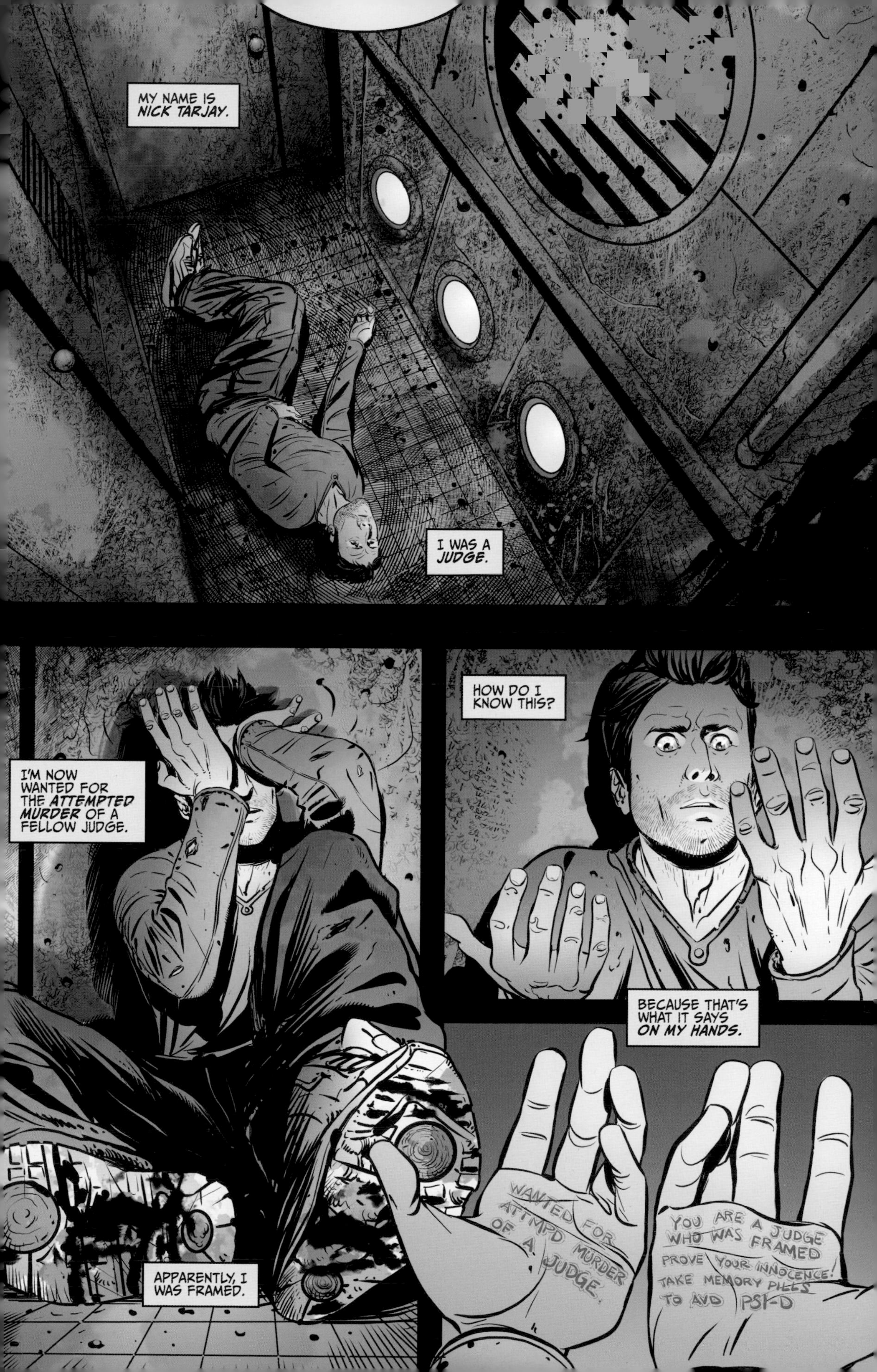
MY NAME IS NICK TARJAY.
I WAS A JUDGE.
I'M NOW WANTED FOR THE ATTEMPTED MURDER OF A FELLOW JUDGE.
HOW DO I KNOW THIS?
BECAUSE THAT'S WHAT IT SAYS ON MY HANDS.
WANTED FOR ATTMPD MURDER OF A JUDGE.
YOU ARE A JUDGE WHO WAS FRAMED
PROVE YOUR INNOCENCE!
TAKE MEMORY PILLS TO AVD PSI-D
APPARENTLY, I WAS FRAMED.

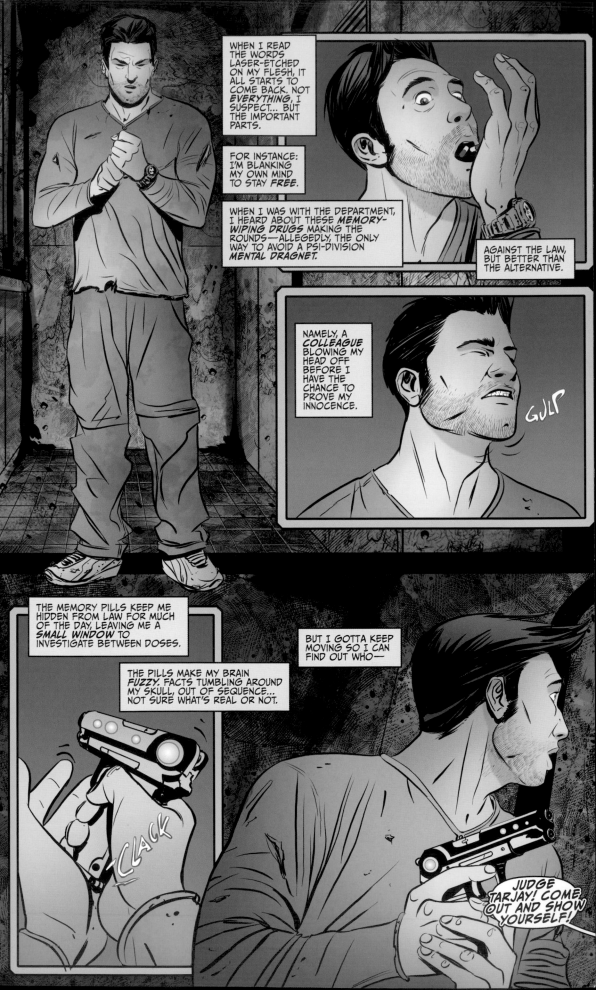

WHEN I READ THE WORDS LASER-ETCHED ON MY FLESH, IT ALL STARTS TO COME BACK. NOT *EVERYTHING*, I SUSPECT... BUT THE IMPORTANT PARTS.

FOR INSTANCE: I'M BLANKING MY OWN MIND TO STAY *FREE*.

WHEN I WAS WITH THE DEPARTMENT, I HEARD ABOUT THESE *MEMORY-WIPING DRUGS* MAKING THE ROUNDS—ALLEGEDLY, THE ONLY WAY TO AVOID A PSI-DIVISION *MENTAL DRAGNET*.

AGAINST THE LAW, BUT BETTER THAN THE ALTERNATIVE.

NAMELY, A *COLLEAGUE* BLOWING MY HEAD OFF BEFORE I HAVE THE CHANCE TO PROVE MY INNOCENCE.

GULP

THE MEMORY PILLS KEEP ME HIDDEN FROM LAW FOR MUCH OF THE DAY, LEAVING ME A *SMALL WINDOW* TO INVESTIGATE BETWEEN DOSES.

THE PILLS MAKE MY BRAIN *FUZZY*. FACTS TUMBLING AROUND MY SKULL, OUT OF SEQUENCE... NOT SURE WHAT'S REAL OR NOT.

BUT I GOTTA KEEP MOVING SO I CAN FIND OUT WHO—

CLACK

JUDGE TARJAY! COME OUT AND SHOW YOURSELF!

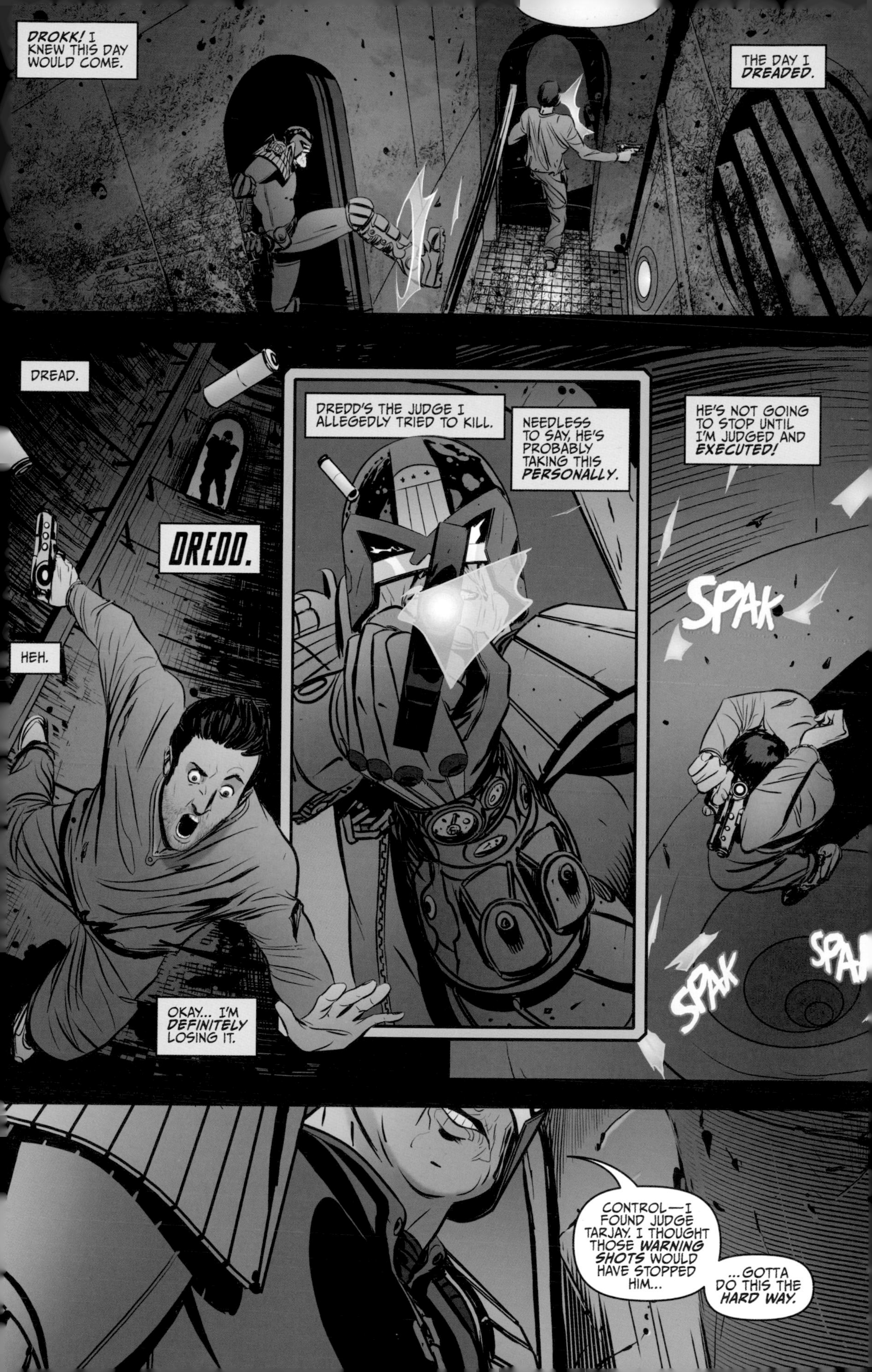
DROKK! I KNEW THIS DAY WOULD COME.
THE DAY I DREADED.
DREAD.
DREDD'S THE JUDGE I ALLEGEDLY TRIED TO KILL.
NEEDLESS TO SAY, HE'S PROBABLY TAKING THIS PERSONALLY.
HE'S NOT GOING TO STOP UNTIL I'M JUDGED AND EXECUTED!
DREDD.
SPAK
HEH.
SPAK
OKAY... I'M DEFINITELY LOSING IT.
CONTROL—I FOUND JUDGE TARJAY. I THOUGHT THOSE WARNING SHOTS WOULD HAVE STOPPED HIM...
...GOTTA DO THIS THE HARD WAY.

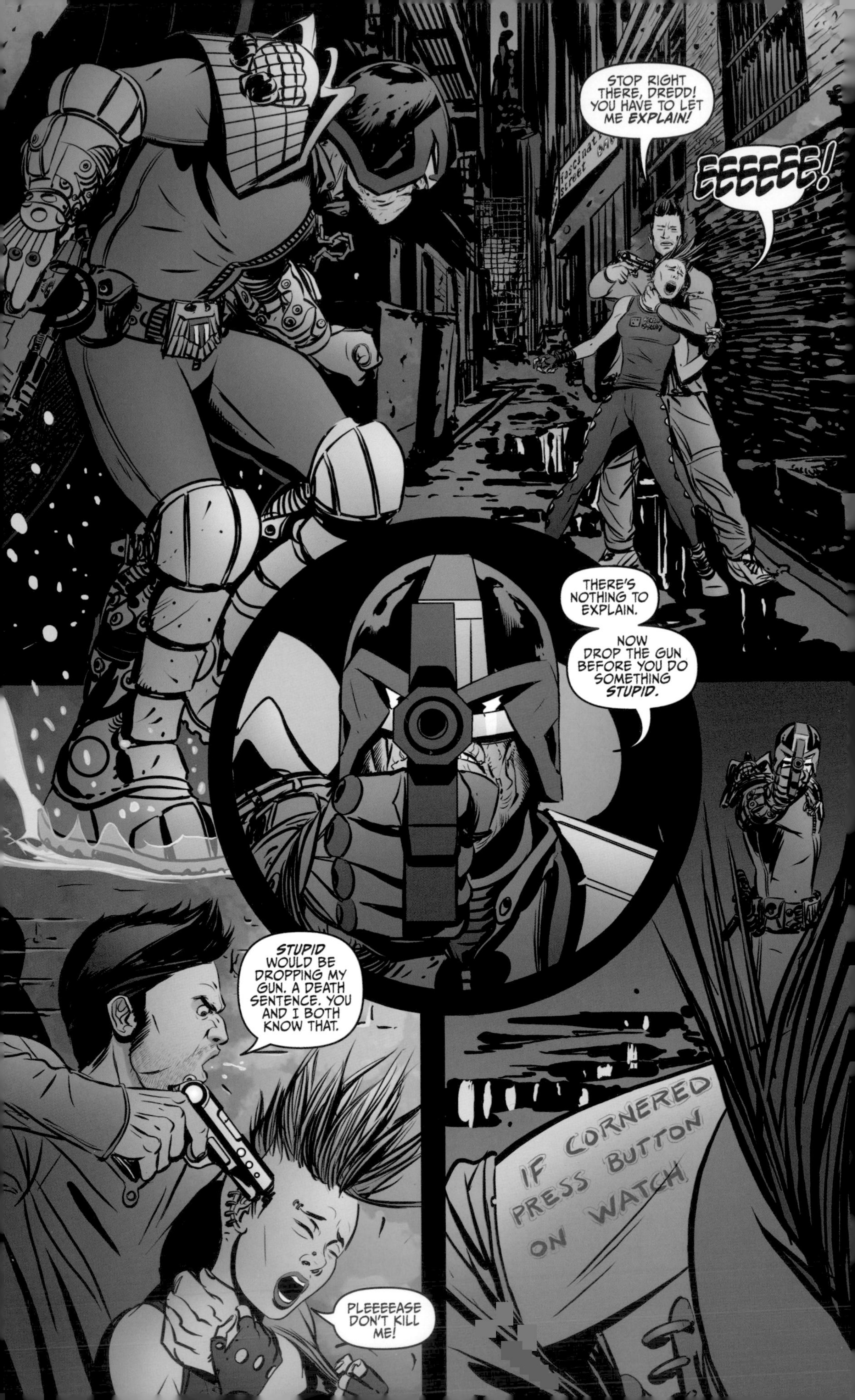
STOP RIGHT THERE, DREDD! YOU HAVE TO LET ME EXPLAIN!
EEEEEE!
THERE'S NOTHING TO EXPLAIN.
NOW DROP THE GUN BEFORE YOU DO SOMETHING STUPID.
STUPID WOULD BE DROPPING MY GUN. A DEATH SENTENCE. YOU AND I BOTH KNOW THAT.
PLEEEEASE DON'T KILL ME!
IF CORNERED PRESS BUTTON ON WATCH

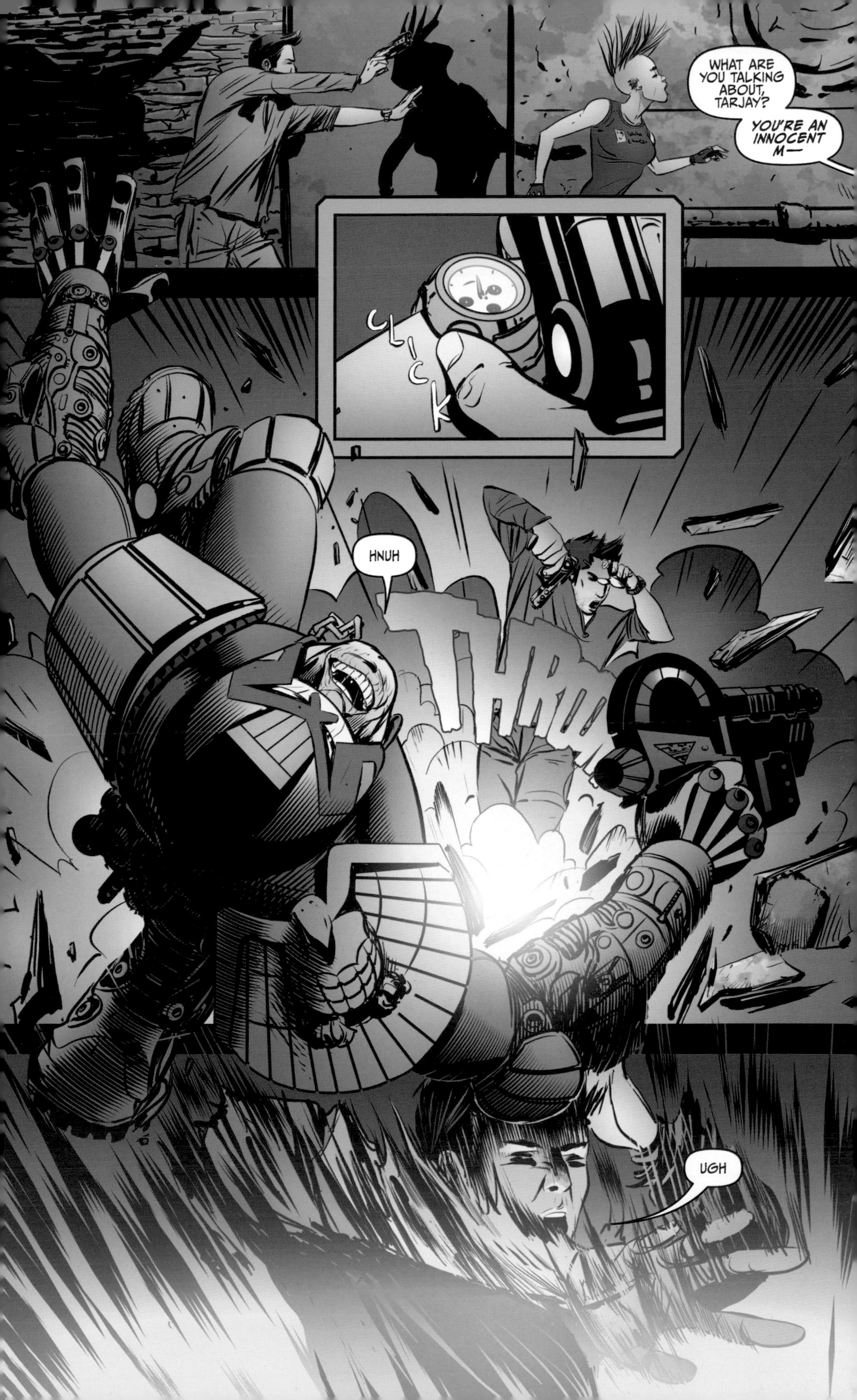
WHAT ARE YOU TALKING ABOUT, TARJAY?
YOU'RE AN INNOCENT M—
CLICK
HNUH
THRO
UGH

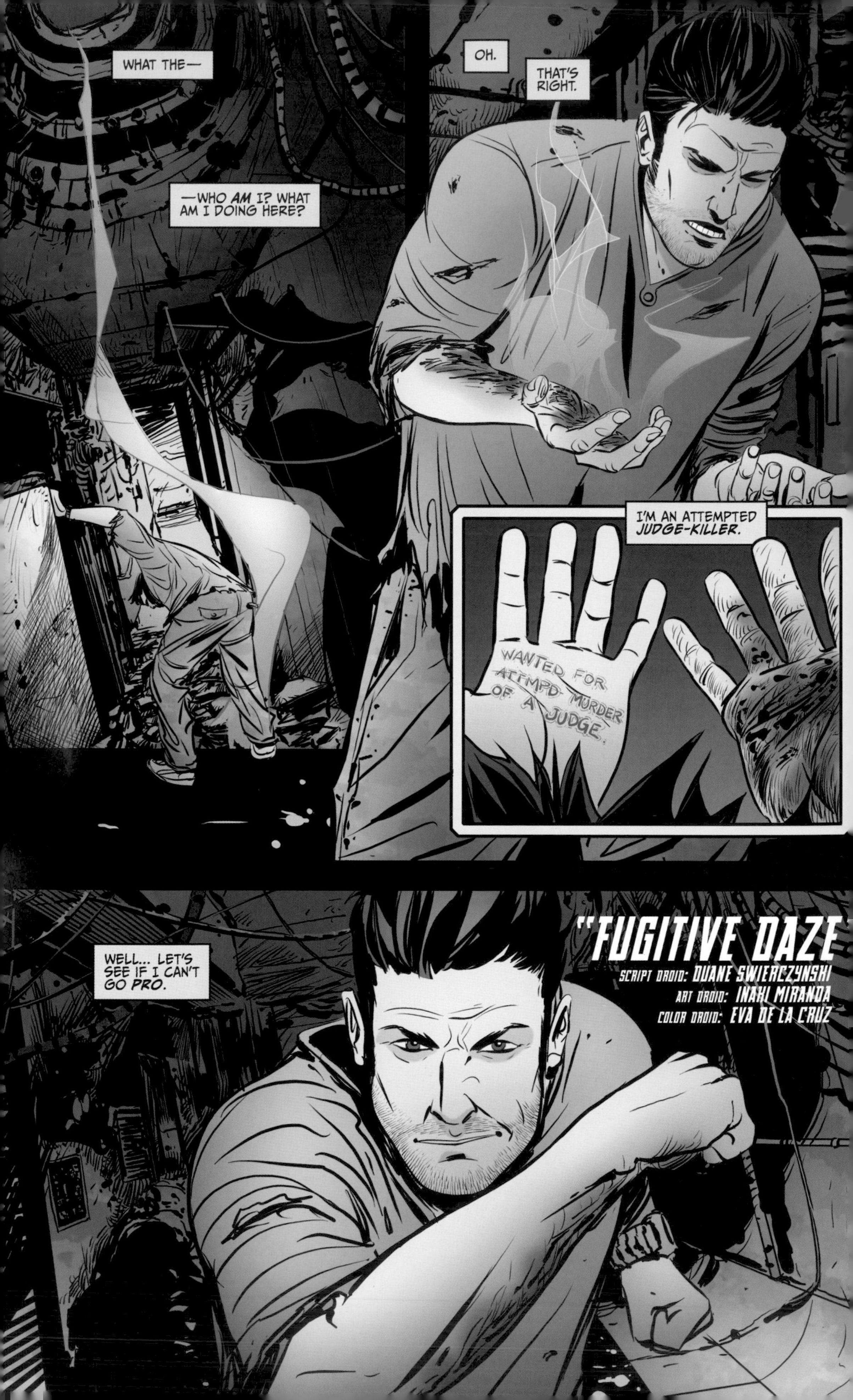
WHAT THE—
—WHO AM I? WHAT AM I DOING HERE?
OH.
THAT'S RIGHT.
I'M AN ATTEMPTED JUDGE-KILLER.
WANTED FOR ATTMPD MURDER OF A JUDGE.
WELL... LET'S SEE IF I CAN'T GO PRO.
"FUGITIVE DAZE"
SCRIPT DROID: DUANE SWIERCZYNSKI
ART DROID: INAKI MIRANDA
COLOR DROID: EVA DE LA CRUZ

JUDGE DREDD®

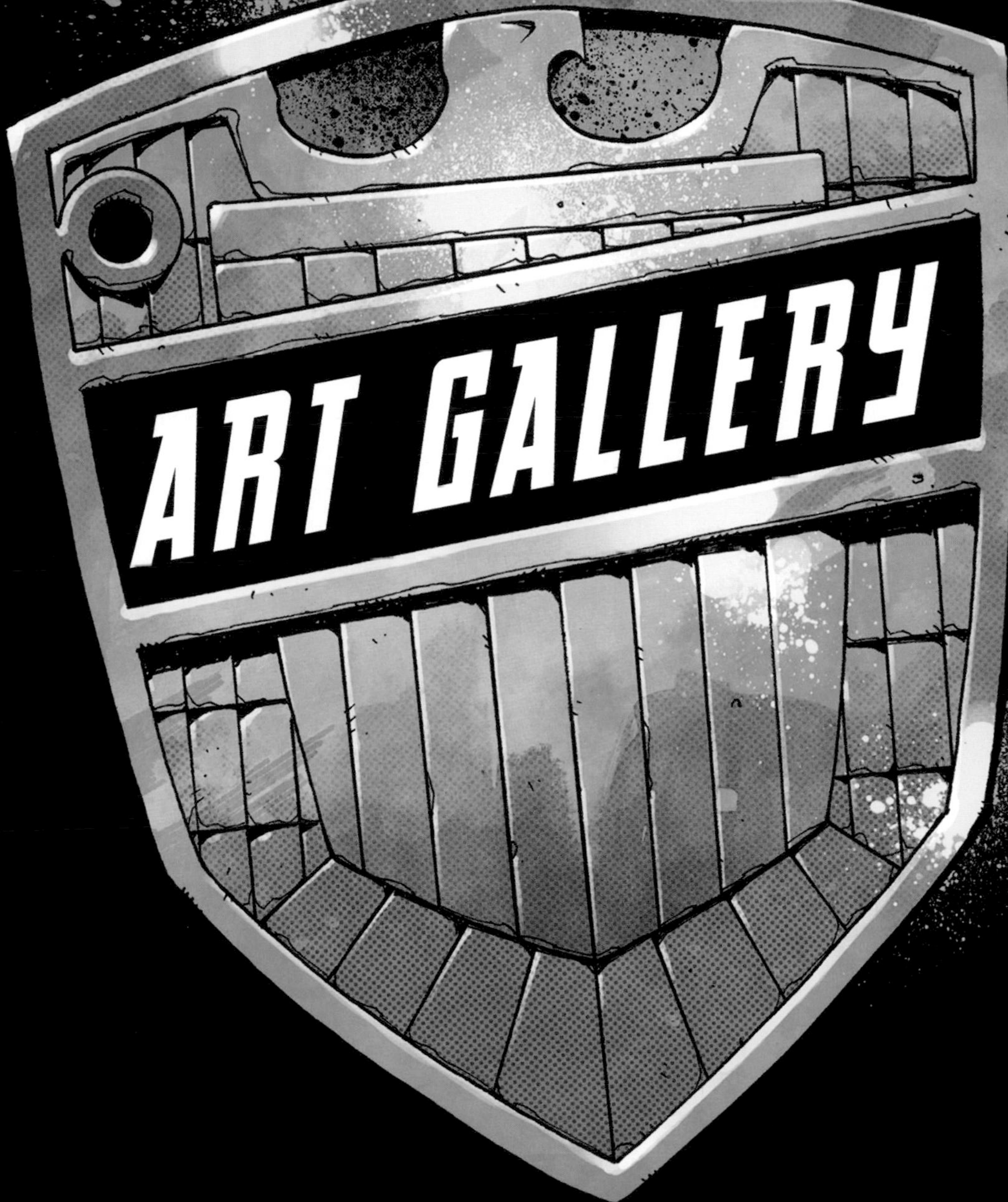
ART GALLERY

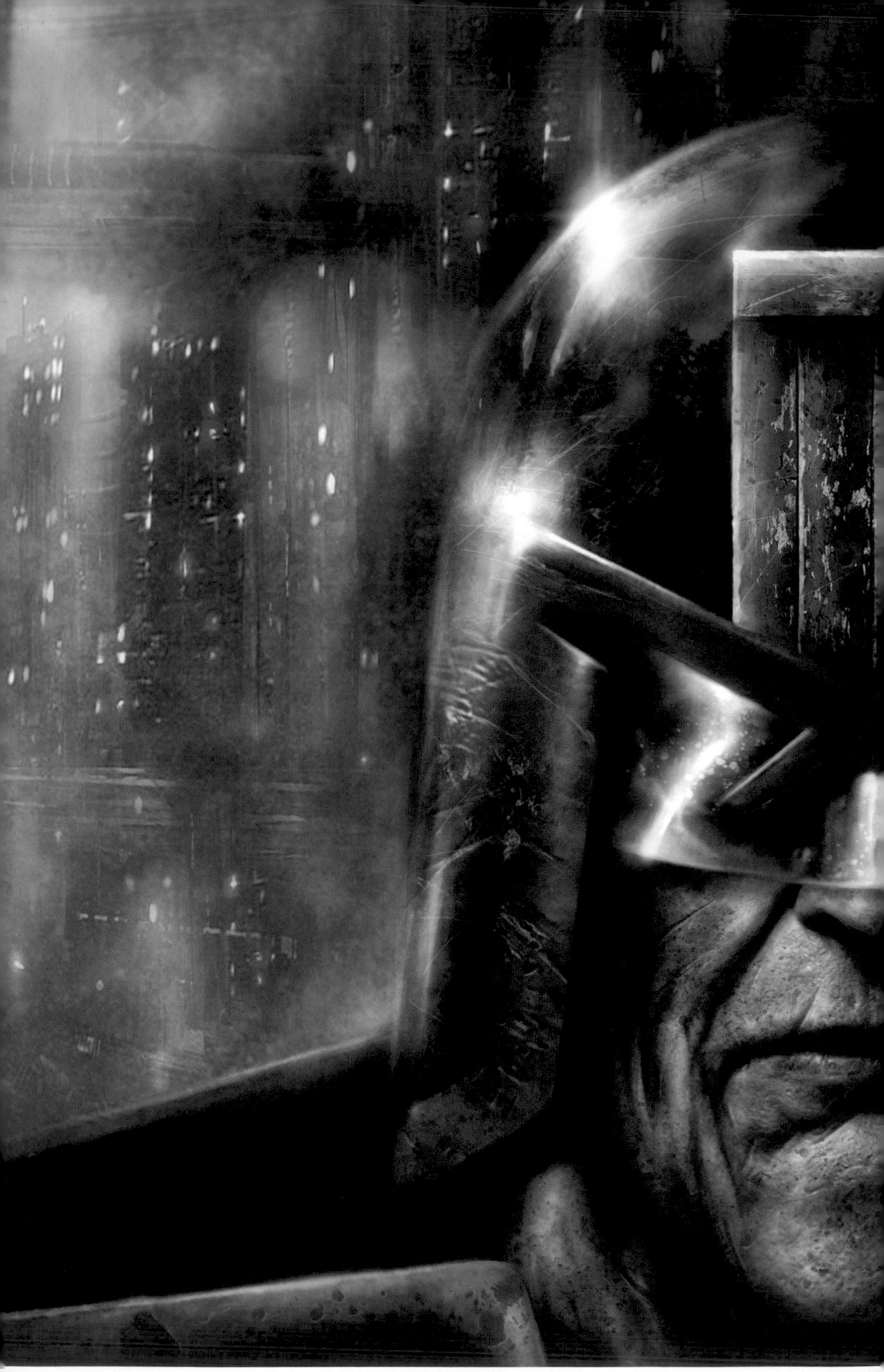

ART BY NICK PERCIVAL

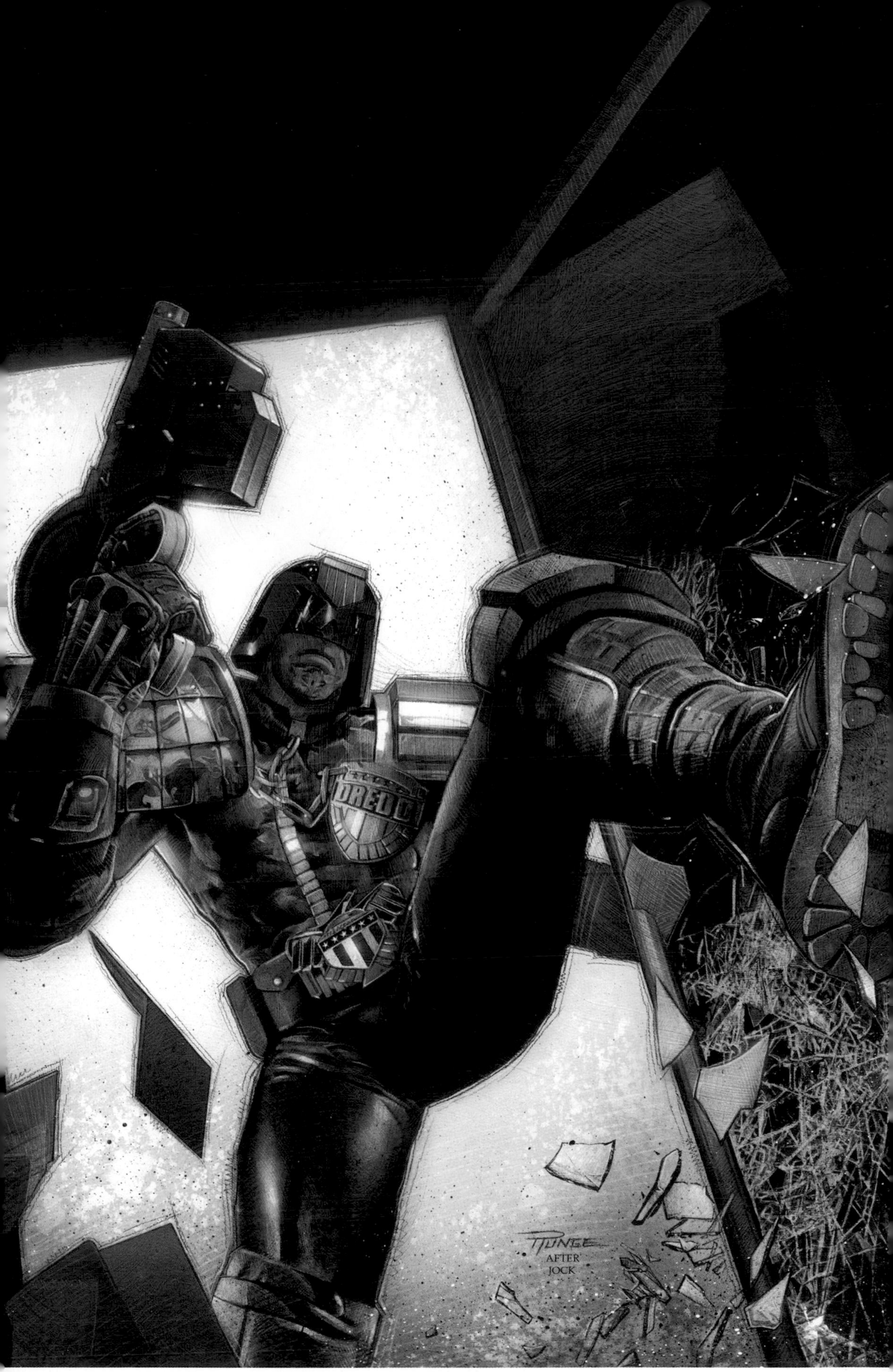
RUNGE
AFTER
JOCK

ART BY **NICK RUNGE**

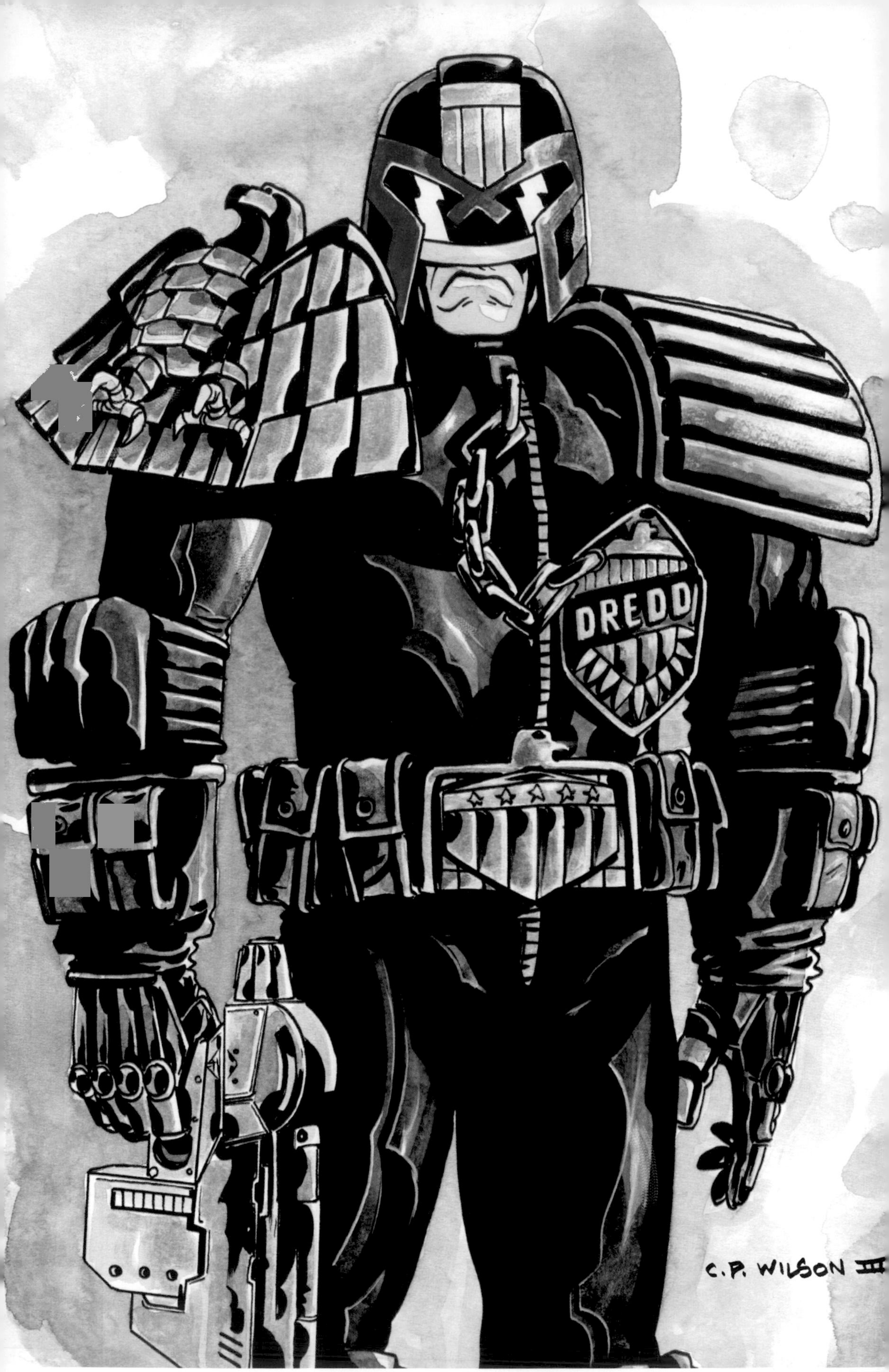
DREDD
C.P. WILSON III

ART BY CHARLES PAUL WILSON III

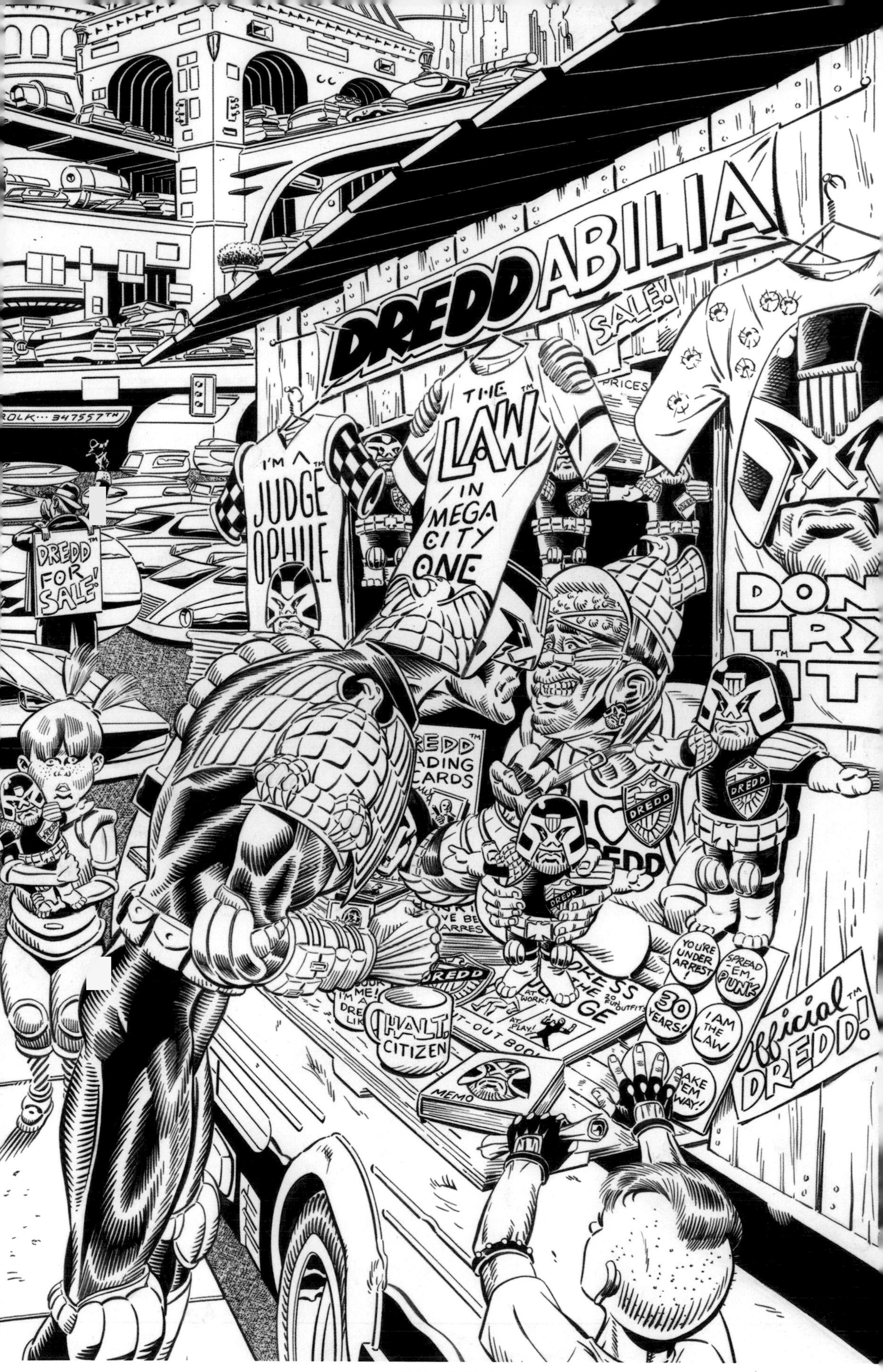
DREDDABILIA
SALE!
PRICES
THE LAW IN MEGA CITY ONE
I'M A JUDGE OPHILE
DREDD FOR SALE!
HALT, CITIZEN
MEMO
YOU'RE UNDER ARREST!
SPREAD 'EM, PUNK
30 YEARS!
I AM THE LAW
Official DREDD!

ART BY **RICH LARSON**

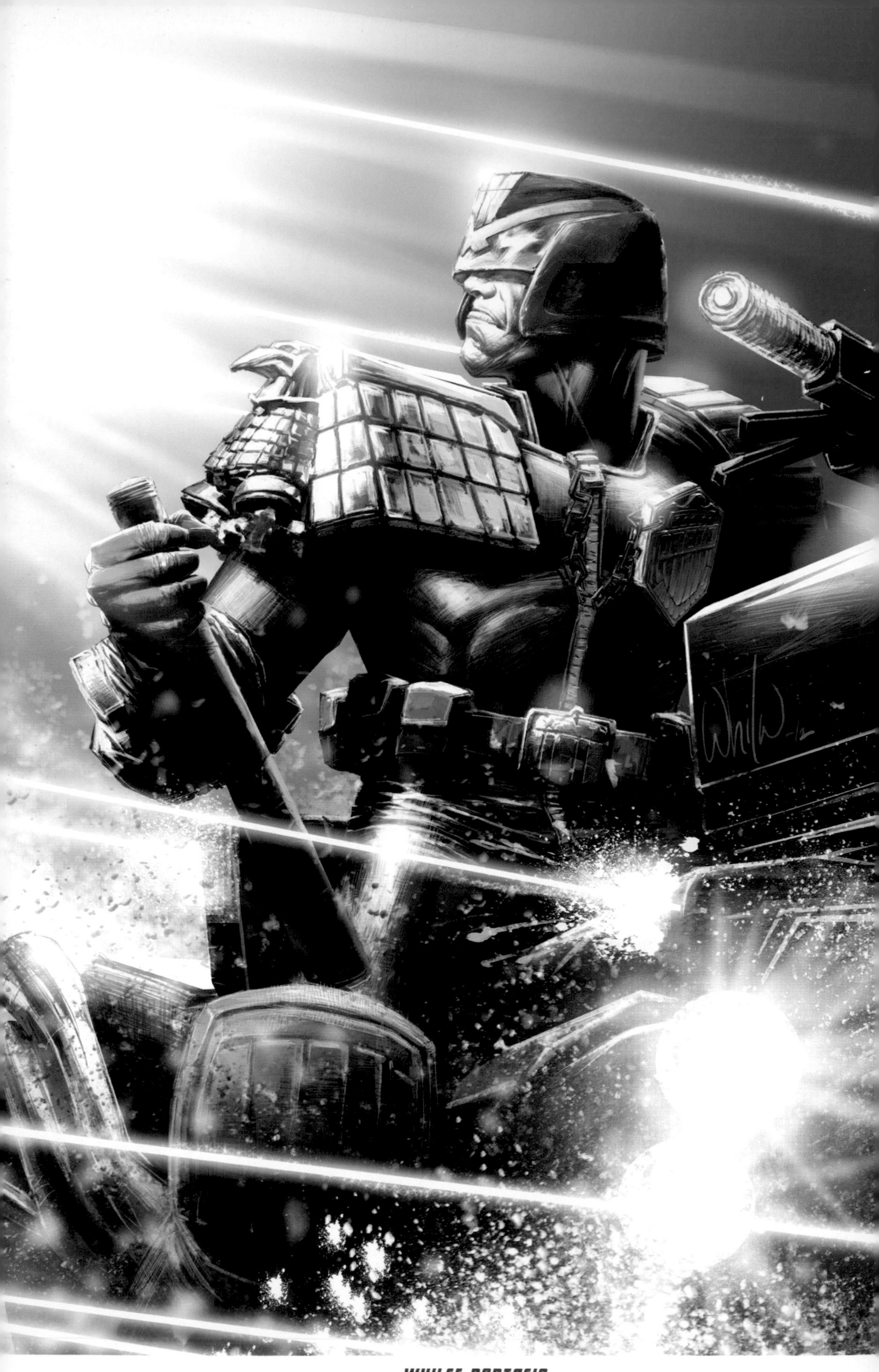

ART BY **WHILCE PORTACIO**

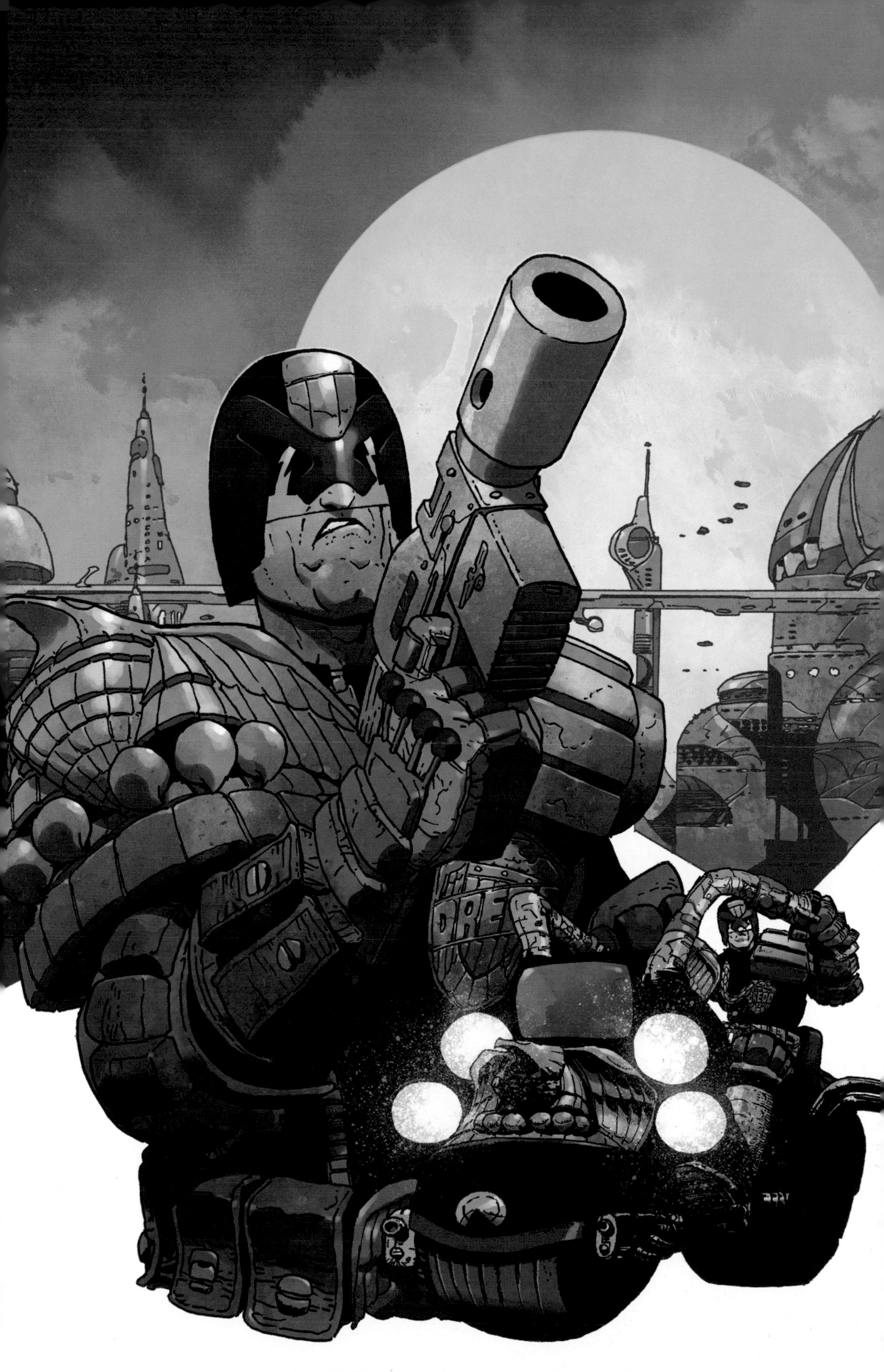

ART BY **CARLOS EZQUERRA** ★ COLORS BY **NELSON DANIEL**

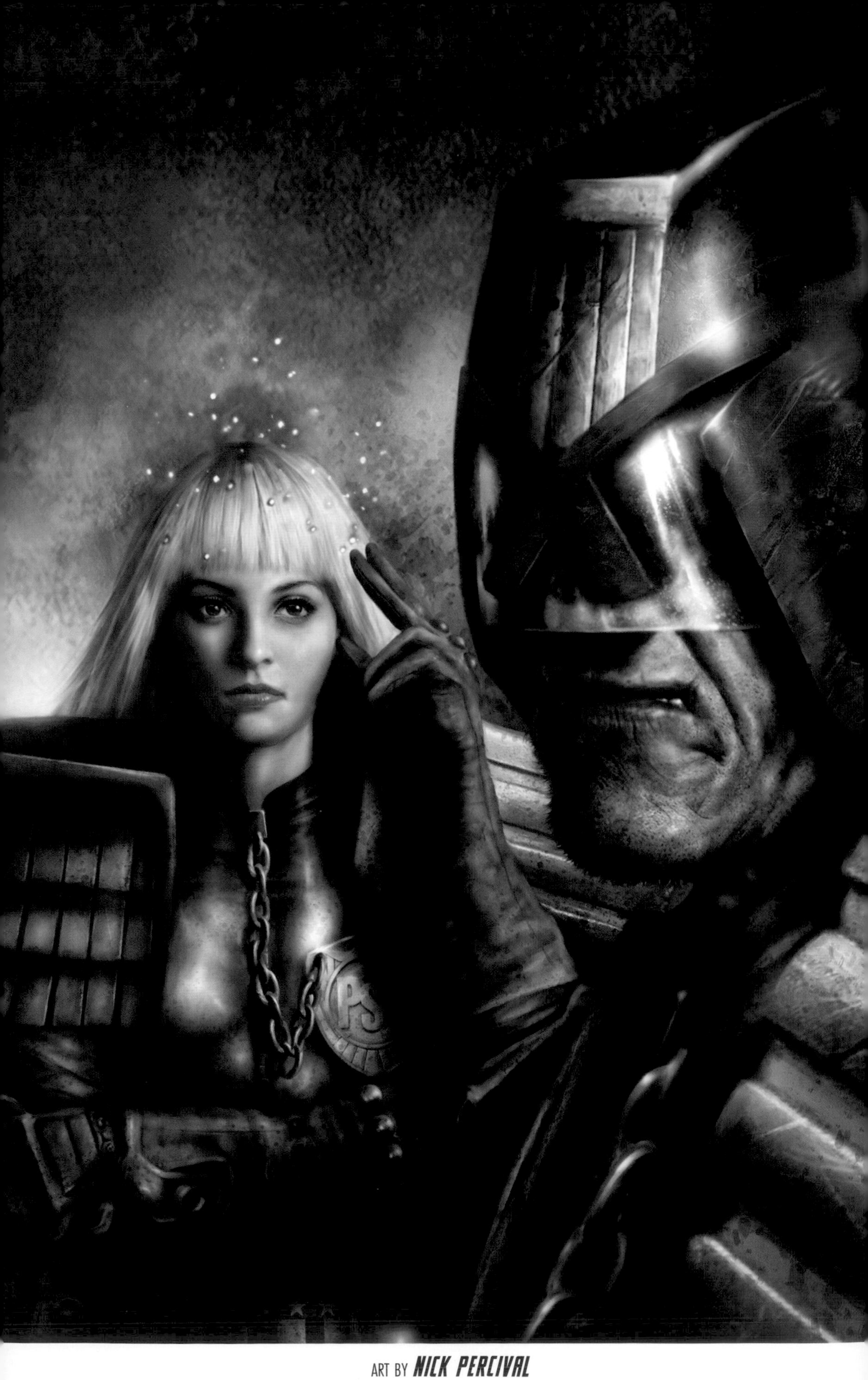

ART BY **NICK PERCIVAL**

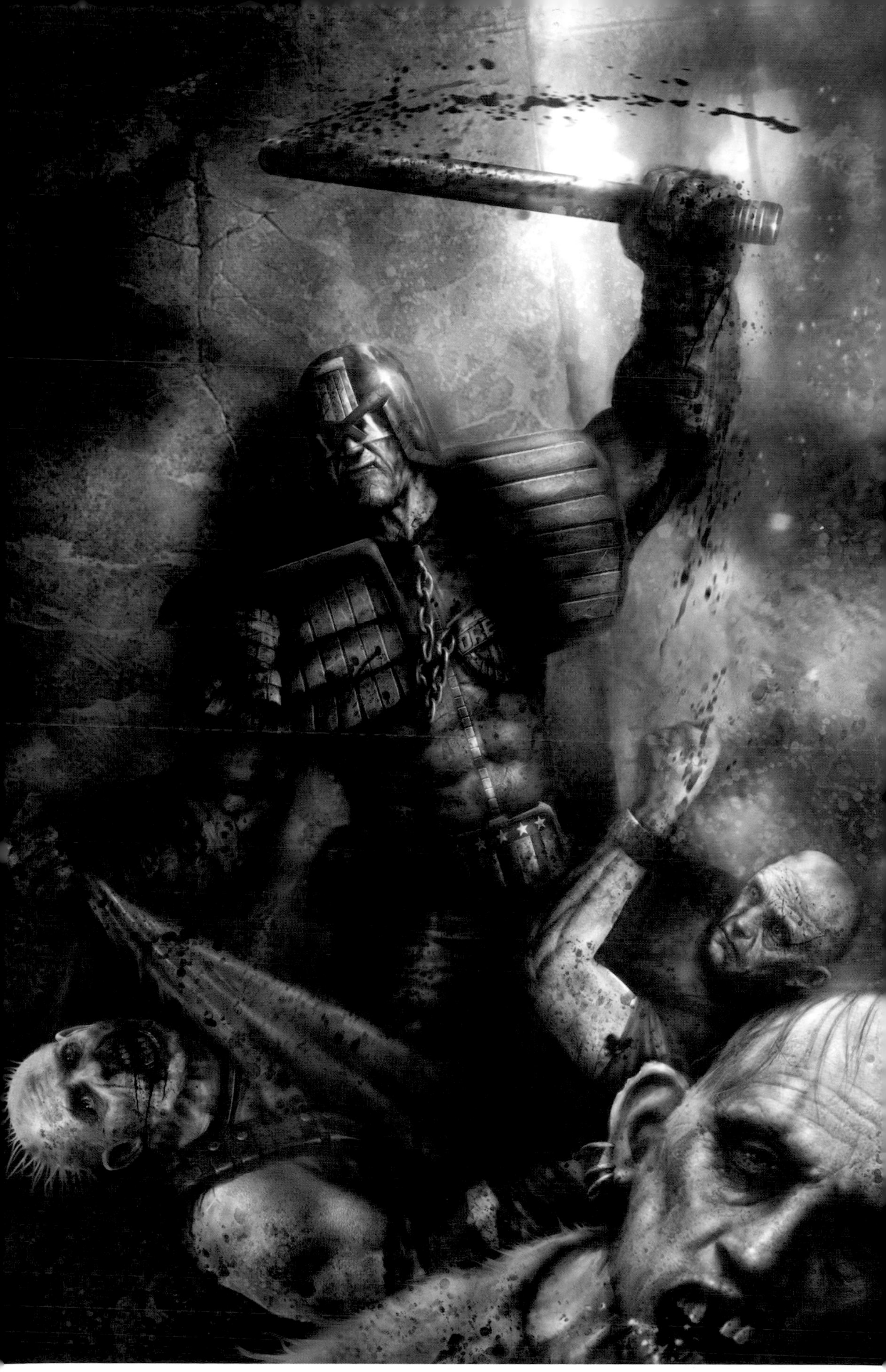

ART BY **NICK PERCIVAL**

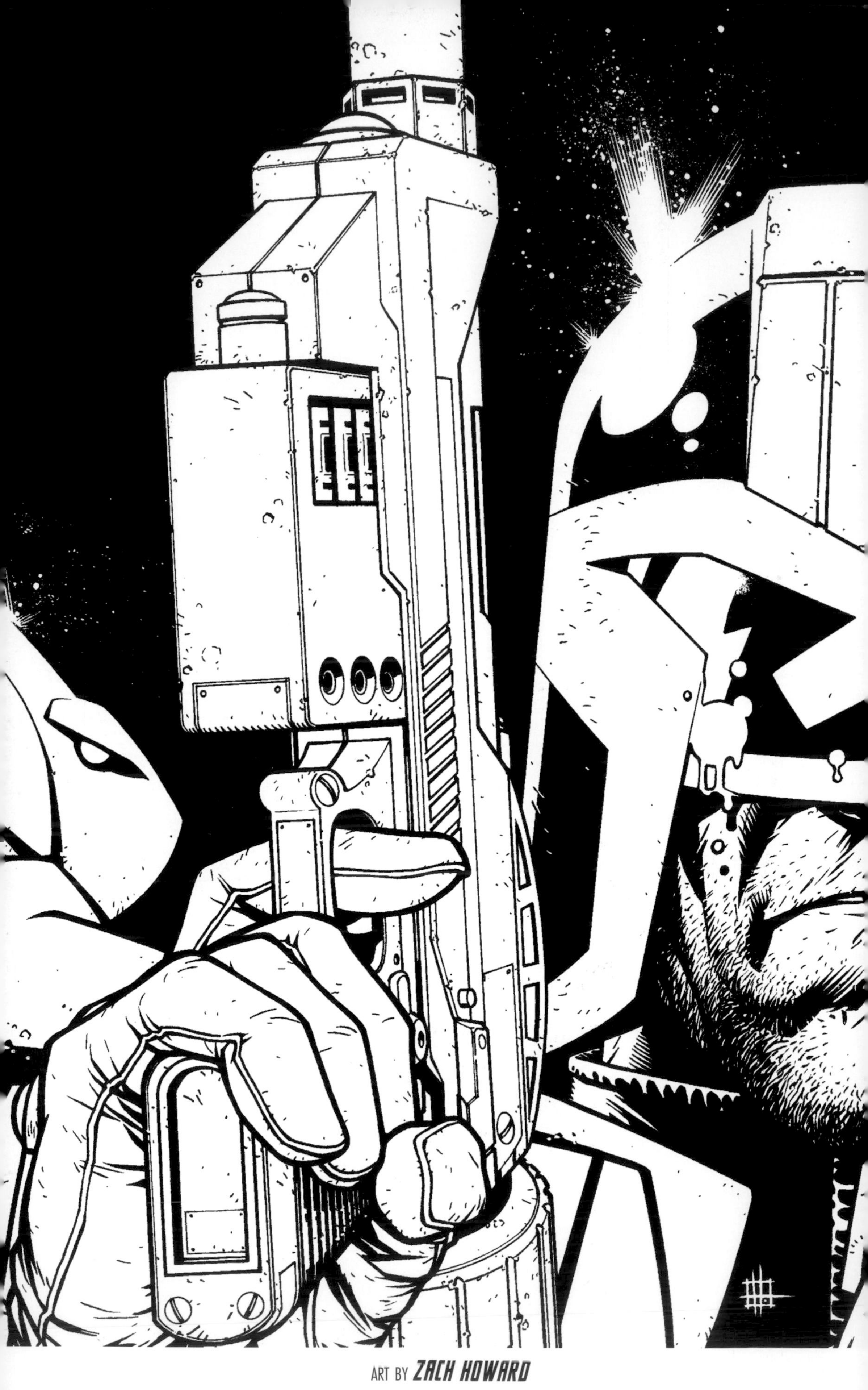

ART BY ZACH HOWARD

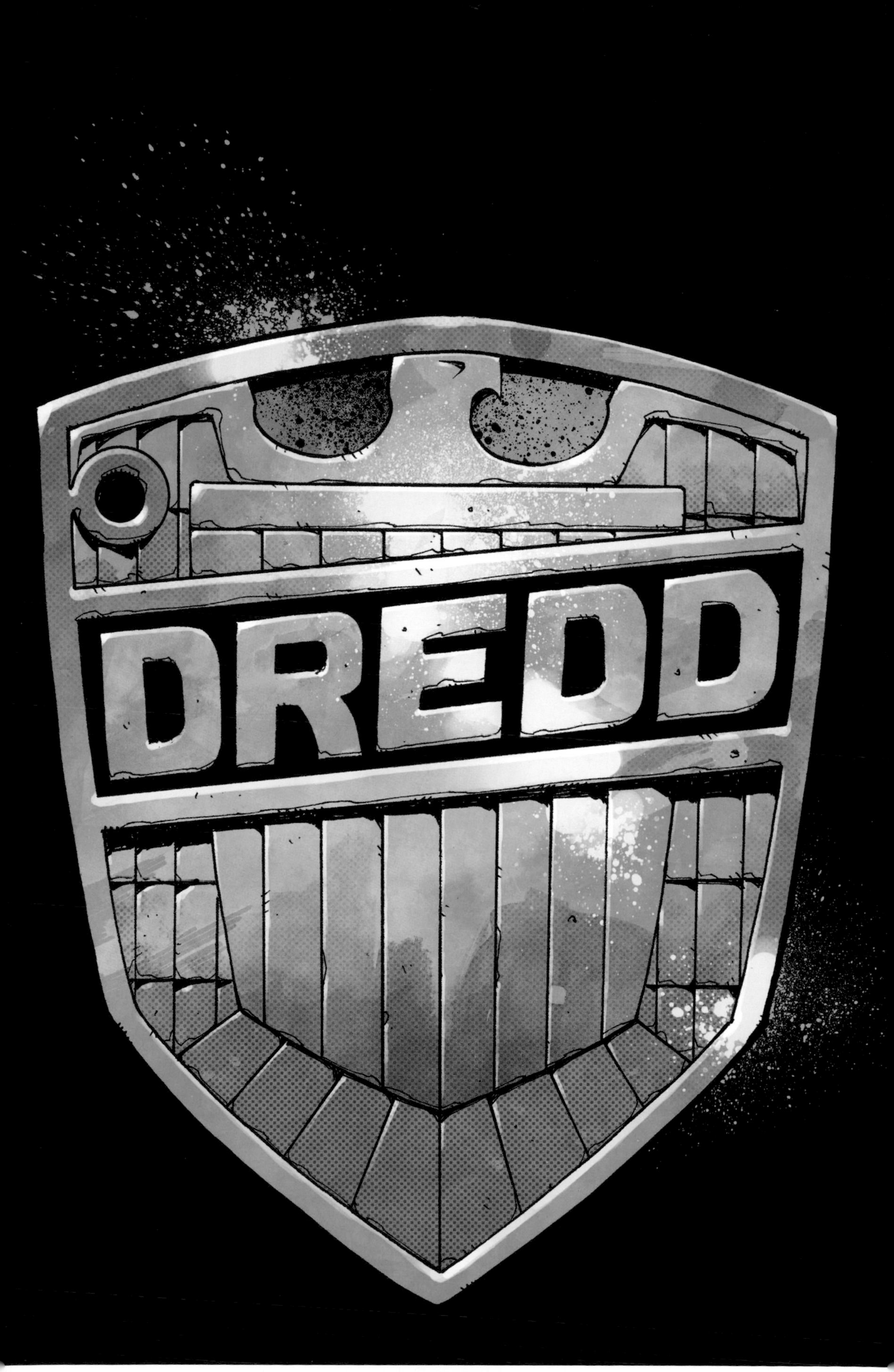
DREDD

ART BY **NELSON DANIEL**

RETAILER EXCLUSIVE
ISSUE #1 COVER CHECKLIST

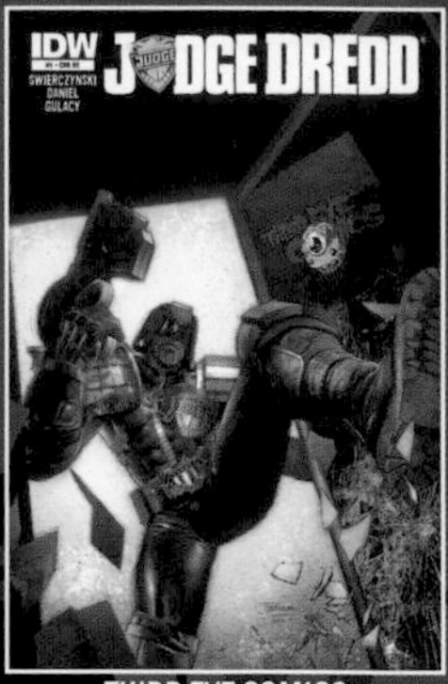
IDW
JUDGE DREDD
SWIERCZYNSKI
DANIEL
GULACY
THIRD EYE COMICS
www.thirdeyecomics.com

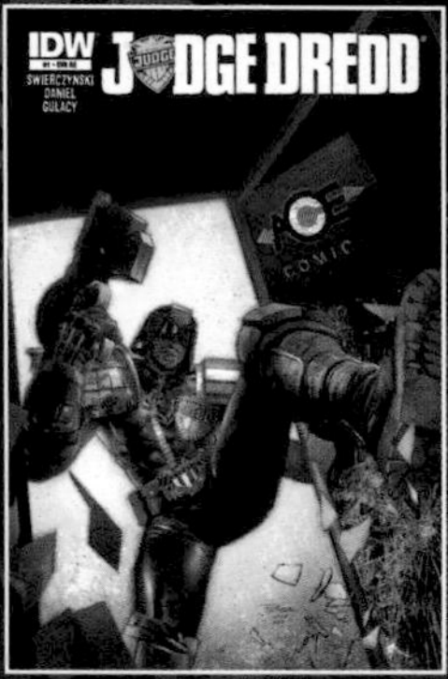
IDW
JUDGE DREDD
SWIERCZYNSKI
DANIEL
GULACY
ACE COMICS
www.acecomics.co.uk

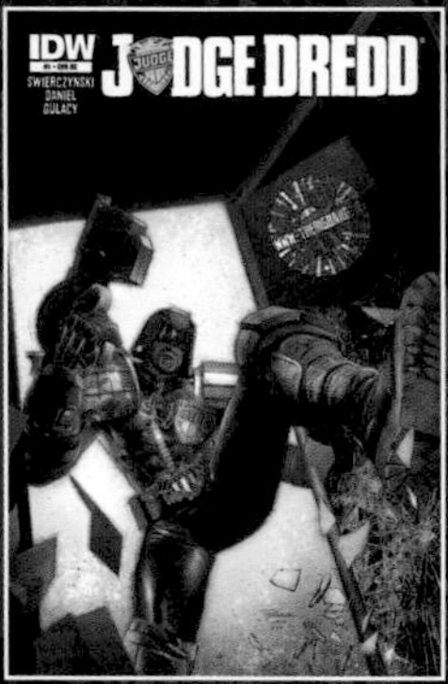
IDW
JUDGE DREDD
SWIERCZYNSKI
DANIEL
GULACY
BIG BANG COMIC SHOP
www.thebigbang.ie

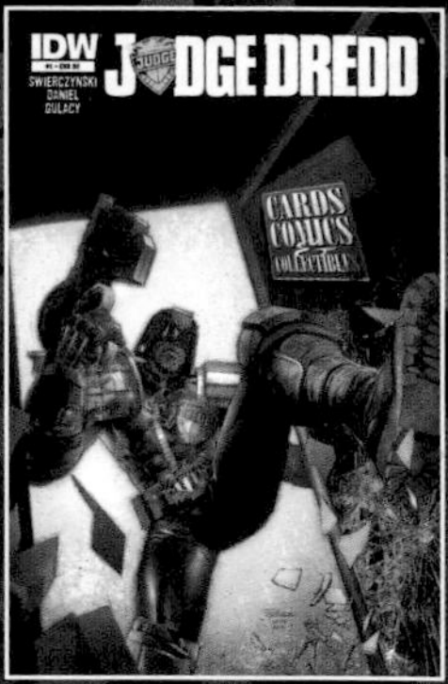
IDW
JUDGE DREDD
SWIERCZYNSKI
DANIEL
GULACY
CARDS
COMICS
COLLECTIBLES
CARDS, COMICS, AND COLLECTIBLES
www.cardscomicscollectibles.com

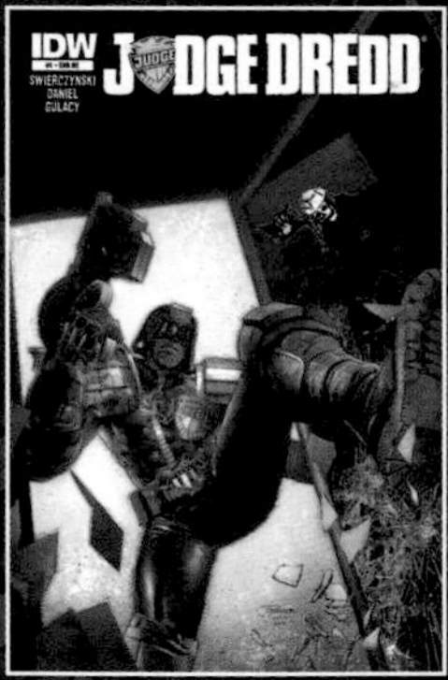
IDW
JUDGE DREDD
SWIERCZYNSKI
DANIEL
GULACY
DISPOSABLE HEROES
www.disposableheroes.co.uk

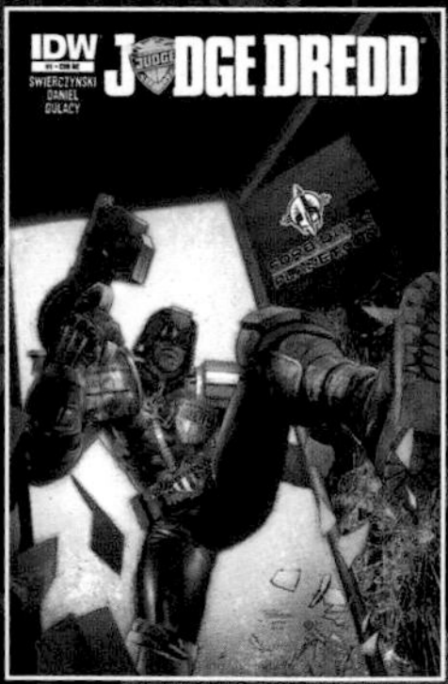
IDW
JUDGE DREDD
SWIERCZYNSKI
DANIEL
GULACY
FORBIDDEN PLANET
www.forbiddenplanet.com

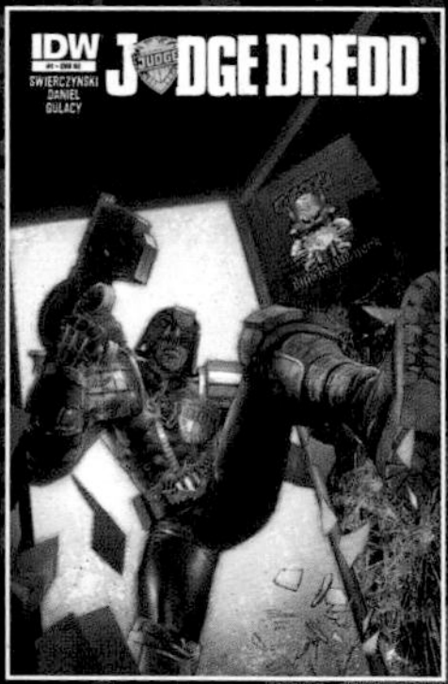
IDW
JUDGE DREDD
SWIERCZYNSKI
DANIEL
GULACY
GIFTS FOR THE GEEK
www.giftsforthegeek.com.au

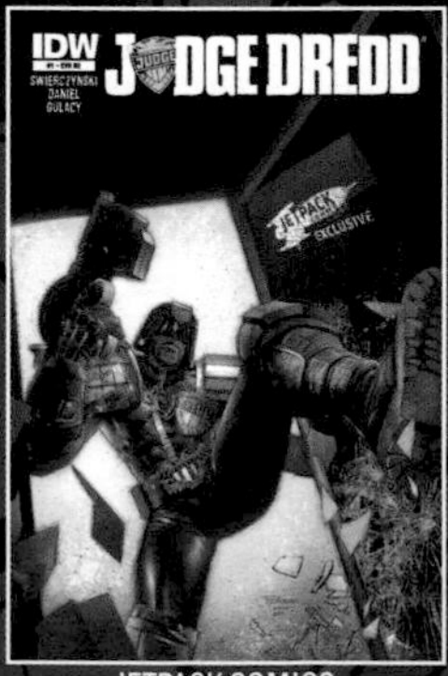
IDW
JUDGE DREDD
SWIERCZYNSKI
DANIEL
GULACY
EXCLUSIVE
JETPACK COMICS
www.jetpackcomics.com

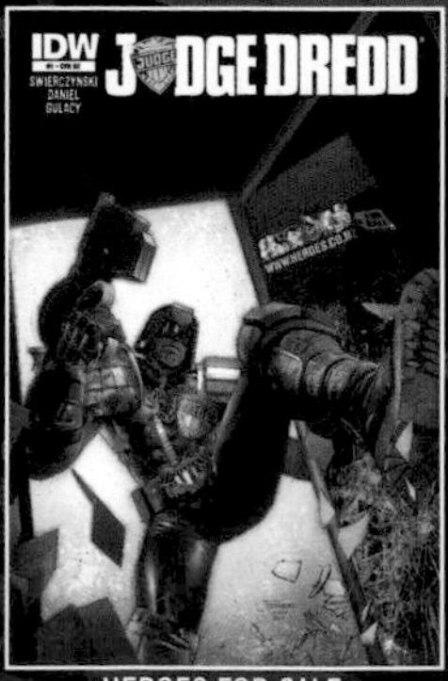
IDW
JUDGE DREDD
SWIERCZYNSKI
DANIEL
GULACY
HEROES FOR SALE
www.heroes4sale.co.nz

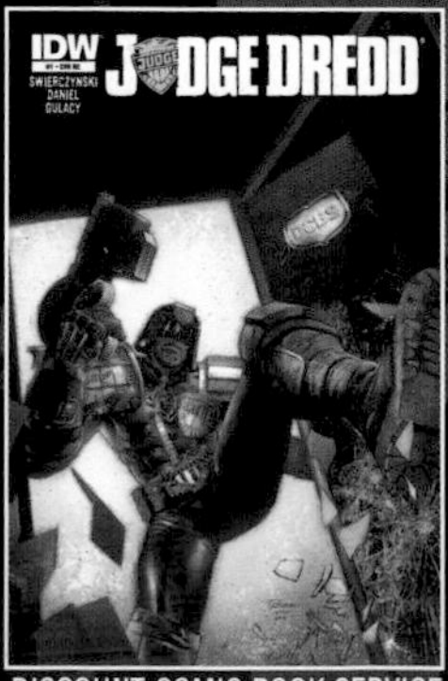
IDW
JUDGE DREDD
SWIERCZYNSKI
DANIEL
GULACY
DISCOUNT COMIC BOOK SERVICE
www.dcbservice.com

IDW
JUDGE DREDD
DREDDABILIA
DON'T TRY IT!
JETPACK COMICS
www.jetpackcomics.com

IDW
JUDGE DREDD
SWIERCZYNSKI
DANIEL
GULACY
JETPACK COMICS
www.jetpackcomics.com

IDW
JUDGE DREDD
SWIERCZYNSKI
DANIEL
GULACY
PLANET COMICS
PLANET COMICS
www.planetcomics.net

IDW
JUDGE DREDD
SWIERCZYNSKI
DANIEL
GULACY
LARRYS
LARRY'S COMICS
www.larryscomics.net

IDW
JUDGE DREDD
SWIERCZYNSKI
DANIEL • GULACY
LARRYS
DREDD
LARRY'S COMICS
www.larryscomics.net

IDW
JUDGE DREDD
SWIERCZYNSKI
DANIEL
GULACY
MIDTOWN COMICS
MIDTOWN COMICS
EXCLUSIVE
MIDTOWN COMICS
www.midtowncomics.com

IDW
JUDGE DREDD
SWIERCZYNSKI
DANIEL
GULACY
COMIX
PULP NOUVEAU COMIX
www.pulpnouveau.com

IDW
JUDGE DREDD
SWIERCZYNSKI
DANIEL
GULACY
SERIEBORSEN
SERIEBORSEN
www.serieborsen.se/english/english.html

IDW
JUDGE DREDD
SWIERCZYNSKI
DANIEL
GULACY
TATE'S
TATE'S COMICS
www.tatescomics.com

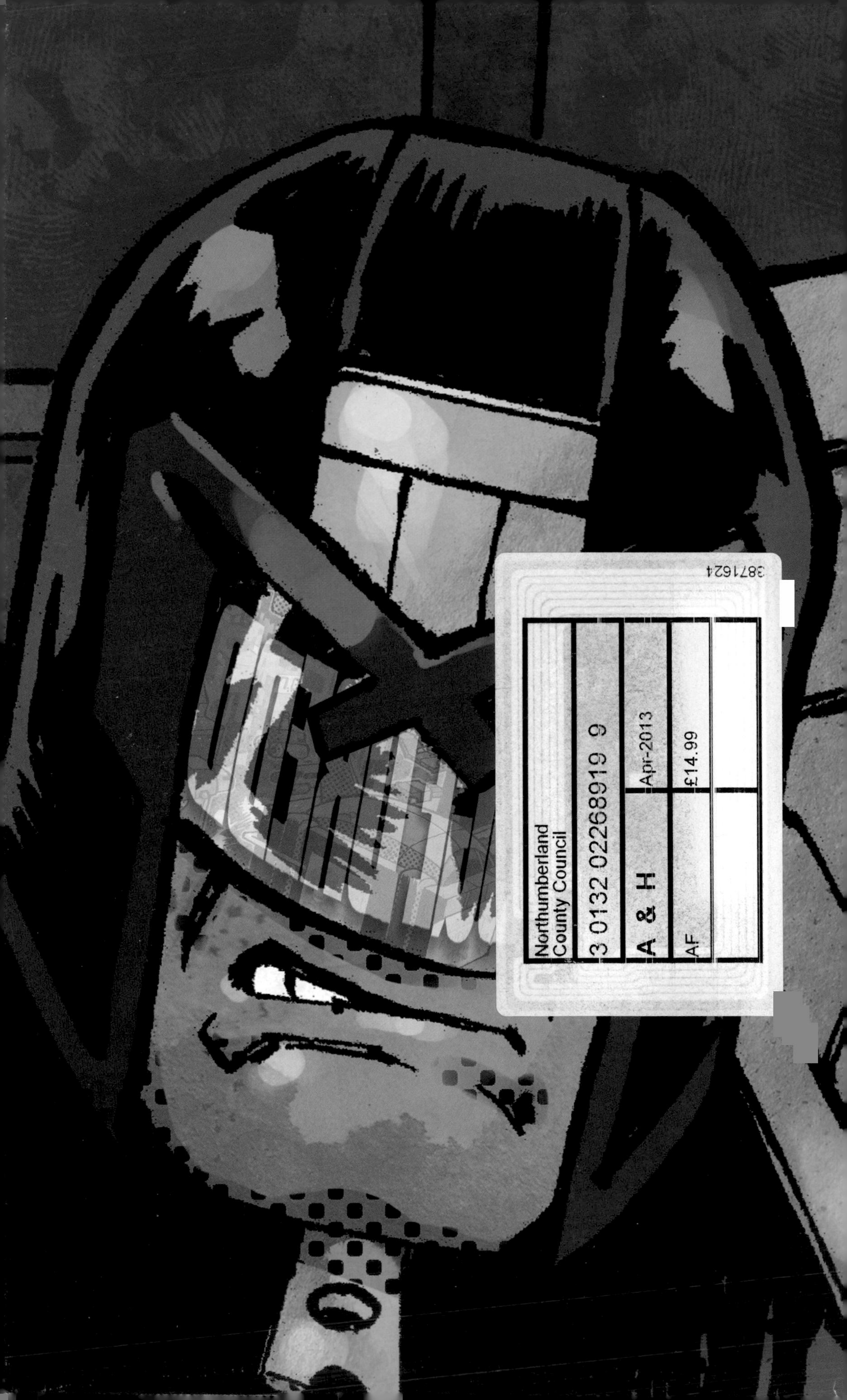